U.S. MORAL THEOLOGY FROM THE MARGINS

Readings in Moral Theology No. 19

PREVIOUS VOLUMES IN THIS SERIES

Readings in Moral Theology No. 1:
Moral Norms and Catholic Tradition (out of print)

Readings in Moral Theology No. 2:
The Distinctiveness of Christian Ethics (out of print)

Readings in Moral Theology No. 3:
The Magisterium and Morality (out of print)

Readings in Moral Theology No. 4:
The Use of Scripture in Moral Theology (out of print)

Readings in Moral Theology No. 5:
Official Catholic Social Teaching (out of print)

Readings in Moral Theology No. 6:
Dissent in the Church

Readings in Moral Theology No. 7:
Natural Law and Theology (out of print)

Readings in Moral Theology No. 8:
Dialogue about Catholic Sexual Teaching (out of print)

Readings in Moral Theology No. 9:
Feminist Ethics and the Catholic Moral Tradition (out of print)

Readings in Moral Theology No. 10:
John Paul II and Moral Theology

Readings in Moral Theology No. 11:
The Historical Development of Fundamental
Moral Theology in the United States

Readings in Moral Theology No. 12:
The Catholic Church, Morality and Politics

Readings in Moral Theology No. 13:
Change in Official Catholic Moral Teachings

Readings in Moral Theology No. 14:
Conscience

Readings in Moral Theology No. 15:
Marriage

Readings in Moral Theology No. 16:
Virtue

Readings in Moral Theology No. 17:
Ethics and Spirituality

Readings in Moral Theology No. 18:
The *Sensus Fidelium* and Moral Theology

U.S. MORAL THEOLOGY FROM THE MARGINS

Readings in Moral Theology No. 19

Edited by
Charles E. Curran
and
Lisa A. Fullam

Paulist Press
New York / Mahwah, NJ

Permissions for previously published material may be found in the Acknowledgments.

Library of Congress Control Number: 2019941899

ISBN 978-0-8091-5486-9 (paperback)
ISBN 978-1-58768-882-9 (e-book)

Published by Paulist Press
997 Macarthur Boulevard
Mahwah, New Jersey 07430
www.paulistpress.com

Printed and bound in the
United States of America

Contents

Acknowledgments

We are grateful to the following authors and publishers for permission to reprint the articles in this volume. Dean Baker, "Rising Inequality: It's Not the Market," *Journal of Catholic Social Thought* 12, no. 1 (Winter 2015): 5–17. Permission to reprint granted by *Journal of Catholic Social Thought*, Villanova University. Mary Jo Bane, "Social Conscience and Politics in the United States of America: Reflections," *International Journal of Public Theology* 5 (2011): 352–65. Permission to reprint granted by *International Journal of Public Theology*. Alison Benders, "Reconstructing the Moral Claim of Racially Unjust Incarceration," in *Today I Gave Myself Permission to Dream: Race and Incarceration in America*, ed. Erin Brigham and Kimberly Rae Connor (San Francisco: University of San Francisco Press, 2018), 47–57. Reprinted with permission. M. Shawn Copeland, "Anti-Blackness and White Supremacy in the Making of American Catholicism," *American Catholic Studies* 127, no. 3 (Fall 2016): 6–8. Reprinted with permission. Charles E. Curran, "Facing Up to Privilege Requires Conversion," *National Catholic Reporter*, June 18, 2016, 18–19. Robert DeFina and Lance Hannon, "Engaging the US Bishops' Pastoral on Crime and Criminal Justice: From Atomism to Community Justice," *Journal of Catholic Social Thought* 8, no. 1 (2011): 77–91. Permission to reprint granted by *Journal of Catholic Social Thought*, Villanova University. Lisa A. Fullam, "Pope Francis, Women, and the Church for the Poor," in *Pope Francis and the Future of Catholicism in the United States: The Challenges of Becoming a Church for the Poor*, ed. Erin Brigham, David E. DeCosse, and Michael Duffy (San Francisco: University of San Francisco Press, 2015), 55–63. Reprinted with permission. Katie M. Grimes, "Theology of Whose Body? Sexual Complementarity, Intersex Conditions, and La Virgin Guadalupe," *Journal of Feminist Studies in Religion* 32, no. 1 (Spring 2016): 75–93. Copyright © 2016, Indiana University Press, reprinted with permission of Indiana University Press; all rights reserved. Diana L. Hayes, "Faith of Our Mothers: Catholic Womanist

God-Talk," in *Uncommon Faithfulness: The Black Catholic Experience* (Maryknoll, NY: Orbis Books, 2009), 129–46. Copyright © 2009 by Orbis Books. Reprinted with permission. Kristin Heyer, "Radical Solidarity: Migration as Challenge for Contemporary Christian Ethics," *Journal of Catholic Social Thought* 14, no. 1 (2017): 87–104. Permission to reprint granted by *Journal of Catholic Social Thought*, Villanova University. Mary E. Hunt, "Catholic Lesbian Feminist Theology," in *Sexual Diversity and Catholicism toward the Development of Moral Theology* (Collegeville, MN: Liturgical Press, 2001), 289–304. Copyright © 2001 by Order of St. Benedict. Published by Liturgical Press, Collegeville, Minnesota. Used with permission. Mary Jo Iozzio, "God Bends Over Backward to Accommodate Human Kind…While Civil Rights Acts and the Americans with Disabilities Act Require [Only] Minimum Effort," *Journal of Moral Theology* 6, special issue 2 (2017): 10–31. Reprinted with permission. Ada María Isasi-Díaz, "*Mujerista* Theology: A Challenge to Traditional Theology," in Isasi-Diaz, *Mujerista Theology: A Theology for the Twenty-First Century* (Maryknoll, NY: Orbis Books, 1996), 59–85. Copyright © 1996 by Orbis Books. Reprinted with permission. Michael Jaycox, "The Black Lives Matter Movement: Justice and Health Equity," *Health Progress* 97, no. 6 (November–December 2016): 42–47. Reprinted with permission. M. Therese Lysaught, "Memory, Funerals, and the Communion of Saints: Growing Old and Practices of Remembering," in *Growing Old in Christ*, ed. Stanley Hauerwas, Carole B. Stoneking, Keith G. Meador, and David Cloutier (Grand Rapids, MI: Wm. B. Eerdmans Publishing Company, 2003), 267–301. Copyright © 2003 Wm. B. Eerdmans Publishing Co., Grand Rapids, MI. Reprinted by permission of the Publisher; all rights reserved. Bryan N. Massingale, "The Systemic Erasure of the Black/Dark-Skinned Body in Catholic Ethics," in *Catholic Theological Ethics: Past, Present, and Future; The Trento Conference* (Maryknoll, NY: Orbis Books, 2011), 116–24. Copyright © 2011 by Orbis Books. Reprinted with permission. Julie A. Mavity Maddalena, "Flood Waters and the Ticking Clock: The Systematic Oppression and Stigmatization of Poor, Single Mothers in American and Christian Theological Responses," *CrossCurrents* 63, no. 2 (June 2013): 158–73. Copyright © 2013 Association for Religion and Intellectual Life, reprinted with permission of Wiley Publications.

Foreword

U.S. Catholic Moral Theology at the Margins is volume 19 of the series Readings in Moral Theology from Paulist Press. Charles E. Curran and Richard A. McCormick, SJ, began editing this series in 1979. Lisa A. Fullam has joined Curran as coeditor of the last three volumes.

This book responds to the contemporary emphasis on the importance of theology at the margins. In the Catholic world, this emphasis began with liberation theology in Latin America and has recently found a home in the United States. Liberation theologians' insistence that the proper starting point for theology is standing with and alongside the poor and marginalized is echoed in another point of increased interest in contemporary moral theology: the role of experience in ethics. While experience has long been recognized as one of the four sources for moral reflection, it has increasingly come to be seen as providing a privileged perspective on moral questions. Margins, then, are frontiers, places of exploration and centers of insight.

It is impossible to cover all the areas involved at the margins, but this volume has chosen eight important issues—aging, disabilities, immigration, LGBTQ, poverty and economic inequality, prison, racism, and women at the margins. In keeping with the ethos of the series, this book brings together previously published materials. Some editing has been done to avoid repetition and to adapt the materials for this volume. Our aim is to recognize those who have made significant contribution in these areas and at the same time to include some younger scholars.

We invite you to think of this as a sampler—each topic is worthy of a volume (or more!) of its own, certainly. Some of our topics are already the subject of a broad literature, and others, we hope, will be. Our task in this volume is not to provide a full exploration of any of our issues, but to provide a glimpse of how moral theology looks when the perspective is not that of the dominant culture. In other words, what might our work look like when we are "recentered" in response to the call of the liberation theologians, when we take experience seriously, when we head to the frontier? The sheer amount of writing from these perspectives influences our decision to restrict this volume to the United States.

Readers may also note considerable respect for intersectionality in this collection: several of the essays could easily fit in more than one of our topics. For example, Heyer's essay on migration engages the gendered nature of that issue, so could also have been listed under our topic "of women at the margins," as well as immigration. Benders's essay on race and mass incarceration reflects both the realities of the contemporary prison-industrial complex and the racial disparities that mass incarceration foments. Several other essays are likewise polyvalent, reflecting two or more interweaving forms of marginalization or oppression.[1] Recognizing intersectionality is intrinsic to adequately engaging structures of oppression.

We editors express our appreciation and thanks to all the people who have assisted us in publishing this volume. The *Journal of Catholic Social Thought* and Orbis Books originally published seven of the articles we have republished here. Above all, we are grateful to Paulist Press for its willingness to sponsor and continue publishing this series. Father Mark-David Janus, CSP, has been most encouraging in supporting our efforts and continuing this long series. The staff of Paulist Press, especially our editor Donna Crilly, continue to assist us both graciously and competently. We also appreciate the work of our associates at our individual institutions who did much of the labor-intensive work of copyediting and reformatting these essays. Mey Saechao with graduate student Madeleine LaForge at the Jesuit School of Theology of Santa Clara University have done their customary excellent work. Lisa Hancock, a doctoral student in systematic theology in the Graduate Program in Religious Studies at Southern Methodist University, has been most helpful. Finally, we are grateful to Santa Clara University for a faculty grant supporting various editorial costs for this volume. Without that grant, this volume would have been greatly limited in scope.

Charles E. Curran
Lisa A. Fullam

Notes

1. *Intersectionality*, a term first coined by legal scholar/civil rights advocate Kimberlé Crenshaw in 1989, is the recognition, for example, that a singular focus on racism can "erase" the experiences of black women, while a singular focus on feminism can likewise render the distinctive challenges of women of color marginal, invisible, or unimportant. In fact, as Crenshaw notes, "Because the intersectional experience is greater than the sum of racism and sexism, any analysis that does not take intersectionality into account cannot sufficiently address the particular manner in which Black women are subordinated." Kimberlé Crenshaw, "Demarginalizing the Intersection of Race and Sex: A Black Feminist Critique of Antidiscrimination Doctrine, Feminist Theory and Antiracist Politics," *University of Chicago Legal Forum* 1989, iss. 1, art. 8 (1989): 140.

Part One

AGING

1. Memory, Funerals, and the Communion of Saints

Growing Old and Practices of Remembering

M. Therese Lysaught

This chapter first appeared in *Growing Old in Christ*. Edited by Stanley Hauerwas, Carole B. Stoneking, Keith G. Meador, and David Cloutier. Grand Rapids: Wm. B. Eerdmans Publishing Company, 2003.

Lord, for your faithful people, life is changed, not ended.[1]

Introduction

When I was ten, I first glimpsed that death and growing old were connected. That June, I spent the first of many three-week summertime visits, *sans* siblings, *sans* parents, with my then eighty-five-year-old great-grandmother, Nonny Dodie, also known as Mary Waldo (hence "Dodie") Nall Thume Foltz. Twice widowed, Nonny was a farm wife who, upon the death of her second husband, Alfred, a few years earlier, had sold the farm and moved into a small house in "town." A wide-eyed girl from a middle-class Chicago suburb, I learned much during those summers in the small, rural community of Sweetser, Indiana (population 967). Life was hard earned. Things wore out before they were thrown out. Nonny taught me how to make egg noodles and oatmeal cookies, applesauce, fried chicken, and wilted lettuce; that the makings of a good meal came mostly out of the cellar or were dropped off by friends; and that bacon grease was a necessary ingredient for making most dishes.

She likewise taught me about aches and pains, support hose, and that teeth could be taken out at night.

These summers also afforded me my first foray amongst Protestants. I not only attended Nonny's Methodist church but, more formatively, spent a good bit of time with the initially forbidding ladies of the church's sewing guild (to whom my mother sternly warned me *not* to broadcast the fact that I was Catholic, for fear of negative repercussions or bringing scandal on my great-grandmother, I don't know which). We sewed bandages for the Red Cross.

It was in this setting that I first learned about obituaries. Each morning, as we sat at the breakfast table with the heavy and already too hot summer breeze blowing the smell of musty wood through adjustable screens, my great-grandmother would pick up the newspaper and, before reading anything else, turn to the obituaries. This was how she started her day. More often than not, she would slowly raise her hand to her mouth, clasping her chin, shaking her head, and say, "Well, Lord have mercy. So-and-so's dead." Then would follow the eulogy—her story of who the dead person was, what kind of work he was in, who he was related to, how long she'd known the family, the troubles and triumphs in their life, some personal anecdote. She would wonder aloud how the family was bearing up, read to me the funeral information, and invariably close with the refrain: "I guess I'm getting old. Every week it seems I lose someone else. God'll be taking me one of these days. I wonder who'll be left to go to my funeral."

At first I thought it was rather morbid to start one's day by seeing who had died. Over time, however, I began to realize that this morning routine and the funerals that Nonny subsequently attended were of a piece with the textures and rhythms of life in Sweetser. It was a rare day that Gladys (her "young," sixty-ish friend) did not come by to pick her up to drive her somewhere: to visit relations, to visit acquaintances, to visit especially those widowed and those whose children had moved away, and to visit Alfred's grave. I, of course, accompanied her. It seemed that most of my time in Sweetser was spent making visits.

What is more, Nonny was far from the only one in Sweetser attending funerals and making visits. How did I know? My great-grandmother also happened to write the "social" column for two local newspapers. Her phone and doorbell rang many times daily with folks calling in or stopping by to report "the news," to report who had gotten married or been born or died, who had come to town, who had come to visit, who they themselves had gone to see, what they'd discovered thereupon, as well as who wore what and what sort of food was served. It soon became clear to me that in Sweetser, Indiana, not only was it nice to be visited; it was newsworthy.

Now, while my Nonny's habits of newspaper reading and visiting were no doubt in part artifacts of life in a farming community as well as semicovert means of gathering information for her column, I am convinced that these interconnected activities signaled something more profound. They bespoke a set of underlying practices that were subtle yet deeply formative and that witnessed to convictions about what mattered most. Indeed, if our beliefs are the way we live—or, rather, if what we believe is known best through the actions and practices that concretely structure our lives—then the citizens of Sweetser, Indiana, in the 1970s believed it to be crucially important to remember others and to be, in turn, remembered.

I tell this story because I think the lives of my Nonny and her community display an alternative to the contemporary professional discourse on aging. Circumscribed as they were by the medical-therapeutic-social work paradigm that dominates analyses of aging, they simply carried on a way of life that witnessed to fundamentally different convictions about growing old. Although my Nonny passed on a dozen years ago and I unfortunately cannot query her directly, I am going to take the liberty of trying to reconstruct the sort of convictions required to sustain the practices in which she participated. I will argue that these convictions challenge both the contemporary demonization of aging and the trend that seeks to counter that demonization by rehabilitating the notion of "memory." Increasingly in the therapeutic and pastoral literature, memory becomes both the primary service the elderly render to the community and the process through which growing old finds meaning. This rehabilitation of memory vis-à-vis aging arises from good intentions. Given that it subscribes to the same anthropological presuppositions as its opponents, however, it fails in the end to provide an adequate bulwark against those forces that would render the reality of growing old and care for the elderly among us unintelligible.

My Nonny's advanced age, her rural piety, and her practice of obituary reading suggest that while memory is certainly not unimportant for understanding what it means to grow old, memory needs to be construed differently. In fact, I believe her life points toward a theological re-reading of memory, encountered concretely through the Christian practice of the funeral liturgy and its affirmation of the communion of saints. Such a re-reading, I will argue, suggests that for Christians, growing old is read best not through "memory" but rather through practices of remembering. Such practices provide Christian communities and those who grow old among them a more adequate response to contemporary realities of aging as well as theologically formed habits of discipleship.

To outline this argument will require a number of steps. I begin with a brief display of the phenomenon of aging and the role of memory as it is presented in contemporary discourse. This leads to a discussion of the notion of memory, both in its philosophically normative mode and theologically re-read. This theological re-reading is displayed through the doctrine of the communion of saints through which Christians learn to remember the dead. These practices, in conjunction with remembering theologically construed, lead finally to an allied set of practices that circumscribes the realities of growing old within the discipleship of the body of Christ.

The Ambiguity of Aging

Aging is ambiguous. As Helen Oppenheimer notes, old age can be characterized as both fruition and decay, a time of both fulfillment and loss.[2] Bernard Nash describes aging as a paradox: "Does it strike you as strange that we all want to live longer but none of us wants to grow old?"[3] Both sides of this ambiguous paradox deserve brief exploration.[4]

What fruits and fulfillment do growing older bring? Why might people rightly desire to live longer? Apart from hopes for a secular sort of immortality, a certain degree of advanced age is simply required in order to experience particular joys and pleasures. These joys come as serendipitous gifts as well as fruit intrinsic to lifelong work in the service of valued practices: seeing one's grandchildren, having "old" friends, celebrating decades of marriage, earning the honor that attends a lifelong career. Growing older provides the opportunity to truly master certain skills, to practice them effortlessly, and to share them with new generations of apprentices. The prospect of retirement, attractive to those whose financial security is assured, promises the leisure to shift one's energies to new pursuits and areas of interest, unfettered by the responsibilities of raising children. And as Oppenheimer notes, "Just to have learnt more, to have seen more and to have more experience to draw upon are benefits bestowed by time which even the brightest youngster will have to wait a while to attain."[5]

As should come as no surprise, many elderly people do not feel "old" but rather maintain "that they still feel the same: perhaps still in their twenties."[6] The poet May Sarton, in her journal *At Seventy*, concurs and further remarks that she *loves* being "old":

> What is it like to be seventy? If someone else had lived so long and could remember things sixty years ago with great clarity, she would seem very old to me. But I do not feel old at all, not as much a survivor as a person still on her way....In the course of [a poetry reading] I said, "This is the best time of life. I love being old." At that point a voice from the audience asked loudly, "Why is it good to be old?" I answered spontaneously and a little on the defensive, for I sensed incredulity in the questioner, "Because I am more myself than I have ever been. There is less conflict. I am happier, more balanced, and, (I heard myself say rather aggressively) "more powerful." I felt it was rather an odd word, "powerful," but I think it is true. It might have been more accurate to say "I am better able to use my powers. I am surer of what my life is *all* about, have less self-doubt to conquer."[7]

Further on in her journal, Sarton extends these reflections in the context of inverting one of the biggest bogeys of aging (especially for women): wrinkled faces.

> Why do we worry about lines in our faces as we grow old? A face without lines that shows no mark of what has been lived through in a long life suggests something unlived, empty, behind it. Still, one mourns one's young face sometimes. It has to be admitted. I now use a night cream for the first time

> in my life. At the same time, as I went over photographs yesterday for a children's book of biographies in which I am included, I felt that my face is better now, and I like it better. That is because I am a far more complete and richer person than I was at twenty-five, when ambition and personal conflicts were paramount and there was a surface of sophistication that was not true of the person inside. Now I wear the inside person outside and am more comfortable with myself. In some ways, I am younger because I can admit vulnerability and more innocent because I do not have to pretend.[8]

The joys that attend aging, however, vary from person to person, especially as actual realities of growing old are shaped by personal context, class, gender, and culture. Even within the span of an individual life, one who finds seventy a time of fruition may find eighty-two more ambiguous or adverse. Indeed, cultural stereotypes generally construe growing old only in terms of its myriad possibilities for physical, mental, economic, and social diminishment. Not only is aging accompanied for many by real financial impoverishment, the disappointments of dreams unattained, betrayal by children or spouses, and the burdens of caring for physically and mentally diminished parents, spouses, and friends, but it also carries with it the threat of "dementia, deafness, blindness, arthritis, helplessness, even repulsiveness; and worst of all the loneliness of outliving one's contemporaries."[9] We see in the elderly around us that

> aging restricts mobility, diminishes senses, and impairs speech and thinking. It leads to a withdrawal from active public life and forces us in time to rely on the help of others to carry out the most basic daily activities;...the loss, suffering, and diminishment of old age [entail] disengagement, isolation, and dependence.[10]

Those who grow old inevitably find their lives becoming undone on a number of levels—their bodies and their minds begin shockingly to fail; capacities diminish; former proficiencies fade; youthful appearance disappears. Identity transmutes, as the former centers of their lives—either career or home—are literally taken away. Their communities unravel in a particularly poignant way, as they find themselves facing again and again the deaths of those with whom they have lived for decades, with whom their entire lives have been intertwined: parents, siblings, spouses, children, mentors, friends. It seems—with all of this taken together—that as one grows old, one's very self dissolves.

This latter dynamic lies at the root of contemporary constructions of aging. Just as Sarton describes the bounty of growing old in terms of the full bloom of her true "self," it is the dissolution of the self that is aging's bane. Given the modern positioning of the self as the source and end of all meaning, anything that threatens it will be feared. Indeed, even the most cursory survey of contemporary literature on aging reveals fear to be a dominant motif. The nature of this fear, however, is culturally determined. As Lucien Richard notes, "The fear of becoming old in our society is determined by the fear of losing those elements which constitute life's goal, and are perceived as the foundation of self-worth and personhood."[11] Thus behind the "problems" that aging poses within late-capitalistic, technologically hyperdriven, liberal Western culture lies a set of anthropological assumptions, convictions about what it means to be a "person."

The clearest and most compelling display of this anthropology can be found in H. Tristram Engelhardt's unvarnished articulation of the logic of liberal capitalist culture, *The Foundations of Bioethics*. Here Engelhardt identifies those elements required for personhood, namely that an entity be "self-conscious, rational, free to choose, and in possession of a sense of moral concern."[12] While others might name these characteristics slightly differently (as autonomy, freedom, self-sufficiency, etc.), a review of the traumas of aging listed above suggests that aging ultimately attacks and impairs personhood: rationality and self-consciousness are effaced via dementia and the impairment of speech and thinking, economic impoverishment, physical afflictions such as the restriction of mobility, blindness, deafness, arthritis, and the need to rely on others ravage freedom-to-choose and self-sufficiency.[13]

That aging can so dismantle the constituents of personhood has led Drew Christiansen to identify "the twin fears" of aging as the fear of dependence and the fear of abandonment and neglect.[14] While these may seem to point in different directions, they are integrally related. The prospect of dependence—whether it be physical, financial, or decisional—

entails the loss of autonomy and therefore, in our culture, compromises one's status as a person. To not be a "person" is to be vulnerable; civil and social protections apply almost exclusively to persons. In fact, Engelhardt describes how the loss of the above abilities moves one from being a "person in the strict sense," to whom the full gamut of rights and protections applies, to being a person "in the social sense." Persons in the social sense find no intrinsic basis for protection and are accorded such rights only insofar as they are important to "full" persons or serve some socially useful function. If they are not or do not, the further they slip away from the norm, the more open they are to any sort of treatment, including the ultimate in abandonment, namely, "being killed painlessly at non-malevolent whim."[15] Thus, it is not unreasonable to fear dependence, abandonment, and neglect under current cultural circumstances.

Memory or Remembering?

A recent move designed to temper the realities of dependency and stave off the threat of abandonment and neglect has been to relocate the center of the geriatric self not in rationality and autonomy but rather in "memory."

Indeed, memory has become one of the major motifs for giving meaning to the process of growing old. Whether it provides the basis for the recently developed pastorally or psychologically mediated therapeutic practice of "life review" or constitutes the elderly's specific contribution to society, the relationship between memory and aging is often depicted as follows:

> When we reach the "noon of life," the movement is toward the "twilight"; there is a turning inward. Our consciousness naturally reflects upon who we are, and we search for a vision of what we might become. Most of us are familiar with the proclivity of old people to tell stories about the past....What a pity it is that so many of us are loath to "waste the time" to listen....The story telling of the aging is a source for enriched memory and a stimulus for the imagination.... Another way to say this is that as we grow older the time

> we have (or appear to have) diminishes, but the space of our world should expand. Death comes closer and we can no longer think in terms of time measured in many years ahead, but we can gain more freedom to explore the space of our inner world. This is one way to describe a "second childhood," which is a bit like Paul Ricoeur's "second naivete." We move into what some have called a receptive mode of consciousness—as opposed to a mode of action—where images and free association within space take precedence over temporal, logical thinking, with its desire for prediction and control. We become like the little child, not in the literal foolishness of pretending to be one, but in the graceful wisdom of one who has recovered the capacity of wonder and surprise.[16]

Through memory, the elderly both have something to contribute to those who would only listen and find a place to explore their very selves in creative freedom.

This rehabilitation of memory in the service of aging stems from a number of sources. Historical memory seems to be primarily the reserve of the elderly—thus, it is something of value that they, and they alone, possess. Phenomenologically, the turn to memory finds validation in stereotypes—the "proclivity of old people to tell stories about the past" or the sense that elders tend to "live in the past." Biologically, short-term recall seems to become less reliable as one grows old but long-term memory often seems to sharpen.

But can "memory" so construed, and the practices it engenders, transmute the distress of dependency or provide a new status for the elderly among the community that will deter the threat of abandonment and neglect? Can it provide an account that makes our continued care for the elderly intelligible? Unfortunately, I think it cannot. Memory as it functions in this discourse serves simply as another way to shore up the disintegrating self; it seeks to establish a new basis for value and identity, apart from job or family, rooted in the individual. And for many who grow old, this will simply be insufficient. To show how this is the case requires a display of how memory is constructed within this discourse. For that we turn, of course, to Augustine.

From Augustine to Alzheimer's

The classic starting point for contemporary understandings of memory is Augustine's *Confessions*.[17] In Book Ten, his reflections on memory span no fewer than thirteen chapters (chaps. 8—20). The conclusions that he reaches in the course of these meditations seem rather obvious, indicating their commonsense nature as well as their historic influence on millennia of Western thought. Augustine begins in chapter 8 with a simple and straightforward observation, that memory is basically an archive—of images, knowledge, and experiences accumulated over a lifetime. It is "like a great field or a spacious palace," he notes, "a storehouse for countless images," a cloister, a vast sanctuary (X.8). This archive is definitely private, something within us, "an inner place" (X.9). But this description is not sufficient, he notes, for memory is surely more than merely a place; it is also an ability, a capacity. The idea of memory, then, implies not only the sum total of stored images but also the capacity to store and retrieve these images.

Augustine's study of memory continues in this vein, momentum building, and in chapter fourteen he makes a very important shift. Not only does he render memory as an archival faculty merely possessed by an individual; memory becomes equated with the self:

> But the mind and the memory are one and the same. We even call the memory the mind....Yet I do not understand the power of memory that is in myself, although without it I could not even speak of myself....The power of the memory is great, O Lord. It is awe-inspiring in its profound and incalculable complexity. Yet it is my mind; it is my self. (X.14, 16, 17)[18]

At this climax, two points become clear. First, memory is cognitive, an intellectual faculty and process, located *within* ourselves—"it is my mind." Second, "it is my self," the very essence of one's identity and being; or as Brian Horne notes, for Augustine "memory and personhood are coterminous...without memory the person cannot exist."[19]

This Augustinian position, that memory is internal, individual, a private storehouse of images and the ability to retrieve them, constitutive of self and identity, continues to powerfully dominate contemporary thought.[20] Richard Schaeffler, for example, reflecting on the memorial/anamnetic dimension of the Eucharist, attributes three powers to memory, one of which is

> to *discover* ourselves among our shifting experiences, so that we may construct, out of the abundance of stories we could tell, that one story of our own individual and social life that allows us to attribute that abundance of experiences to ourselves as their "subjects." This task is controlled by the idea of the "self," that is, by the conscious purpose of discovering within our life-situations the one characteristic way in which we have appropriated the external circumstances and their changes as *our own story*; how, in an equally characteristic way, we may have failed in that task; or how we have lost ourselves in the flood of events and retrieved ourselves from it.[21]

Thus, according to this account, memory is the vehicle through which I construct myself, through which I grasp my identity. It is the existential essence of the individual.

Reflections on memory and aging likewise reflect this standard account of memory. In Urban Holmes's earlier comments, for example, memory is found by turning inward to the space of our inner world. It is an intellectual process, an exercise of reflective consciousness, the function of which is to discover or construct our self and identity.

This way of construing memory vis-à-vis aging is troubling, however, in a number of ways. First, it may mask a latent focus on productivity as the locus of individual worth; pacifying a utilitarian calculus, those with memories have something to offer.[22] Second, as reflected in Holmes's comments, memory is situated as that activity particularly fitting to those who have no future. Dale Schlitt, likewise, in a reflection on aging and memory states, "Imperceptibly the threshold is crossed where one tends to locate one's primary point of reference no longer in the future or in those with whom one presently lives and works but in persons and events now recalled from the past."[23] But a third point is most problematic. If memory plays such an important role in the meaning of aging and is so crucial for personal identity, what do we make of the fact that as people age, memory is often precisely that which they lose? We are familiar with phrases like "she's not who she once was," "he's really no longer himself," and how those with diminished capacity are referred to as "shells of their former selves." Insofar as memory, premised as the foundation of the self that is internal and intellectual, recapitulates the terms of the liberal construction of the self that gives rise to the threats of dependence, abandonment, and neglect, it cannot withstand aging's ultimate threat.

Memory as remedy for the meaninglessness of aging fails most dramatically when faced with the dreaded loss of mental ability, captured most vividly in the possibility of Alzheimer's disease. Not only does Alzheimer's entail the most radical sort of dependence over a period of years or decades; the victim's very self disintegrates before the eyes of those who care for and love him as he loses not only his abilities and personality but even his very memories. This radical loss of self no appeal to memory can salve. Consequently, caring for those with Alzheimer's becomes completely unintelligible.

This is precisely the issue taken up by David Keck in his compelling book *Forgetting Whose We Are: Alzheimer's Disease and the Love of God.*[24] Like Augustine, Keck finds memory to be awe-inspiring in its power and complexity, and key to individual identity. But at the same time, through caring for his mother as Alzheimer's disease deconstructs her self, he finds that the reality of the disease challenges deeply held convictions about memory and selfhood that further challenges theological beliefs grounded in this anthropology:

> Ontologically, what happens in Alzheimer's? What becomes of a person and her memories? Is there a metaphysical basis for the human person which this disease does not destroy? The human subject in many ways lies at the center of contemporary theological reflection; we are presumed to be rational, self-actualizing, and intentional. But can we be confident about theologies predicated on a self-conscious, decision-making subject when a person may live for over ten years without any subjecthood?...How is it possible to speak of a personal relationship with God, when there seems

> to be no person left? Does the Holy Spirit depend on a conscious subject in order to be present or to provide comfort to a person?[25]

The above perspectives on memory emerge from anthropological reflection—Augustine's reflections on the working of his own mind, philosophical reflection on the construction of one's own personal narrative, and ethnographic reflection on the behavior and opportunities of those who grow old. But Keck's questions raise theological issues and as such require a theological starting point. A theological account of memory should begin with God's way of remembering, a thick description of which is found best, of course, in Scripture.

Memory Theologically Re-read

In Scripture we find that God remembers. From the beginning, God's remembering emerges as radically different from human memory as described above. First, God's remembering is crucial for human existence. To be remembered by God is to be held in existence, to live. To be forgotten, on the other hand, means death: "not to be remembered," Keck notes, "is 'not to exist.'...In Psalm 88, the person whom God has forgotten has no strength, is already in the grave, already in 'the regions dark and deep.'"[26]

But God's remembering is not simply the generic substrate of existence, a philosophical concept of "being." It is concrete, particular, pervasive.[27] To be remembered by God is to be healed, to have one's prayers heard and answered, and "to be assured of God's tender concern." Yahweh remembers specific individuals; God "remembered" Rachel (Gen 30:22) and Hannah (1 Sam 1:11, 19–20) and answered their prayers for children. The blinded Samson's strength is reborn when God answers his prayer to be remembered (Judg 16:28–30). God remembers not *only* individuals but Israel as well, as God remembers the covenant (e.g., Gen 9:16; 19:29; Lev 26:42–43; Deut 9:27; Ps 104:8–10; 105:45; 110:4–5; Ezek 16:60–63).[28]

Thus, a number of characteristics differentiate God's remembering from human memory. To begin with, it is cast as a verb rather than as a noun. Scripture rarely speaks of God's memory per se; God's memory is known only through God's acts. For God, therefore, remembering is not a cognitive, mental operation; rather, it entails efficacious, "providential, salvific activity."[29] As such, while God may remember the past (or remember it not, an act characterized as forgiveness), God's remembering primarily implies presence; when God remembers, God becomes present to individuals and to Israel. Consequently, God's remembering is other-oriented. We do not find God reviewing images in the divine mind in order to construct the divine "personal" identity; rather, God's acts of remembering, while contributing to God's identity, are primarily acts that constitute God's relationship with another. Thus, to speak of God's memory is not to speak first of identity but, as Keck notes, "to speak of God's fidelity."[30]

As relational, moreover, God's remembering calls forth a response.[31] As God faithfully remembers individuals, Israel, and the covenant, God likewise calls and expects Israel to faithfully remember as well. Keck notes, "After the great work of liberation wrought by God in the Exodus, itself a manifestation of God's faithful memory, it is Israel's duty to remember these deeds and to employ this communal memory as a spur to the fulfillment of the law."[32] Again, God does not want simple mental recall on the part of Israel; remembering entails action, namely, observance of the law, the remembering of God and others. "To remember God is a commandment," writes Keck, "but likewise so is remembering human beings. 'Remember those who are in prison' (Heb 13:3) and 'remember the poor' (Gal 2:10)."[33] Such remembering on the part of Israel and the early church entails not mental recollection but rather concrete acts of presence and service.

In practicing the law, the lives of the faithful become a tapestry of remembering. Although the memory of God's deeds and the observance of the law are essential to who they are as a people, however, Israel knows that the root of its identity lies not in its own memory but in the acts through which God remembered the Israelites, liberated them, covenanted with them, and constituted them as a people. It is God's remembering, therefore, that confers identity.

But while it is characteristic of God to remember, it is characteristic of humanity to forget. Time and again, Israel forgets the Lord, despite the imprecations of the psalmists and prophets ("Do not forget the works of the Lord," Ps 78:7), and forgets the widows, orphans, and strangers among them. Such forgetfulness of God and neighbor is equated with the descent into sin—either the sin of idolatry or the sin of injustice. Such forgetfulness of God and neighbor, time and again, sunders Israel's relation with God and precipitates its demise.

Yet although Israel and humanity forget, God remains faithful. God continues to remember even when forgotten. This is the essence of the paschal mystery, God's penultimate act of remembering. Here, the character of God's remembering as faithful, life-giving, efficacious, other-oriented, relationship-constituting, and identity-conferring is seen in all its fullness. God remembers us to the point of assuming human flesh and living among us, suffering our forgetfulness in his very body, and in rising, forgiving—or remembering our sins no more. Through God's act of remembering in Jesus we are given life anew; our enslavement to the tyranny of existential forgottenness—death—is vanquished.

Our task is then very simple: "Do this in remembrance of me." Thus, at the center of the life of discipleship, itself a tapestry of remembering, we remember God's great act of remembering that confers our identity; we celebrate the Eucharist. This remembering is not simply recall of a past event but is instead *anamnetic*, "an effective remembering that makes something genuinely past to be present and active in the community today."[34] We experience God's great act of remembering as present.

With this presence, eucharistic remembrance transforms our identity as we become a member of the one who is remembering us, a member of the body of Christ. As Merold Westphal notes, looking at remembrance from the obverse:

> To forget…is to prevent the forgotten from shaping our thought, feeling, and action as it should….When Jesus invites us to eat the bread and drink the wine "in remembrance of me"…here memory is not the ability to answer questions but *the openness to having our lives (trans)formed by what we attend to.*[35]

The key to this transformation is inherent in remembering itself. When we "remember," for Westphal, "the remembered event is to be renewed, or better, allowed to renew itself upon us in order that we may be renewed in a variety of senses that include regeneration and conversion."[36] As the elements are transformed into the body of Christ, eucharistic remembrance embeds our relationship with the divine, our renewed identities, in our very bodies. As our bodies become transformed by the events and Person we attend to, liturgical remembrance reveals that God remembers through the material, that the material world and indeed our very bodies—both individual and corporate—mediate God's grace. As Marjorie Proctor-Smith notes,

> Liturgical anamnesis involves not only remembering with the mind but also remembering with the body (individual and collective). More than the repetition of words, liturgical anamnesis involves the use of the body in gesture and movement, sometimes familiar, sometimes awkward. This bodiliness reminds us of the embodiment of divine activity in history, the Word made flesh. It also brings, experientially and dramatically, divine activity in to the present, not only in time but in space. The human body and human community then are seen as the locus for all this activity. This embodied remembering is found at the center of all Christian liturgy insofar as that liturgy remembers, and remembering celebrates, the paschal mystery of Jesus Christ crucified, dead, risen and present in the power of the Spirit.[37]

Through the Eucharist, our bodies shaped and transformed by God's remembering become enabled to mediate God's remembering to others, as we, through lives of discipleship, engage in concrete acts of remembering.

Theologically construed, therefore, the relationship between memory, selfhood, and identity emerges very differently from the Augustinian-based liberal account with which we began. It is not, primarily, that identity and the self reside in one's own personal recollection of one's own history; rather, identity is conferred through God's remembering of us and, correlatively, through our faithful remembering of God and each other. But it is clear that many of us are far more adept at forgetting than at remembering. The next question, then, is where do we learn how to remember? More specifically, where do we learn how to remember each other in the way that God remembers?

Oddly enough, within the Christian community, one of the primary places we learn how to remember the living is where we learn to remember the dead—through that remarkable Christian practice of remembering, namely, the practice of funerals.[38]

Funerals and the Communion of Saints

That Christians hold funerals seems neither particularly remarkable nor unique. But what Christians do and proclaim in the course of funeral rites is rather extraordinary. For here Christians remember those whose minds and bodies have disintegrated in the most radical of ways, whose lives have certainly "changed but not ended." In doing so, funerals shape and train us to remember each other, particularly those whose minds and bodies have begun to diminish, those who grow old among us, whose lives likewise are changing but not ended. As they proclaim that the dead are indeed alive, the funeral rites remind us that what is determinative for our identity is not that we are selves but that we are saints. In doing so, they provide a radically different lens through which to see—and thereby remember—those among us who are isolated and marginalized. Finally, as we participate in the rites, we learn to remember as God remembers—as concrete, particular, active, other-oriented, present, eucharistic, embodied, life-giving, relationshipconstituting, and reconciling.

Remembering with the Angels and Martyrs

Not only is God present to the one who has died, but the rite summons the hosts of heaven to accompany and welcome the dead: "May the angels lead you to paradise; May the martyrs come to welcome you and take you to the holy city, the new and eternal Jerusalem" ("Order of Christian Funerals," no. 176).[39] The rites ask God to "admit him/her to the joyful company of your saints" (no. 64). The dead, we believe, are alive in the company or, better, the "communion of saints."

In popular parlance, the notion of the communion of saints seems primarily eschatological; it says something about what happens to people when they die. But, as Elizabeth Johnson demonstrates in her valuable retrieval of the doctrine in *Friends of God and Prophets: A Feminist Theological Reading of the Communion of Saints*, historically it is rather first and more centrally ecclesiological. The concept indicates as much—or more—about the nature of the church as it does about the nature of the afterlife.

The doctrine emerges out of Paul's use of the term "the saints" (*hagioi*). For Paul, the term *saint* refers not primarily to the dead, nor primarily to individuals, nor even to morally or spiritually righteous exemplars, but rather to the community as a whole, a community made holy by the presence and activity of God.[40] As Johnson notes,

> The net effect of being part of this community is that all members are considered participants in the holy life of God. This comes about not because of a state of life they choose or a set of virtues they practice, not because of their innocence or perfection, but because of the gift of the Spirit who is given to all. The Spirit of life who raised Jesus from the dead is poured out on them and they are clothed with Christ, being transformed into the very image of Christ. As always, this is a gift freely given. Its effect is to create a community in grace....Its extensive use in reference to the community of living Christians reflects the heat and vigor of their sense of the presence and action of God in their midst through the life, death, and resurrection of Jesus Christ, which leads to a sharing of physical and spiritual goods among themselves.[41]

Thus, the term *saint* is a theological and ecclesial claim. Through God's gracious action and vital, ongoing presence within the community, God has rendered those baptized into the church as "saints" and has rendered the church as a whole a "communion of saints." The term further indicates the scope of the church, confidently positing "a bond of companionship among living persons themselves who, though widely separated geographically, form one church community."[42]

Likewise, it confidently posits a bond of companionship between the living and the dead, a confidence rooted not in a naive realism or an archaic cosmology but in an ecclesial and sacramental ontology. The practical and theological foundation for the communion of saints is baptism and the Eucharist. Through baptism we become members of the church; through the Eucharist we become members of one body, the bonds of which death's destructive power cannot sever.

Thus, through the Eucharist, through the communion of holy things, not only are the living rendered a communion of saints, but insofar as death cannot separate us from the love of God and membership in the body of Christ, the dead remain with us, tied to us in one church, one body, one communion. As the *Order of Christian Funerals* affirms,

> In partaking in the body of Christ, all are given a foretaste of eternal life in Christ and are united with Christ, with each other, and with all the faithful, living and dead: "Because there is one bread, we who are many are one body, for we all partake of the one bread" (1 Corinthians 10:17). (no.143)

Bonded together in communion, the living and dead continue to care for each other through practices of remembrance. The earliest evidence of Christian funerary practices indicates that prayer of the living for the dead has been considered part of appropriate care for the dead since the beginning. Early Christians offered prayers of praise and thanksgiving, prayed to accompany the deceased on their journeys, and asked God that the deceased would find rest. The church continues this prayer today. As eucharistic and anamnetic, through prayer we come into each other's presence in an active, embodied way, speaking concretely, going out of ourselves toward the other in a way that is creative, healing, life-giving, and salvific. Keck concurs:

> Such a prayer affirms that our responsibilities as caregivers do not cease. Prayer then is not just a mental act of memory and commemoration. It is a real work of the soul which links the living, the dead, and their God. It is a real work of caregiving. (We may add, that in the churches which believe in intercessory saints, caregiving prayer is offered both for the dead and by the dead—the deceased, too, are care-givers).[43]

The doctrine of the communion of saints echoes this belief that the deceased act as caregivers as well; they remain active in prayer in remembering the living. According to Johnson, with the practice of remembering and venerating the martyrs arose the practice of directly calling on them for prayers. Within this context, the martyrs were seen as partners, co-disciples, mutual companions in Christ, reflecting a vigorous sense of continuing companionship between the dead and the living. Just as living members of the church would pray for each other in their struggles to be faithful disciples, so the martyrs were called upon for their prayers as "a specific way of evoking the solidarity that existed between pilgrims on earth and those who had been sealed with the victory of Christ. These latter were asked to participate in Christ's continuing intercession and remember before God their brothers and sisters who had not yet run the whole course."[44] This understanding of the prayer of the dead was simply an extension of the ordinary Christian practice of the church as communion, the practice of praying for others, for support and specific intentions. As Johnson notes,

> Scripture encourages persons to pray for all human beings and for specific needs and is replete with examples of people praying for each other....Such prayer functions as a key way of expressing love and concern for others....If living persons can and do ask each other for the encouragement of prayer, must that stop when persons die?
>
> The saints in heaven...are with their companions on earth in one community of grace. [If so], then calling on a saint in heaven to "pray for us" is one particular, limited, concrete expression of this solidarity in the Spirit.[45]

Keck further observes, in reflecting imaginatively on the afterlife: "Indeed, we may wonder if it is possible for someone to have experiences of God's presence and not desire to share them with others, just as the Triune God who is self-communicating love seeks to share his love with his creation."[46] The dead pray for the living, we believe, because they are immersed in the joyous presence of God, which their souls, shaped as self-communicating love, cannot help but impart, but also because they remain disciples, wayfarers with us on the journey toward the kingdom.

One specific form of caregiving in particular is worth mentioning, namely, forgiveness and reconciliation. Given that central to God's remembering is the forgetting of our sin in reconciling us to himself, one of the concrete ways in which our remembering of the deceased is normed by God's prior act is as reconciliation. Bishop Kallistos Ware makes this point well:

> All too easily it can happen that we postpone seeking a reconciliation with someone whom we have alienated, and death intervenes before we have forgiven each other. In bitter remorse, we are tempted to say to ourselves: "Too late, too late, the chance has gone forever; there is nothing more to be done." But we are altogether mistaken, for it is *not* too late. On the contrary, we can go home this very day, and in our evening prayers we can speak directly to the dead friend from whom we were estranged. Using the same words that we would employ if they were still alive and we were meeting them face to face, we can ask their forgiveness and reaffirm our love. And from that very moment our mutual relationship will be changed.[47]

Thus, remembering as reconciliation can be a transformative, renewing, even conversional practice of mutual caregiving. Moreover, it may take different forms. It might entail acting to foster reconciliation between the deceased and another person or to make practical amends for a wrong one committed against the deceased. And beyond prayer and reconciliation, acts of remembering might also include attending to the deceased's former responsibilities—for example, visiting the deceased's elderly parents; carrying on the work of those martyred; providing companionship to those who mourn the loss.

And so, the Christian practice of funerals boldly immerses us in a theological reality—one comprised of a vibrant community between the living and those diminished to the point of death, sustained by God's gracious remembering. Through the rites we discover that the deceased remain present with us in the communion of saints, engaged together with us in mutual practices of remembrance as care. And if this is true for the deceased, how much more is it the case for those visibly among us? In learning to remember the dead and that we are remembered by them, we are simultaneously reoriented toward those among us, living but diminished. We learn to remember those who grow old.

Saints and Disciples: Remembering Those Who Grow Old

And so it turns out that making visits is a profoundly theological practice.[48] Through unassuming, everyday activities, ordinary folks in Sweetser, Indiana, engaged in an important mode of discipleship. They remembered the dead, through funerals and cemetery visits, and they remembered each other; they remembered those among them who had "grown old." In doing so, their lives gave witness to fundamentally different convictions about what it means to grow old and to what practices are appropriate for caring for the elderly among us.

Fundamental to these practices is a basic affirmation: that what is determinative for the elderly is not whether they qualify as "persons," nor their individual memory of their personal story, nor that they can share historical memories with others, but rather simply that they, as much as any other member of the body of Christ, are in fact "saints." To be clear, the term *saint* refers not to some degree of moral or spiritual perfection, implying that the elderly, because they have more time for spiritual introspection and prayer, are somehow closer to God. Indeed, as many age they seem to become the antithesis of our narrow notions of saints. Personal eccentricities magnify into embarrassing or frustrating obsessions; they become set in their ways, critical of innovation, cantankerous, loudly complaining of their loneliness and bodily afflictions. Moreover, little perfection or spiritual depth seems to be found in those who suffer dementia, who must be watched, fed, helped in the bathroom, and dressed, as hostility, obscenity, and irrational mutterings are tolerated. What might it mean, then, to look anew at our aging neighbors—indeed, our parents—and see them as saints? It means that the Spirit of Life who raised Jesus from the dead has been poured out on them and has transformed them into the very image of Christ. It means that God remains present and active with them, among us, in a vital and vigorous way, so that among us there is mutual sharing of physical and spiritual goods.

Now, in some ways, this may not seem like a terribly profound claim. But I would argue that it has profound implications both for how the elderly construe themselves and for how the Christian community understands the status of growing old. As the relationship among the members of the communion of saints is constituted by practices of remembrance as care, so it should be with regard to those who grow old. While it is difficult to specify such practices in too much detail apart from their display in a concrete community, the broad outlines of such an approach can be sketched.

Growing Old in Discipleship

Turning first to the elderly themselves, redescribing them as saints suggests that, even as they grow old, the elderly remain disciples. For those who grow old in Christian community, "retirement" is not an option. Just as death does not dispense one from continuing to follow the call to discipleship, the elderly, as members of the ecclesial community, remain called to a vocation, a ministry, to concrete practices of care modeled on God's remembering. They remain called equally to the practices of the corporal and spiritual works of mercy, to theological reflection, to prayer and worship, to liturgical ministry, to sharing the faith with the young, and to the promotion of social justice. The elderly minister to others in the community in a variety of ways, offering their historical memories, their example and wisdom, to those who seek to navigate paths they have already traversed—the struggles of marriage, child-rearing, or forgiveness and reconciliation. In continuing to follow the call of discipleship, they witness to the fact that identity is rooted not in employment or autonomous self-achievement, challenging the perspective of those of us preoccupied with these pursuits. Given the diversity and individuality among those who grow old, the vocations and ministries to which they are called will be as varied as for those at any other stage of life. The elderly, with the community, must continually discern how they can persist in the work of discipleship as their circumstances change.[49] The community must likewise foster this call and welcome their gifts of ministry and service, especially in public sacramental ministries.[50] And as importantly, the church must discern the vocation of those who are diminished, those with Alzheimer's, for example, who seem to have nothing to offer. They remain, after all, saints.

Thus, the communion of saints not only "forges intergenerational bonds across time that sustain faith in strange new times and places."[51] In recasting the elderly as saints and disciples, the communion of saints forges intergenerational bonds among those in the community. It challenges those approaches to "religion and aging" that situate the elderly in a passive, receptive position, as primarily recipients of the ministrations of others.

Construing the elderly as saints and disciples likewise challenges another troubling tenet of contemporary discourse on aging. As Mary M. Knutsen comments, "A common and influential image of human development in aging is that of an upward and then downward curve centered on work and economic productivity and characterized by a 'mid-life crisis' (the beginning of the downward curve) and finding its final denouement in retirement."[52] As was noted earlier, those who are in the "twilight" of their lives are characterized as spending a greater proportion of their time reminiscing about the past, since the past is all they have in terms of either identity or what they have to offer.[53] Understanding the elderly as members of the communion of saints, however, means, at minimum, that they have a future. While that future surely includes the experience of their own death, more importantly, it is a future that includes those who will remain behind. In that future, they will be reunited in a new and concrete way with those who have preceded them in death. And, although they may feel alone now, grieving the loss of their parents, spouse, siblings, and friends, the communion of saints reminds them that they are not—those who have gone before us remain with us.

Remembering as a Communal Practice

Given the realities of aging, however, the elderly are not only disciples but need to be ministered to as well. As disciples, we are called to remember as God remembers—as concrete, particular, active, other-oriented, present, eucharistic, embodied, life-giving, relationship-constituting, faithful, and reconciling. This challenges human tendencies to count good intentions or mental recollection as remembering or to value interactions with the elderly that are primarily self-oriented and controlling.

To remember is to act; thus, remembering the elderly will be embodied in concrete activities.[54] As often as these activities may be meaningful and enjoyable, they may also be onerous, boring, painful, unpleasant, constraining, and take valuable time away from our schedules and priorities. As Keck reminds us, "Remembering, after *all*, takes time, and…entails distinct responsibilities."[55]

The most basic act of remembering, and fundamental to all others, is simply the act of being present. As Keck astutely observes, "As anyone in a nursing home will tell us, not only is it important be remembered, it is also crucial to be visited."[56] Those who have visited nursing homes know how valuable a commodity such visits are for the residents and how devastating it is for those whose children never come. Like God's remembering of us, our presence to the elderly as we remember them sustains them.

Beyond visiting, remembering takes as many forms as there are people who grow old. But certain common practices are important. Growing old invariably entails the loss of those who structure one's life—spouses, siblings, parents, friends. An important concrete act of remembering is that of consolation and ministry to the grieving in times of death. We are called to the sometimes-uncomfortable task of encouraging the elderly to talk about one who has died and of being present and listening as they do so, as they cry, not just during a "legitimate" period of mourning but on an ongoing basis.

Beyond simply listening, the "Order of Christian Funerals" counsels continuous, concrete practices of care for those who mourn, extending to "act[s] of kindness, for example, assisting them with some of the routine tasks of daily living" (no. 10). Assistance with the mundane and everyday is no less crucial for the elderly, examples of which could multiply: "assistance in activities that are a routine part of living: shopping, cooking, cleaning, banking, and so on…nursing chores, such as bathing, grooming, and supervising medication…sharing social activities such as visiting, listening to stories, sharing feelings, and so on…and [facilitating] the authority competent adults exercise over fundamental aspects of their lives."[57]

All too often, these activities are assumed to be the sole responsibility of family members. As such, they can be overwhelming. The funeral rite, however, reminds us that remembering is a communal activity, that responsibility for remembering lies not only with family members but rather with the whole church. At minimum, dispersing the concrete, mundane tasks of care required to sustain the elderly makes the burden of doing so less onerous; but it also concretely renders the community as the body of Christ. As David Keck notes,

> Supporting this Herculean (or better, Samsonian) task of the caregivers is one of the ways in which non-caregivers can most clearly fulfill their call to join the body of Christ. In 1 Corinthians 12, Paul describes the diversity of the body's parts as a way of describing the different gifts of the Spirit and tasks of diverse Christians. So too can we see that those who come by for visits with caregivers, perhaps bringing home-made soup, or who serve as part-time caregivers in their different roles help to form the body of Christ into which Christians are baptized. These seemingly simple tasks (which require so much effort and are not done frequently) help make us one.[58]

But remembering as a communal practice can encompass more than the mundane. A wonderful display of a community that took seriously this responsibility can be found in Curtis Freeman's essay "What Shall We Do about Norman?"[59] Freeman recounts how his parish, "Norman's church family," found themselves charged unexpectedly with the task of deciding whether Norman, a seventy-nine-year-old friend and member who suffered a heart attack and fell into a permanent vegetative state (PVS), should be sustained with medical treatment or allowed to die. A task generally reserved as almost sacred for family members or special appointees, proxy consent became proper to them not only because of their friendship but because of Norman's "identity as a member of the community of God's new creation which we witnessed in his Christian baptism on May 9, 1926."[60] As he was one of the saints among them, the community found that remembering Norman took the form not only of keeping vigil with him in the hospital as he lay dying but also of an extended and deliberative communal process of discernment and eventually decision-making.

Freeman's account of his community's care for Norman also reminds us that from baptism to death, the community assumes responsibility for the faith of its members. The central moral question became for them,

> How could we as a community of discernment assist Norman to live with integrity the life which he owned in baptism?... Even in a PVS Norman remained part of the community he joined in baptism, and he was still responsible for living his life in keeping with that baptismal pledge. Our role was to support and sustain him in those decisions which we understood to be consistent with faithful discipleship.[61]

Freeman's account renders the community as co-disciples, responsible not for helping its members to achieve the personal fulfillment of an autonomous self but rather for helping them to be faithful to the life embraced in baptism. Keck takes this claim one step further, suggesting that an important task in remembering the elderly may be to assume the responsibility of believing for them. While this certainly defies understandings of faith that privilege individual rationality and autonomy, it gains credence within a framework of communal identity premised in the resurrection:

> Because the patient seems to lose all capacities of subjecthood, it is the work done by others for him which becomes crucial. As the community accepts the responsibility of believing for a newly-baptized infant, so too at the end of life does the church accept this task for those in end-stage dementia....In light of Alzheimer's we come to recognize that we sometimes must do the believing for others. As we assume this heavy responsibility, we should consider that we have a particular responsibility not to underbelieve. That is, as we bear the fullness of a person through the last years of dementia, so too should we bear the abundance of the resurrection and God's work for us. Not everyone can bear this plenitude—either as a caregiver or a Christian—but, as

> caregivers strive to sustain the fullness of a person, so should the body of Christ seek to bear the fullness of his work.[62]

Thus, through concrete practices of remembering, the Christian community rescues the elderly—even those with Alzheimer's or those in a persistent vegetative state—from abandonment and neglect. It is in this context especially that failure to remember—or forgetting of the elderly—correlates with alienation and death, and thus becomes an act of sin. Forgetfulness sunders not only our relationship with God but also human relationships: "the adulterer forgets the spouse, the rich forget the poor, the friend forgets the friend. We forget the simplest acts of writing thank you and birthday cards. Perhaps we are too busy to remember."[63] For the elderly especially, "not to be remembered," to be forgotten, is a cause of deep pain and despair, sometimes even making them wish they no longer existed.

But we do forget. Perhaps we are too busy. The structures of aging, which remove the sick and elderly to places like nursing homes, facilitate our forgetfulness. Thus, crucial to practices of remembering are practices of forgiveness and reconciliation. In all the relationships entailed in this communion of saints, significant need remains for reconciliation: between the elderly and their companions who have died as well as between the elderly and those who comprise their communities. Remembering the elderly as an act of presence will require the painful remembering of harms they have committed against us and we against them. To be a people capable of remembering as God remembers, we must remember our sins, committed in the past, as well as our ongoing failures, and in remembering seek forgiveness and reconciliation.

Such reconciliation will be not be easy, nor will it be superficial, simply therapeutic, or painless. The remembered acts of sin, failure, and harm in all their ugliness will renew themselves upon us, released from where they have festered. We will recognize them as part of our mutual identities; we will recognize that the past cannot be changed nor, in most instances, made right. On their own such acts would continue to sunder the very relationship for whose sake we remember them. Thus, reconciliation must be normed and made possible by the act of remembering that constitutes our unity, namely, the Eucharist. Only in this context, when the act of God's forgiveness in Jesus Christ likewise renews itself on us, can practices of reconciliation as remembrance be transformative.[64]

Not only does the Eucharist provide a context for enabling reconciliation, it also provides the center from which further liturgical practices of remembrance spring. The prayer of the community is a form of remembering that makes present and thereby unites those separated with the community. In the prayers of petition or intercession, the community prays for those who are sick and for those absent from the worship gathering. As the funeral liturgy attends to the grief that accompanies death, so the Christian community needs to attend to the fears, diminishment, and grief that accompany the losses and illnesses of aging, praying for the specific needs of those in their midst. Related sacramental activities, such as commissioning ministers to bring Communion to the sick and shut-ins and the practice of anointing of the sick, are further acts whereby the community as ecclesia makes itself present to those who are separated.

This eucharistic context suggests one final dimension of practices of remembering. As noted earlier regarding the dead, an important part of the refusal to deny death is the attention to the body during the funeral rites—from the personal care of the bodies of the dead to the presence of the body at the funeral liturgy, the materiality of the eucharistic celebration, and the affirmation that resurrection is indeed bodily. Likewise, learning to read aging through the baptismal and eucharistic context of funerals helps to challenge cultural tendencies to deny the bodies of the elderly: to treat them as a medical problem to be solved, as undignified failures from the norm of which we should be ashamed, or, in a dualist modality, as separable from a brain-centered notion of personhood. These ways of situating aging bodies each suggest that real bodies might be expendable: if the "problems" they present cannot be solved with technology, if they compromise dignity individually defined, or if specific intellectual faculties become impaired.

Over against these constructs, the affirmation of the resurrection of the body situates aging bodies differently. The resurrection affirms that our bodies, our very materiality given to us in our creation, are integral to who we are as persons. Our bodies are members of the body of Christ, a capacity or character that aging cannot erase. God has entered into this very materiality and so, even in a diminished capacity, our bodies remain vehicles of God's grace. Contrary to accounts that construe aging bodies as falling away from the human norm, Mary Knutsen suggests that aging bodies be read rather as an actualization of the incarnation and paschal mystery:

> Bodies are the very medium of communion with God, with others, and with the earth—and so the medium of all joy.... At the center of God's own triune life [is] the incarnation of God in Jesus Christ, God "deep in the flesh" of bodily, finite, cruciform human life. For Christians, growth into the actuality of particular, finite bodies with age is an ever-deepening journey into God "deep in the flesh" in Jesus Christ, an ever-deepening actualization of our baptism into the corporeal and communal body of Christ. Hence aging and death need to be seen not just as part of the "downward slope" of human life but in light of the paschal mystery of Christ.[65]

That this light is the paschal mystery is important, for as crucial as the resurrection is in affirming the intrinsic value and importance of our bodies as they age, the crucified, suffering body of Christ cannot yet be dismissed. The embodied experience of growing old is often one of significant physical infirmity, illness, loss, and suffering, and the "fear of pain and suffering" could be added as a third to Drew Christiansen's twin fears of aging mentioned earlier (the fear of dependence and the fear of abandonment and neglect). The journey into actuality described by Knutsen is one in which we enter increasingly into our finitude and the fallen nature of creation. Although we trust that our bodies will be taken up into the resurrection and ultimately transformed when creation is renewed, for now the diminishment and disintegration of our bodies—even unto death—must be seen "as intimately connected with sin, which crucified Christ and which violates and rips life with each other and God."[66] Thus, while such diminishment is not to be welcomed and can legitimately be addressed, neither is it to be escaped by eliminating or devaluing the bodies of the elderly. Situated within the paschal mystery, the elderly in their bodies, and we as we tend to them, meet Christ who suffers the depths of pain, suffering, sickness, and death.[67] Thus, the practices of remembering, especially those that entail particular attention to the bodies of the aging, take on new significance. Normed by the Eucharist, they take on a sacramental dimension in their own right.

Lord, for Your Faithful People, Life Is Changed, Not Ended

Thus we find that theological re-reading of memory, practiced through funerals and the communion of saints, challenges the dominant ideology of the self that so devastates us as we grow old. It challenges the ideology of personhood as comprised solely of rationality and autonomy. The communion of saints reminds us that dependence, or rather interdependence,[68] is not a developmental and alien challenge to the foundation of our personhood but rather is constitutive of Christian identity from the beginning.[69] At the same time, the reality of the communion of saints situates the elderly as equal partners in the body of Christ; without the elderly, the church is not complete.[70] Thus, abandonment and neglect of the elderly are not only unfortunate afflictions attendant upon aging; when present within Christian communities they stand as indictments of sinfulness and of the communities' failure to be the church.

Likewise, this account challenges the ideology of memory, critiquing its continued privileging of a notion of the self individually construed. A theological reading of growing old locates identity not individually but rather communally. One's identity as a member of the body of Christ comes not as an individual achievement but rather as a gift, as God remembers us and makes us saints, participants in the holy life of the Trinity. Such an identity, such a foundation for who we are, the ravages of aging cannot efface, not even unto death.

What becomes important, then, is not so much that those who grow old can remember but rather that we, as a community, actively and concretely remember them. In so doing, we become a people of memory, faithful to God's way of sustaining his creation—a people for whom life will always change but never end. This my great-grandmother began to teach me when I was ten years old.[71]

Notes

1. International Commission on English in the Liturgy, "Preface of Christian Death I," in *The Sacramentary: The Roman Missal*, English translation prepared by the International Commission on English in the Liturgy (New York: Collins World, 1974), 493.

2. Helen Oppenheimer, "Reflections on the Experience of Aging," in *Aging*, ed. Lisa Sowle Cahill and Dietmar Mieth (Philadelphia: Trinity Press International, 1996), 41–44.

3. Bernard Nash, "Reworking the Image," *The Witness* 76 (January/February1993): 11.

4. Given that the social construction of aging has already been well described by previous essays (in *Growing Old in Christ*), I shall here note only the most general contours.

5. Oppenheimer, "Reflections on the Experience of Aging," 41.

6. Oppenheimer, "Reflections on the Experience of Aging," 41.

7. May Sarton, *At Seventy: A Journal* (New York: W. W. Norton, 1984), 10.

8. Sarton, *At Seventy*, 60–61.

9. Oppenheimer, "Reflections on the Experience of Aging," 43.

10. Drew Christiansen, "A Catholic Perspective," in *Aging, Spirituality and Religion: A Handbook*, ed. Melvin A. Kimble et al. (Minneapolis: Fortress, 1995), 404.

11. Lucien Richard, "Toward a Theology of Aging," *Science et Esprit* 34, no. 3 (1982): 274.

12. H. Tristram Engelhardt Jr., *The Foundations of Bioethics*, 2nd ed. (New York: Oxford University Press, 1996), 136.

13. Apart from discussions of Alzheimer's and other forms of dementia, there is little or no sense that aging impacts one's "possession of a sense of moral concern." In fact, the elderly are often described in terms that render them guardians of "morality" or spirituality.

14. Christiansen, "A Catholic Perspective," 406.

15. Engelhardt, *Foundations of Bioethics*, 146.

16. Urban T. Holmes, "Worship and Aging: Memory and Repentance," in *Ministry with the Aging*, ed. William M. Clements (San Francisco: Harper and Row, 1991), 96–97. One of my, shall we say, "older" colleagues, Father Jack McGrath, remarked upon reading this passage that "many, many older people *love* prediction and control." I think Father McGrath's response points to the possibility that many, many older people would not recognize themselves in the literature on aging. This leads one to speculate on how this professional discourse

seeks to shape the elderly in specific normative ways, and to postulate what ends such formation may serve.

17. Augustine, *Confessions*, trans. R. S. Pine-Coffin (New York: Penguin, 1961). References will be given parenthetically within the text.

18. David Keck observes that "many, perhaps most, modern theologians follow Hume in his shift from talk of a soul to concentration on a 'self.' This 'self' becomes the referent of bundles of impressions, ideas, and thoughts which exhibit continuity over time in each person's own consciousness" (*Forgetting Whose We Are: Alzheimer's Disease and the Love of God* [Nashville: Abingdon,1996], 106). Given Augustine's reflections on memory, we might trace this back farther than Hume.

19. Brian L. Horne, "Person as Confession: Augustine of Hippo," in *Persons, Divine and Human*, ed. Christoph Schwobel and Colin E. Gunton (Edinburgh: T&T Clark, 1991), 71.

20. See, e.g., K. Brynolf Lyon, "The Unwelcome Presence: The Practical Moral Intention of Remembering," *Encounter* 48, no. 1 (Winter 1987): 139; Keck, *Forgetting Whose We Are*, 126; Marjorie Proctor-Smith, "Liturgical Anamnesis and Women's Memory: 'Something Missing,'" *Worship* 61 (September 1987): 407–8; Dale M. Schlitt, "Temporality, Experience, and Memory: Theological Reflections on Aging," *Eglise et Théologie* 16 (1985): 89; and Richard Schaeffler, "'Therefore We Remember...': The Connection between Remembrance and Hope in the Present of the Liturgical Celebration; Religious-Philosophical Reflections on a Religious Understanding of Time," in *The Meaning of the Liturgy*, ed. A. Haussling (Collegeville, MN: Liturgical Press, 1991), 15–16.

21. Schaeffler, "Therefore We Remember," 20.

22. In other words, to caricature this position: the elderly no longer have anything to contribute to society except their memories or "wisdom," which, as a valuable commodity under a market model, can be traded for our continued support of them.

23. Schlitt, "Temporality, Experience, and Memory," 99. It is interesting that this observation occurs in a subsection entitled "The Aging from an Augustinian Perspective on Memory."

24. As may be clear, I am deeply indebted to David Keck's remarkable reflections on memory in the second chapter of this exceptional book.

25. Keck, *Forgetting Whose We Are*, 39–40. Rabbi Hershel Matt, a nursing home chaplain, casts this question in terms of the *imago Dei*. Noting that traditionally the notion of creation-in-the-image refers to intellectual, rational, psychological, or spiritual human faculties, he asks, "What can be said, however, when mind itself falters and regresses, and when such mental capacities as reason, logic, memory, recognition, response, imagination, anticipation—all

of them surely aspects of the 'image'—begin to deteriorate and function only feebly or intermittently?" ("Fading Image of God? Theological Reflections of a Nursing Home Chaplain," *Judaism* 36 [Winter 1987]: 78). His conclusion is that the image of God is indeed effaced.

26. Keck, *Forgetting Whose We Are*, 43. See also Proctor-Smith: "To be forgotten by God is to die; to be remembered by God is to live" ("Liturgical Anamnesis and Women's Memory," 412).

27. Merold Westphal's account of Christian memory likewise emphasizes this particularity: "Christian memory is radically different from Platonic recollection....Christian memory opens itself to an historical event in all of its unique particularity....The term *event* is appropriate here because it signifies that Christian memory resists the dissolution of the temporal and particular in the eternal and universal" ("Lest We Forget," *Perspectives* [February 1996]:11).

28. Keck, *Forgetting Whose We Are*, 43–48, and Proctor-Smith, "Liturgical Anamnesis and Women's Memory," 410.

29. Keck, *Forgetting Whose We Are*, 47.

30. Keck, *Forgetting Whose We Are*, 45.

31. As Proctor-Smith notes: "The notion of remembrance found in the Hebrew Scriptures is dialogical, effective and concrete (or embodied). It is dialogical because it presumes a relationship between God and people; effective because the remembering calls forth a response, whether from God or from people; concrete because it involves specifics such as names, people, actions, and objects" ("Liturgical Anamnesis and Women's Memory," 410).

32. Keck, *Forgetting Whose We Are*, 46.

33. Keck, *Forgetting Whose We Are*, 55.

34. Elizabeth Johnson, *Friends of God and Prophets: A Feminist Theological Reading of the Communion of Saints* (New York: Continuum, 1998), 234.

35. Westphal, "Lest We Forget," 11.

36. Westphal, "Lest We Forget," 11.

37. Proctor-Smith, "Liturgical Anamnesis and Women's Memory," 409.

38. Other liturgical practices would be worth exploring in this regard, including the practice of reconciliation, the kiss of peace, the sacrament of anointing of the sick, prayers of petition, the litany of saints, and marriage.

39. International Commission on English in the Liturgy, "Order of Christian Funerals," in *The Rites of the Catholic Church*, vol. 1, ICEL (New York: Catholic Book Publishing, 1989). (Cited hereafter by number.) It is important to note, however, that the Roman Catholic rites, in their revised form, are quite similar to those used within other Christian denominations, especially insofar as the various rites retrieve early church practices and root their prayers in Scripture. See, e.g., discussions of the Lutheran *Burial of the Dead* in H. P. V. Rezner, "A Christian Rite of Burial: An Instrument of Pastoral Care," *Lutheran Theological*

Journal 26 (May 1992): 72–77, and Eric E. Dyck, "*Lex Orandi*, a New *Lex Credendi*: *The Burial of the Dead*, 1978 from an Historical Perspective," *Consensus* 18, no. 2 (1991): 63–73; of the Presbyterian rite in the 1993 *Book of Common Worship* in Stanley Hall, "Renewing the Rites of Death," *Insights: A Journal of the Faculty of Austin Seminary* (Fall 1994): 39–50; and of the Orthodox Rite in Kallistos Ware, "'One Body in Christ': Death and the Communion of Saints," *Sobornost/ECR* 3, no. 2 (1981): 179–91.

40. As Johnson notes, this is the term's most extensive meaning in the New Testament, occurring some sixty times. The term is multivalent as well, however, "referring on different occasions in the New Testament to the angels, to pious Jews who have already died, or to Christians who die under persecution.…In addition to the general notion of Israel as the holy people of God, some scholars believe that the specific background for [its referent to the Christian community as a whole] is found in late Jewish apocalyptic literature where 'the saints' describe the elect who will share in the blessings of the messianic age" (Johnson, *Friends of God and Prophets*, 60).

41. Johnson, *Friends of God and Prophets*, 60.

42. Johnson, *Friends of God and Prophets*, 7.

43. Keck, *Forgetting Whose We Are*, 145.

44. Johnson, *Friends of God and Prophets*, 78.

45. Johnson, *Friends of God and Prophets*, 132. For a wonderful reflection on the intersection of these practices in the Orthodox tradition, see Ware, "One Body in Christ," 188–91. Mutual prayer is a fundamental relational practice of discipleship among the living; therefore, construing the church as the communion of saints suggests mutual prayer between the living and the dead. As Ware notes, "If, then, as members of a single family we are united by the bond of mutual prayer, and if within this family there is no division between living and departed, then it should surely be considered normal and natural that we pray for the departed, and ask the saints to pray on our behalf. Whether alive or dead, we belong to the same family: therefore, whether alive or dead, we pray for one another. Here on earth we pray for others: why should we not continue to pray for them after their death? Do they cease to exist, that we should cease to intercede for them? Here on earth we likewise request others to remember us in their prayers: and since in the risen Christ the saints are not divided from us but belong still to the same family, why should we not continue to ask them for their intercessions?" (Ware, "One Body in Christ," 189).

46. Keck, *Forgetting Whose We Are*, 152.

47. Kallistos Ware, "Go Joyfully: The Mystery of Death and Resurrection," in *Beyond Death: Theological and Philosophical Reflections on Life after Death*, ed. Dan Cohn-Sherbok and Christopher Lewis (London: Macmillan, 1995), 38.

48. That visiting is a "practice" follows from Alasdair MacIntyre's well-known definition of *practice* in *After Virtue* (Notre Dame, IN: University of Notre Dame Press, 1981), 175. Visiting certainly is a "coherent and complex form of socially established cooperative human activity," as my great-grandmother's news network would attest. There are certainly goods internal to it, standards of excellence that define it and systematically form participants in the virtues. These might include friendship, hospitality, being present to the other, patience, and, often, fortitude. Unlike many activities advanced as practices (e.g., chess-playing), visiting is a locally embodied practice open to all and engaged in by regular folks (mostly women). That this is the case speaks not against its status as a practice but may instead provide a corrective against elitist, universalized, and competitive accounts of practices. That it is theological as well is apparent from Jesus' own life, the corporal works of mercy, and the prophetic and Pauline injunctions to remember the widows.

49. Marius L. Bressoud's moving and compelling reflection on his own "personal" spiritual journey in his "eighth decade" highlights this well. He finds that he is not merely called to a comfortable process of introspective personal reflection on his own spirituality but rather finds himself called to minister concretely, in a way he never would have anticipated, to a dying homeless man called Ramon. See Marius L. Bressaud, "A Slow Dying," *Second Opinion* 21, no. 1 (July 1995): 43–47.

50. This public, sacramental role is important to overcome the all-too-frequent marginalization of the elderly within their communities and to remind the church that without the elderly it is incomplete. This might mean, of course, that the "efficiency" of our public rituals may need to be sacrificed; the elderly may read the Scriptures more slowly as lectors; they may need assistance in distributing Communion and may take much longer than their crack, thirty-something counterpart. But their presence at the altar is crucial in challenging the fear of growing old and the devaluing of the elderly, outweighing the importance of completing Mass or worship in fifty-five minutes.

51. Johnson, *Friends of God and Prophets*, 85.

52. Mary M. Knutsen, "A Feminist Theology of Aging," in *Aging, Spirituality and Religion: A Handbook*, ed. Melvin A. Kimble et al. (Minneapolis: Augsburg Fortress Press, 2003), 466.

53. See, e.g., the discussion of the practice of "life review" in David G. Hawkins, "Memory, Hold the Door," *Journal of Religion and Aging* 3, nos. 3–4 (Spring–Summer 1987):13–21, and Drew Christiansen, "Creative Social Responses to Aging," in Cahill and Mieth, *Aging*, 114–22. It is this construct of aging that fuels the ubiquitous practice of "life review," one that is "characterized by the progressive return to the consciousness of past experiences and, particularly, the resurgence of unresolved conflicts" (Hawkins, "Memory," 18, quoting

Robert N. Butler, "Life Review Therapy," *Geriatrics* 8 [November 1974]: 165). As a therapeutic technique aimed at the maintenance and preservation of the elderly's "self-image," it is unclear what role "life review" has in an ecclesial or pastoral context; it might be more properly located, and therefore modified, as a component of an ongoing practice of reconciliation.

54. It could also be suggested that concrete activities and encounters are required to sustain our very ability to remember anyone or anything. Moreover, we will find as we engage in concrete activities of remembering with the elderly that they become much more a part of who we are. This, then, will indeed make their deaths more painful, but at the same time we will find that "remembering" them when they are gone has become second nature.

55. Keck, *Forgetting Whose We Are*, 58. For a realistic display of the fact that remembering (in this case, waiting on someone as he dies) takes time and challenges our desires for efficiency and control, see Curtis W. Freeman, "What Shall We Do about Norman? An Experiment in Communal Discernment," *Christian Bioethics* 2, no. 1 (1996): 34–36.

56. Keck, *Forgetting Whose We Are*, 47.

57. Christiansen, "Creative Social Responses to Aging," 117.

58. Keck, *Forgetting Whose We Are*, 137.

59. Freeman's description of the parish's discernment process, and his theological analysis, resonates with many of the points made in this section.

60. Freeman, "What Shall We Do about Norman?," 26.

61. Freeman, "What Shall We Do about Norman?," 26, 30.

62. Keck, *Forgetting Whose We Are*, 91, 134.

63. Keck, *Forgetting Whose We Are*, 58.

64. As Westphal notes, such practices of reconciliation are not only individual but require communal repentance as well: "Those who stand in this perpetual need of revitalization and redirection include not only the individual believers who make up the community of faith but the community itself as a corporate body. Remembrance involves personal and collective renewal at the same time" (Westphal, "Lest We Forget," 11). In the context of communities who have marginalized the aging or who have sinned against an individual member, acts of reconciliation as practices of remembering would be indicated.

65. Knutsen, "A Feminist Theology of Aging," 473.

66. Knutsen, "A Feminist Theology of Aging," 474.

67. It is important to remain cautious when mapping suffering on to Christ's Passion. As Curtis Freeman aptly states, "The connection between the suffering of Christ and our own suffering is not an easy one to make. Nevertheless, when guided by the spiritual disciplines of worship, prayer, reading and ministry it is possible for the Christian to envision her pain as the sacramental *anamnesis* of the cross" ("Redeeming Love and Suicide: An 'Evangelical Catholic' Response to

Amundsen," *Christian Bioethics* 1, no. 3 [December 1995]: 320n5; Freeman here cites Stanley Hauerwas, *Naming the Silences* [Grand Rapids: Eerdmans, 1990], 86–89). Such a reading should be available in the community to those so habituated through practices of *askesis* (as were the martyrs) who are thereby capable of taking it upon themselves; when forced upon another, it becomes a weapon of torture. Lucien Richard, in "Toward a Theology of Aging," and others also explore the relationship between the suffering of aging and the Passion through the concept of *kenosis*. See also Christiansen, "A Catholic Perspective."

68. The use of the term *interdependence* is not simply a matter of semantics but rather one of accuracy. The use of the language of "dependence" regarding the elderly severs their present situation from the larger context of their overall life, which when viewed more broadly would reveal a complex tapestry of interdependence construed over a lifetime.

69. More broadly speaking, such interdependence is likewise constitutive of human identity as well, if one affirms the conviction that humans are created in the *imago Dei*. The image of God as Trinitarian suggests that identity is not located within an individual but rather is located in the spaces between myself and others, constructed through the relational actions of remembering that occur in those spaces. In short, my identity is comprised in my relationship with others. As Knutsen notes, "Within the life of the triune God, and among all created life in God, relationality generates each personal identity, and the personal identities thus generated in turn constitute and transform the dynamics of their relationality" (Knutsen, "A Feminist Theology of Aging," 471). Similarly see Freeman: "Sacredness…is not an ontic category *within the self* but a dialogic notion *between the self and others*" (Freeman, "What Shall We Do about Norman?," 24).

70. The reality of the communion of saints also reminds us that the church is equally comprised of others who may be marginalized or excluded from our communities—the disabled, the poor, the mentally ill, those of different racial or ethnic backgrounds—and likewise calls us to redefine their roles among us. Many of the reflections in this essay would apply equally to other constituencies.

71. That this essay exists is certainly a testimony to the communion of saints. It could not have been written without the material assistance of my Nonny and others who inspired me as I wrote; my colleagues Terrence W. Tilley, Sandra Yocum Mize, Michael Barnes, Dennis Doyle, Una Cadegan, James Heft, Jack McGrath, and Maureen Tilley who read earlier drafts of the essay; Stanley Hauerwas who called it into existence; and my friends who are gracious enough to remember me (even and especially when I'm not so good at remembering) and, in so doing, sustain my work and my life.

Part Two

DISABILITIES

2. God Bends Over Backward to Accommodate Humankind… While the Civil Rights Acts and the Americans with Disabilities Act Require [Only] Minimum Effort

Mary Jo Iozzio

This chapter first appeared in *Journal of Moral Theology* 6 (September 1, 2017): 10–31.

The civil rights and ADA laws in the United States represent some of the results of the interrogations of privilege that attempt to ameliorate the disadvantages of servitude, marginalization, and the institutionalization of minoritized people with proactive measures for equality and access. However, these laws, like most laws, are limited in their ability to influence a change of heart among many. In this essay I consider some of the contours of these laws, I look at Catholic social teaching for insight on how to be with and for those who are poor or otherwise marginalized, and I reflect on what I think God wills we would do.

In 2015, the United States celebrated the fiftieth anniversary of the Voting Rights Act (1965) and the twenty-fifth anniversary of the Americans with Disabilities Act (1990). Some people in the United States and elsewhere celebrated these legislative measures that ensure legal protections against discrimination on the bases of race or disability; some did not. One of the concerns on the periphery of this essay is the apparent failure, if not outright hostility, that those not celebrating these legislative successes harbor against people belonging to one or both of these minorities in the United States and elsewhere. Another of my concerns is the failure to recognize that these and other laws require only a minimalist or anemic justice to avoid discriminatory behavior and other harms upon individuals and communities and the violation of citizens' exercise of their rights to common liberties and access to common goods. Mostly, while these laws are critically important for the real lives of those who are vulnerable, I am concerned about the theological implications of following or ignoring God's lead in accommodating humankind in all its diverse incarnations.

Why are these initiatives important? Because not one of us should have to wait for the Kingdom to know that we are loved, lovable, and capable of loving in return. Not one of us should have to witness another lynching, rape, institutionalization, sterilization, or insult to the humanity of another. Not one of us should ever think ourselves above or untouched by the fray in advantage or disadvantage. Moreover, we Christians may be especially indictable when we have failed to welcome strangers, clothe those naked, feed those hungry, shelter those without safe places to rest, visit those imprisoned—in jails, asylums, hospitals, detention centers, camps, and reservations—or announce the Good News.

From most accounts in Christian traditions and to the extent that it can be known, God's will for what God has wrought is that all creation flourish from the least to the greatest. God's lead goes far further than these laws in promoting the common goods they seek to distribute, and I find myself wanting to push law to its limits to accommodate people who have been left out of the goods that constitute the relationships with the One and the many. Insofar as God bends over backward toward humankind and identifies especially with those who are vulnerable in the share of those goods, we Christians must go and do likewise.[1] I invoke the image of "bending over backward" for its sense of no limit in terms of the extra mile, cloak, or other cheek that Jesus asks of those who would follow him as well as for its sense of exposure by the one so bending/bent to vulnerability. To the extent that God's will can be known in God's becoming human, God has clearly gone the extra mile and experienced exposure even to an excruciating death. Since then, not one other person needs to so bend, except by her or his own choice and where or when injustice prevails.

In a time when suspicions about who count as legal members of our communities and who are protected by the laws of the land are raised by isolationist political camps, the image of God bending over backward suggests another way to be with and to accommodate people in need of both justice and mercy. God's justice is not punitive; it is reconciliatory. God's mercy is scandalously generous; it is kenotic and favorably disposed to those who are marginalized on account of their deviance from assumed norms and privilege.

I engage this concern about God's designs for humankind from the perspective of disability studies at the intersections of theological ethics, race and anti-racism activism, and gender minority studies. I am committed to members of minoritized communities, particularly to those designated by hegemonic normativity—subsequent to an unrecognized or unacknowledged complacence by dominant "majoritized" others—as undesirable on the basis of race and disability. These designations about some human beings offend justice at large and, in particular, their dignity as members of the one human community. That offense against the dignity of so many people disturbs the peace and ultimately offends the Creator in whose image each and every person is created and loved. I take the opportunity of these anniversaries to examine the nature of anti-discrimination laws and the protections they afford and to place those initiatives in dialogue with an ethics of virtue, the tools that the law has at its disposal to embrace as a teacher. I remain accountable to those about whom I write—people with disabilities and people of color—as well as to the guild of Catholic ethicists that turns to the implications of the Incarnation above all to find the means and the meanings of God's justice and mercy in a world distorted by sin.

The Civil Rights Acts (1964 and 1965) and the Americans with Disabilities Act (1990) offer protections against discrimination and, to a lesser extent, encourage opportunities for development and the participation of individuals and communities belonging to these protected classes in the local, state, national, and international communities of human commerce. These Acts represent landmark legislation and progress in fostering a sense of "liberty and justice for all" in pursuit of activities that bring people together in economic, educational, commercial, health, housing, legal, political, public, recreational, religious, and social venues. Unfortunately, both people identified with racial minorities and people with disabilities in the United States (and elsewhere) continue to experience limits to their liberty and justice. These limits are saturated by the long-lasting residue of bias maintained by unexamined and unearned dominant white, male, hetero, Christian, and ableist privilege that remains preserved (covertly and well) in the systems from which human economies operate.[2] While charges are filed in the court systems and claims of multiple types of violation against these protected classes have been argued successfully in US courts,[3] the perpetuation of discrimination on the basis of race and disability reveals the limitations inherent to these laws. Those limitations point directly to an anemic conception of law where a more robust appreciation of the laws' pedagogical function better serves the commonweal.

Although the laws of a land serve as a guide in the development of individuals' and society's virtue, in forming upright and decent citizens and communities, laws today more often than not represent only a minimum (of decency let alone justice for the moment) owed between parties in human commerce. The notion of the law as a teacher is nearly lost.[4] As she builds upon the work of Aristotle and Aquinas, Cathleen Kaveny instructs that the key virtues about which law should teach are autonomy and solidarity.[5] Not coincidentally, these virtues are two of the most often referenced in calls for justice by advocacy groups. Yet for those who belong to or stand with communities of color and people with disabilities, recognition of their experiences exposes the laws' inadequacies and demonstrates that more than minimum is necessary, particularly when being black or having a disability is the reality questioned. When "being" is questioned, whose lives matter? It is simply "Not OK" to denigrate, discriminate, or disrespect any longer.[6]

It is all too clear that history has not been kind to people who differ from the dominant populations among which they are present and are presented by their families and friends to be acknowledged, recognized, and welcomed. While the United States experiment in democracy through the Constitution and more inclusively in subsequent Amendments purported (and still purports) equal opportunities and freedom for all, not everyone enjoys this equality among their neighbors, except on the papers that define the nation as sovereign and in the cultural imagination set in "The New Colossus" (aka Lady Liberty) and "Manifest Destiny."[7] Sadly and scandalously, the nation's Original Sin of the theft of this land from and the near extinction of its Native Peoples, coupled with the slave trade and enshrined in its quintessential beliefs and myths about exceptionalism and democratic ideals,[8] is played out nearly daily in public and private spaces as news is told in the reports of promising and not-so-promising black lives lost to violence and complacence.[9] More than 50% of homicides committed in the United States are perpetrated against racialized minorities, with African Americans overwhelmingly among the dead. Similar violence against people with disabilities, though not as frequently reported on account of a cloak of invisibility or presumed rarity, plays on the vulnerability to the same losses from dominant narratives suspicious of danger to a mentality that assumes the victim is an easy target. Like crimes against black men, a variety of hate crimes toward people with disabilities occur with impunity, and many are particularly vicious toward those with developmental or behavioral disabilities.[10] Moreover, women with disabilities are especially vulnerable to more kinds of, and more severe, sexual assaults, by more distinct perpetrators, and over a longer period of time than their non-disabled peers. The most recent report of the Federal Office of Justice Programs confirms the rate of violent crime against people with disabilities as two times greater than crimes against people without disabilities: at 14% of the total US population in 2013, people with disabilities numbered more than 21% of all violent crime victims.[11] This sinful history—from its original theft to its contemporary oppressive expressions—must not be ignored or glossed over, rather it must be exposed, reparations made, and its residue rejected. If our laws are to teach civility and virtue, then the hope of equal regard as fully human and of equal access to human flourishing and to the nation's common goods—assuring the violence-free and hate-free exercise of personal autonomy as well as supporting solidarity in the work of community and national pride—will inform the intents and the effects of the Civil Rights and Americans with Disabilities Acts.

A Primer on the Civil Rights and Americans with Disabilities Acts

The Civil Rights Act of 1964 outlaws discrimination against and segregation of people on the basis of race, color, religion, sex, and national origin.[12] The former ways of separate and unequal access to education, healthcare, transportation, dining, and other public facilities as well as employment discrimination would no longer suffice. The Voting Rights

Act of 1965 outlaws racial discrimination in voting and (moderately) effectively enfranchised racial minorities. This legislation and subsequent amendments that clarify and extend provisions of the Act give local, state, and federal law enforcement agencies the capabilities that point back to the Civil Rights Act, to ensure thereby that the right of US citizens to vote is inviolable.[13] Overt and other more subtle disenfranchisement ploys, such as gerrymandering that manipulatively influences poll populations and precincts' results, and poll taxes were deemed illegal. The Americans with Disabilities Act of 1990 prohibits discrimination against persons with disabilities with protections similar to the Civil Rights Acts, as well as requiring employers to provide reasonable accommodations to employees with disabilities and public venues to provide accessibility to patrons with disabilities.[14] The days of warehousing people with disabilities in asylums and the like or consigning them to substandard housing, inhumane and abusive treatment, and widespread exclusion in human work, other commerce, and play are no longer tolerated.

Each of these Acts reflects a major step in the direction of justice for many in the US. Those early steps followed the nation's widespread witness—through the increasingly available media outlets of newspapers, radio broadcasts, and both public and in-home television sets—of the struggles for freedom and fair play.[15] The discrimination against being black or another racial minority or having a disability, which these laws seek to jettison, exposes the intersections of common experience among individuals in the US belonging to non-dominant communities. In what follows I focus on ways to dismantle the edifice of dominant narratives and the power they wield through the strategic naming of injustice as these laws identify them.[16] I offer the terms of discriminating acts, I consider the elements of accountability the statutes employ, and I look at solidarity as the key to accommodate not only the minimum of rights but the fullness of life, work, and play that is God's way of reconciling perceived differences in the struggles for both racial and disability justice.

The Legal Terms Outlining Discrimination

While racialized skin color is often, though not always, apparent, disabilities may be and perhaps often are hidden and thereby render the categorizing of persons who would be protected by law both difficult and fungible. While, hopefully, the question of personhood is not asked, the question of "who" qualifies is asked, at times with impunity. These kinds of questions go to the heart of human dignity and raise suspicions about the presumptions that are based on philosophical and theological anthropologies in regard to who counts as human and who qualifies thereby for the protections offered in law.[17] Invisibilities or doubts that authorities may harbor about the real (or in their view imagined) condition or experience of disability(ies) influence the determinations those authorities consider about the applicability of the law.

The Civil Rights Acts and the Americans with Disabilities Act serve to extend consciousness of widespread discrimination in human commerce and to enforce compliance that protects people from the injustices of humanity denied in terms of employment and access to other forms of human commerce. These acts use similar language to enfranchise and protect against discrimination. However, the legal terms point almost singularly to a denial of access based on presumptions of worth in comparison to those whose access is taken for granted. This is, discrimination will end only when access to voting, schooling, healthcare, employment, religious/social/recreational activities, and movement about the commons will be equal to those whose access is at present unencumbered and free. The Equal Employment Opportunity Commission (EEOC) identifies eleven bases of employment discrimination:[18] race, sex, age, disability,[19] gender, pregnancy, national origin, religion, compensation, genetic information, and retaliation (termination, censure, demotion or failure to promote).

Unlike the Civil Rights Acts, which does not "qualify" what constitutes race or color, the Americans with Disabilities Act (hereafter ADA) does qualify what constitutes conditions that compel compliance. Title I Regulations of the ADA define the extent to which employers and public venues are to provide reasonable accommodations to people with disabilities (hereafter PWD). Title II of the ADA defines the conditions or impairments, with respect to an individual, that qualify or do not qualify for the protections against discrimination and recourse to the law as a champion of civil rights. Title II, Subpart A, "prohibits...[and] protects qualified individuals with disabilities from discrimination on the basis of disabilities." Title III, Subpart A, offers that, "Disability means, with respect to an individual, a physical or mental impairment that substantially limits one or more of the major life activities of such individual; a record of such impairment; or being regarded as having such an impairment."[20] As a result, the ADA allows "qualifications" (as well as minimum requirements incumbent upon and minimum compliance by employers, public and private institutions, and commercial venues) to make a way for and forward for PWD to enter into the determinations of discriminations against, equal opportunity for, or denied access to PWD. More often than not, these determined qualifications have undermined the intent to democratize employment of and social practices for PWD and have made recourse to the legal system all the more difficult for them and for their advocates and allies.[21]

The Elements of Accountability

Like the exacting force of definitions that determine the categories (e.g., race and gender) or classes of persons (e.g., children, elderly, PWD, patients), which the laws are designed to protect, coverage formulae outline the reach of the Federal Government to impose upon or relieve juridic persons from this or that requirement. Coverage formulae are most often used in the legal sphere on matters of voting rights and require a state or local municipality to seek permission of the courts before changing current practice regarding voting laws for protected classes of people. Coverage formulae are useful also in protecting the increase of access that PWD might experience across the spectrum of human commerce, including voting rights. Unfortunately, coverage formulae for the ADA are bound to factors of "qualified" entities as well as to their cost-to-revenue percentages (a mere 1% change in cost-to-revenue balances can be sufficient reason for disqualification on compliance and an opt-out to accommodate modifications for individuals and PWD) that grant a fairly widespread safe harbor exemption from being required to comply (i.e., to enjoy a status of non-compliance).[22] Similarly unfortunate, these formulae favor and protect the status quo of non-disabled/normate privilege.[23]

In community organizing, accountability has a meaning quite different from the legal definitions and assignments of responsibility for compliance used in federal, state, and local law. Social activists—to whom many of us are indebted in reference to the fifty-one (Voting Rights), fifty (Civil Rights), and twenty-five (ADA) year anniversaries of anti-discrimination acts celebrated in 2015—identify accountability as one of the measures used to ensure honesty and success in achieving the aims of liberty, access, and opportunity (that is, justice) for those whose capabilities to be agents of their own making have been systematically obstructed.[24] In the law, coverage formulae determine what entities must engage these and other laws and the extent to which anti-discrimination and reasonable accommodations laws are to reach; however, as the exemptions to compliance demonstrate, the law often betrays and even undermines its purpose to lead and teach as it remains a protectorate over a minimum measure of human dignity.

For example, in reference to the Voting Rights Act, following a series of legal challenges, coverage formulae were designed as a measure of accountability to prevent voter suppression through discriminatory testing, registration processes, language bias, identification cards, and precincts' boundaries through carefully crafted political gerrymandering.[25] In light of the ADA, PWD were added to the voting rolls and thereby covered by the Voting Rights Act as a specific class with previously limited enfranchisement. Regrettably, the US Supreme Court decision in "Shelby County v. Holder" (2013) eliminated the requirement of states, counties, and municipalities to request and wait to receive Department of Justice (D.O.J.) approval before changing any local voting rules and practices.[26] D.O.J. oversight of safeguards against voter suppression designed to protect minority voters is unraveling. Since Shelby County v. Holder and in time for the 2016 Presidential election, fourteen states instituted new voting restrictions, reducing both safeguards and D.O.J. oversight. For all intents and purposes, coverage formulae requirements have been annulled.[27]

In reference to the Civil Rights Acts inclusive of civil rights extended in the ADA, the coverage requirements of compliance against employment discrimination and access is limited. Accountability in the context of the ADA leans in favor of "entities" and away from PWD, exempting many entities from accommodations on account of an entity's employee base and on the determination of "reasonable" accommodations. Under the EEOC and authorized by the Civil Rights Acts and the

ADA, businesses with fewer than fifteen employees are exempt from compliance in matters of both non-discrimination and reasonable accommodations, as are private "clubs" and religious organizations. Unfortunately, these formulary mechanisms of accountability demonstrate attention to only a minimum standard for recruitment and retention, a minimum that fails the tests of the nation's concern for those intangible yet inalienable rights to life, liberty, and the pursuit of happiness. Just as the challenges that conservative legislators have raised in as many as 20 states and as the Supreme Court ruled on June 25, 2013, to dismantle a key piece of the formula of Section 4(b) that identifies jurisdictions in need of a preclearance to make changes,[28] the ADA is similarly subject to revision and loss. Moreover, unlike civil rights laws, the ADA is perhaps more properly considered as a voluntary compliance law: employers are expected to comply even though they are not required to report on the raw data indicating the number of employees with disabilities, or the requests they may have received or fulfilled for reasonable accommodations or their fulfillment of those requests. Nevertheless, and like the path to a restoration of voting rights denied through political machinations and district gerrymandering, resort after the fact to the courts may be the only recourse to result in remedies.[29]

Solidarity in Reconciling Disability Justice and Racial Justice

Aside from the fact that these laws hold a minimum of expectations by which institutions—whether governmental, commercial, educational, recreational, or religious—are required to abide, the Civil Rights and Disability Rights movements call for more than protections from harms. Many people who belong to racial minorities or are PWD remain in need of programs and services that genuinely respond to opportunities for the development of their capabilities and talents that anti-discrimination laws and reasonable accommodations simply do not provide. Further, as made clear in the all-too-frequent harms inflicted upon and the murders of black folk and the under-reported violence against PWD,[30] the minimum has failed in law's original intent to teach and guide in the ways of virtue and decency. Instead, witnesses learn something—first-hand

and through media outlets—from violent crime and assault suffered by a person or group whom they resemble in terms of race, sex, gender, class, or religion: to fear the "other." If the other resembles the witnesses in one way or another, they may internalize self-hate or hate the other, an experience reinforced with graphic images instigating post-traumatic stress.[31]

Yet Aquinas, building on Aristotle about the law as teacher, argues, "Every law is ordained to the common good" (ST I–II q. 90, a. 2c). Moreover, "It is evident that the proper effect of law is to lead its subjects to their proper virtue; and since virtue is 'that which makes its subject good,' it follows that the proper effect of law is to make those to whom it is given, good, either simply or in some particular respect" (ST I–II q. 92, a. 1c). Further, "[Women and] men who are well disposed are led willingly to virtue by being admonished better than by coercion, but [women and] men who are evilly disposed are not led to virtue unless they are compelled" by the discipline of law (ST I–II q. 95, a .1, ad. 1).[32] Anti-discrimination laws protect, but, in theory, they could also inspire more noble qualities. That is (and I may be asking more than is reasonable), the law has failed to advance the cause of justice in policies that will reach into the consciousness and consciences of the polity to reject any denial of the humanity and the dignity with which all persons have been endowed. Many may argue that the law is not designed to advance these kinds of changes. However, as the tradition bears out, laws do encourage by means of external legislation the internal dispositions and the cultivation of the virtues toward right and just behavior between and among the people of the polis.

From ancient and pre-industrialized texts unearthed by archaeology—papyri, tablets, manuscripts, architecture, burial sites, battlefields, and other artifacts—to the contemporary and ubiquitous media, the norms of an imperial past that signal "best" and "most admired" and their opposites can be inferred. Influential agents of the past, who assigned norms and normative status to dominant group identifiers, relied on the force of physical power and prowess to silence the subaltern, the different, the "other."[33] Though fewer in number, other influential agents—the prophets of old, Jesus, and the early Christian communities among them—proffered norms of inclusivity and a welcome of diversity. As a result of a postcolonial consciousness, today these norms both proliferate and weaken as standards of superiority—on the basis of race, sex, gender, religion, and ability—are raised on a trajectory parallel to the disadvantages and implied inferiority to the very being and achievement of minority populations. The norms proliferate in overt and covert ways as more people become aware of a status that has been assigned as privileged or not, and paradoxically weaken as more people in both dominant and minority populations begin to interrogate why and how a dominant "better" and minority "worse" emerged.[34] In the meantime, the Civil Rights and ADA laws, among the results of those interrogations, attempt to ameliorate the disadvantages of past servitude, marginalization, and institutionalization (imprisonment/incarceration for black and other racialized minorities, asylum or imprisonment for PWD[35]) with proactive measures for equality and access.

More is yet needed, particularly when people who are non-white, non-heterosexual, non-Christian, living with disabilities, or women are violated with scandalous impunity on account of their being in places and spaces where some members of the dominant culture prefer they not go. This "reluctance" on the part of some members of the dominant and normate culture to "let others be" suggests internalized prejudices against members of the non-dominant communities of a categorical kind that questions entrenched suppositions about who among them qualifies as fully human. It is this line of questioning and thinking that strikes at the heart of the Civil Rights Acts explored here. To whom, if not to everyone, do civil rights belong? Who count as persons, and what remedies are to be applied to overcome and dismantle internalized apathy, unremarked hate speech, and lip service in the face of systemic structural obstacles against initiatives to thrive?

Sadly, racism continues to poison public and private spheres with exasperating frequency in the US and elsewhere, and, just as sadly, ableism too remains as entrenched. While derogatory name-calling may be on the decline, microaggressions against racial minorities and PWD occur far too often in and across a variety of contexts—at work, in school, in formal and informal settings—that make them especially covert, pernicious, and, thereby, ever more insidious. These aggressions "are everyday, seemingly minor verbal, nonverbal, or environmental slights or insults [providing] a glimpse of the communicator's conscious or unconscious assumptions and prejudices."[36]

At this juncture, a hermeneutic of solidarity and accountability, by means of the preferential option for those who are poor and otherwise marginalized, may serve this rights agenda as it reconciles work for justice against the prevailing hegemony of racism and ableism. Catholic social teaching is instructive on many levels for this purpose, with solidarity and the preferential option for the poor as key. With the Second Vatican Council and the popes since, the Church has recognized solidarity as a fact of human life, as a norm of and for the relations on which each of us is interdependent, if not dependent, and as a virtue directed toward the common good.[37] A hermeneutic of solidarity invites dominant communities and their members to interrogate their privilege and share their space and use their power with, always with, those who have been marginalized. In addition, this hermeneutic invites minority communities and their members to interrogate their (self-imposed) silence and reject the stigmatizing otherness that the dominant have imposed. Then, speaking truth to power where the dominant and the minoritized people assemble and hear at once, a new dialogue of respect and care and love for one another can emerge. The ways and means of the preferential option for those who are marginalized requires that their voices and concerns are heard and are placed at the top of the list of what to achieve, where to start, and how to proceed. When solidarity is coupled with this preferential option: (1) an accounting of those who have been marginalized will be reconciled with the reality of human diversity writ large, (2) every individual will be honored as sister and brother of one human family, and (3) the goods of the earth and of human hands will be distributed according to need and the common good.[38]

While God Bends Over Backward

The Civil Rights and Disability Rights movements have paved a way where the going was often steep and rocky and pockmarked and dangerous. Like the prophecy of Isaiah where a voice announces, "Every valley shall be lifted up, and every mountain and hill be made low; the uneven ground shall become level, and the rough places a plain" (Isa 40:4), these movements have sought to tread and, thereby, make a way for the people who have been exiled to assume or to return to their places in human commerce and relationship. However, many obstacles to inclusion and access to the places where the dominant go—work, school, shop, play, and worship—continue to hold sway instead of the fulfillment of Isaiah's prophecy and instead of anti-discrimination laws, equal access, and equal employment opportunities. In the face of God's justice and extraordinary concern for those who are disadvantaged by individuals, communities, and institutions of the dominant corps and the systems that are designed to oppress, the law is inadequate to the task.[39] While God bends over backward to lighten the burdens of difference imposed on account of racism and ableism, complacence about the law and complicity in systemic injustice reveal persistent personal and social/structural sins—from exclusionary practices and microaggressions to outright hostility and violence—in dire need of redress.

In addition to the movements' ongoing efforts to support the advance of minorities, religionists are increasingly aware of the intersections of experience (overlapping discriminations and marginalizations) and concern (for liberation in the present and for the generations to come) among people who have been minoritized on account of race, sex, gender, religion, or disability.[40] Those working in theological or religious ethics give deliberate witness to a way of reconciling the dividing practices that have been institutionalized in the edifice of dominant narratives and the power they wield.[41] Moreover, for those of us who work to expose injustice for liberation purposes in the way that God wills it to be for all people, we have an obligation to witness and to do the work by weaving the multi-colored and variably malleable threads of warp and woof that reveal one and the same creative-created cloth, a tapestry of God's fecund imaginary and kaleidoscopic diversity.

Antithetical to one multi-colored/multi-dimensional tapestry and evident in artifacts from dominant communities in ancient and modern contexts, the stigma attached to minoritized people has traumatized them, literally (often abusively) and figuratively, and segregated them—in asylums to half-way houses to the streets—from the communities in which they ought to number and contribute.[42] Historically, oppression occurred with the exercise of a tyrant and a cohort ruling party over the masses and laborers in their jurisdiction; empire- and religious-tradition building grew into colonizing initiatives recognized today as the disadvantaging injustice that the colonized suffer from the "well-intentioned" practices of paternalist lords and masters or their strong-arm demands. We (descendants of both the "in" and the "out" groups of those practices) have inherited a system maintained by unquestioned norms and structures that "are systematically reproduced in major economic, political, and cultural institutions."[43] Moreover, with the scientific/technological revolutions of the Enlightenment period, an ideology of hegemonic normativity has been insinuated across the globe. Such hegemony confounds the readily observable reality of the diversity of creation as much as it belies God's fecund creative imaginary. This ideological hegemony is evident in institutions of every sort, including our churches and the missions and ministries in which we are engaged.[44] Its hegemony has effectively divided and essentialized humankind into two groups, the normal and the defective, and distributed a power that privileges the one as it disables—by demonizing, marginalizing, and oppressing—the other.[45] Challenges to this normativity result in the assignment of stigma: "an attribute that is deeply discrediting" and ultimately dehumanizing.[46] Consider that 100,000 people with physical and developmental disabilities were the first victims of the Nazi program to eliminate inferior races. In capitalist economies, PWD are considered counter-productive, if not worthless, for profit. Few are employed. In day-to-day human commerce, PWD are regularly infantilized regardless of their age or physical or cognitive or developmental disability. This ideology of segregating exclusion has been inserted into nearly every social structure of human making, including the Church, and has corrupted the proclamation—by its "normative" interpretation—of the Good News in a way that defies the logic of the Incarnation. (Not coincidentally, the crucifixion resulted in the "stigmata." While the Roman practice was certainly stigmatizing and scandalizing, devotion to the risen Christ eliminates the recoil open wounds would ordinarily evoke.) The results of that corruption, the residue of these sins—the ongoing exclusion and oppression of racial minorities and PWD as well as the internalized presumption of superiority (on the part of the dominant) or inferiority (on the part of minorities)—needs to be confessed and purged and vowed to never again dehumanize.

Here I call to mind the images that can be evoked by the idiom to bend over backward. Consider the idiom as a metaphor for doing all that can be done to help someone, to go the extra mile, to be moved to relieve the hardship and the hardness of life among those who have been robbed of the means to thrive. Consider the idiom also as openness to vulnerability. Just think of the exposure of the human torso in such a position and the ease with which vital organs—from throat to pelvis—could be eviscerated. Clearly, this violence also suggests rape, and, considering the vulnerability of rape victims (vulnerable in the face of first violence and vulnerable to another, and another, and another attack), solidarity with and for these victims can be life-saving.

Now consider God so bending…for us.[47] In the *Spiritual Exercises* of St. Ignatius, retreatants are instructed to contemplate the Trinity as the Divine Persons look upon Earth and its human inhabitants to see the mess into which we had gotten ourselves. Pity the people: vicious in word and deed, blasphemous against one another and against the *imago Dei* to be hallowed in each. But no, the Divine Persons proclaim, "Let us work the redemption of the human race."[48] In the Incarnation, in the Divine self-emptying *kenosis*, God bends over backward—so in love with and merciful toward humankind is God for us—so as to become human. No minimum of effort or formulary limit can be found in that *kenosis*. In fact, even to death does Jesus bend—nearly eviscerated, possibly raped/impaled,[49] and rather completely, shamefully, and demonstratively stigmatized—in command and loving all the way to crucifixion and resurrected life. *Kenosis*, folly to the Greeks and blasphemy to the Jews, is shameful and illustrative of the lengths to which God bends for us. God is simply not capable of anything but the most and the best and more, including the self-emptying into human matter and spirit, that God can, would, and does do. Admittedly, we human beings fail to so bend time and again. We begrudge equal employment opportunities, equal access to education and healthcare, equal welcome to our places of gathering and worship, and we fail thereby solidarity and the preferential option: we fail to do what God wills. Nevertheless, we each are called to persevere in aligning our wills to God's will as well as to God's will for others who we do not yet know. We human beings also succeed in bending, I venture, more often than not in spite of the scandalizing horror in war-torn locales, in refugee flight, in mass incarceration, in urban neighborhoods, in environmental degradation.[50]

It is all too clear that the Civil Rights Acts of anti-discrimination and enfranchisement have not lived up to their purposes, as many people had hoped. The unfortunate minimum applications of the law have been structured and institutionalized in deliberately anemic fashion, evident especially in the coverage formulae and, for the benefit of the privileged, without a program to teach and guide the populace how to pursue happiness and the common good with liberty and justice for all. Law's pedagogical value remains underutilized while God's example is often forgotten, even when just a little give-and-take in place of fully backward bending may be sufficient to accommodate an expressed need.

What practical take-away can be used to increase accountability to and solidarity with people so as to live a preferential option for those who are marginalized, to do what is right and just and best? As a start, interrogate the past with a view to interrogate the present.

1) Retrieve the dangerous memories and scandals of the past. Listen to the voices of wisdom with those who have been marginalized on the basis of their "deviance" from the dominant norms and follow their lead for change. PWD in particular experience violent crime—rape, sexual assault, robbery, aggravated assault, and simple assault—at twice the rate of non-disabled people in the US (and young teens with disabilities at three times the rate). More personally, perhaps less violently but marginalizing and oppressive nonetheless, members of minoritized communities have been excluded for far too long. The systemic institutionalized segregations of minority populations from the dominant power is no longer tolerable. Not unlike truth and justice commissions for restorative justice, PWD and other minoritized people must be heeded.
2) Dismantle what those who have been marginalized identify as oppressive and repressive structures and attitudes, inclusive of veiled microaggressions, that lead to internalized inferiority and self-hate among minoritized people while, at the same time, empower and embolden the dominant to dominate again. Regardless of race, sex, gender, class, or (dis)ability, each of us unconsciously learns from our respective places—as if it is in the air we breathe—the stereotypes about groups of people and individuals belonging to that group. Bullying, mocking, dismissing others reinforces assumptions of superiority in

dominant folks while it sadistically reinforces self-doubt and assumptions of inferiority in minoritized people. Dismantling institutionalized and structural oppressions requires a thorough examination of conscious and unconscious speech and behaviors by oppressor and oppressed alike. Success will require moderated conversations to expose the failures to recognize and honor the *imago Dei* present in everyone.

3) Internalize a hermeneutic of solidarity with and a preferential option for those who are marginalized. In the language of social justice movements, become an ally. Regardless of which side of the spectrum you stand on: know yourself, learn about others different from you in formal and informal ways, take chances on friendship, develop empowering communication skills, take action and advocate with and for those who are marginalized.
4) Then, look in and around common spaces—churches, schools, commercial and recreational venues, and government, in every gathering of the people—to note who is there and who is absent. Perform a regular check on inclusion. Where the gatherings are monochrome or mono-abled, there exclusionary practices of physical or attitudinal obstacles persist.
5) Repeat: listen and speak again with equal regard, then together assess results of initiatives to dismantle oppression, brainstorm next steps with additional expertise, and follow the lead of wisdom for solidarity and the preferential option to make change.

Concluding Thoughts

Envisioning justice as God wills it, while weaving in by warp and woof the threads of diversity, reveals the potentials of solidarity and the preferential option for the poor that require instruction on more than the status quo minimum interpretation of civil rights law. Consider too the standard that Jesus presents on fulfillment of the law versus the demands of the Commandments and the Beatitudes.[51] To so weave is to seek justice and mercy, the "two dimensions of a single reality that unfolds progressively until it culminates in the fullness of love" (*Misericordiae Vultus*, no. 20). Surely, God's justice wills the halt of the pervasive recurrence of discriminations, access denied, and violence experienced daily by too many members of minoritized peoples. Just as surely, God, who is Creator, has a plan of flourishing for all creation. That plan, God's will, is that all the parts are welcome, to have a place and role in a future blessedness sustained in and by the "laws" of justice and mercy as found in the parables of, for example, the Lost Coin (Luke 15:8–10), the Prodigal Son (Luke 15:11–32), and, par excellence, the Good Samaritan (Luke 10:25–37).[52] Finally and comprehensively, God's way of reconciling justice and mercy is definitive in the plain words and action of the Paschal Mystery: the whole story begun with the Incarnation through the stigma-scandalizing death and culminating in life restored and forgiveness won.

This kind of justice reflects the right relations between the parts: between persons (one to another), between persons and communities (along with their institutions, systems, and social structures), and between persons/communities and the goods of creation and those made by human hands to be shared not so as to simply survive but to thrive. Understood in Aristotelian terms (and followed by medieval scholars), those relations are determinable according to the being or properties distinguishing the nature(s) of persons and things (ST II–II, q. 57–61). Once those relations are determined, given the fundamental equality with which God creates all that is, moving forward in solidarity requires that we human beings, like God, bend over backward in our efforts to dismantle the systems that assign diminished "property" status and oppress individuals and communities thereby.

Misericordes sicut Pater! As Pope Francis and the tradition teach:

> Mercy: the word reveals the very mystery of the Most Holy Trinity. Mercy: the ultimate and supreme act by which God comes to meet us. Mercy: the fundamental law that dwells in the heart of every person who looks sincerely into the eyes of...brothers and sisters on the path to life. Mercy: the bridge that connects God and [human beings], opening our hearts

> to the hope of being loved forever despite our sinfulness. (*Misericordiae Vultus*, no. 2)

Mercy, which appears to defy the logic of justice, is its obverse. Mercy calls us to do more always and especially for those who have been downtrodden by the imposition of norms that do not reflect the encounter God wills. Mercy reflects "our willingness to enter into the chaos of another,"[53] including the chaos that is the scandal of stigma, of those who are voiceless, forgotten by indifference, and deliberately not counted, wounded, shot, lynched, bullied, ridiculed, institutionalized, raped, abused, and denied their humanity. "During this Jubilee, the Church will be called even more to heal these wounds, to assuage them with the oil of consolation, to bind them with mercy and cure them with solidarity and vigilant care" (*Misericordiae Vultus*, no. 15). God bends human ineptitude toward justice and mercy, calls humankind to accountability for unearned and unexamined privilege, and accommodates each and every one who has been bowed low so as to take their places and participate in every manner of human commerce. It is scandalous to do anything less.

Notes

1. Of course, other religious traditions have similar concerns for the weal of those in their midst who are vulnerable. Clearly, Judaism, the faith of Jesus of Nazareth, presents care for the widow, orphan, and sojourner as imperatives for the people, as important as the laws of the covenant. Islam too has among the pillars of faith support of those who are in need.

2. Although there are parallels found in the discriminations against women, non-heterosexuals, and religious minorities in the United States, in what follows I confine my argument to the discriminations against and minimums afforded to people of color and people with disabilities.

3. Since Fiscal Year 1997, more than 1.6 million charges have been filed with the EEOC. See "Charge Statistics, FY1997 through FY 2015," *Enforcement and Litigation Statistics*, Equal Employment Opportunity Commission, www.eeoc.gov/eeoc/statistics/enforcement/charges.cfm.

4. Among others, see Thomas Aquinas, "Treatise on Law," *Summa Theologiae*, I–II, q. 90–108; Cathleen Kaveny, *Law's Virtues: Fostering Autonomy and Solidarity in American Society* (Washington, DC: Georgetown

University Press, 2012); and Robert P. George, "Law and Moral Purpose," *First Things*, January 2008, www.firstthings.com/article/2008/01/001-law-and-moral-purpose.

5. See Kaveny, "Law as Moral Teacher," "Autonomy, Solidarity, and Law's Pedagogy," and "Law and Morality: Understanding the Relationship," in *Law's Virtues*.

6. With a single hand up in a sign language stop sign fashion, the Twitter feed #NotOK has "become a rallying cry of righteous indignation…[against] the bland, generic violence of what we, as a patriarchal society, deem acceptable…the ironic challenge to our social complacency and normalized expectations of well-being in the face of injustice." See Laurence Scott, "Not OK: How a Cunningly Terse Phrase Elevates Moral Virtue over a Bad Status Quo," *Boston Globe*, October 30, 2016, www.bostonglobe.com/ideas/2016/10/29/not/mBNeOrNivDfEWxRG072arK/story.html.

7. For an interesting examination of the ambivalent relationship between this cultural imagination and the realities of nation-building, see Edward L. Widmer, *Ark of Liberties: America and the World* (New York: Farrar, Straus and Giroux, 2008), especially chap. 6.

8. Among others, see Kelly Brown Douglas, *Stand Your Ground: Black Bodies and the Justice of God* (Maryknoll, NY: Orbis Books, 2015).

9. The FBI reports that more than 50% of homicide victims in 2015 are black folk in a nation of 321 million where blacks comprise a mere 13.3% of the population. That is, out of 13,455 murders 7,039 were black folk. See Federal Bureau of Investigation, Uniform Crime Reporting, "Murder Victims by Race, Ethnicity, and Sex 2015," ucr.fbi.gov/crime-in-the-u.s/2015/crime-in-the-u.s.-2015/tables/expanded_homicide_data_table_1_murder_victims_by_race_ethnicity_and_sex_2015.xls. Data for 2016 are not yet available; however, the black victim rate continues to rise. For one city's example, there were 798 homicides in Chicago in 2016. Of those 798, 624 are black, 133 Hispanic, 41 white/other. See Hey Jackass! Illustrating Chicago Values, "Stats," heyjackass.com/category/2016-stats/.

10. See Nora J. Baladerian, Thomas F. Coleman, and Jim Stream, *Abuse of People with Disabilities: Victims and Their Families Speak Out* (Los Angeles: Spectrum Institute, 2013), disability-abuse.com/survey/survey-report.pdf. Sadly, most of these crimes go unreported and, thereby, occur with ever-greater empowerment of the perpetrators (possibly with greater frequency) since they go unchallenged.

11. See Erika Harrell, "Crime against Persons with Disabilities, 2009–2013—Statistical Tables," US Department of Justice, Office of Justice Programs, Bureau of Justice Statistics (May 2015), www.bjs.gov/content/pub/pdf/capd0913st.pdf.

12. Civil Rights Act, Public Law 88–352, 88th Congress (July 2, 1964), https://www.govinfo.gov/content/pkg/STATUTE-78/pdf/STATUTE-78-Pg241.pdf: "An act to enforce the constitutional right to vote, to confer jurisdiction upon the district courts of the USA to provide injunctive relief against discrimination in public accommodations, to authorize the Attorney General to institute suits to protect constitutional rights in public facilities and public education, to extend the Commission on Civil Rights, to prevent discrimination in federally assisted programs, to establish a Commission on Equal Employment Opportunity [hereafter, EEOC], and for other purposes."

13. Voting Rights Act, Public Law 89–110, 89th Congress (August 6, 1965), www.archives.gov/historical-docs/doc-content/images/voting-rights-act.pdf: "An act to enforce the Fifteenth Amendment [ratified February 3, 1870, prohibiting denial of a citizen's right to vote on account of 'race, color, or previous condition of servitude'] to the Constitution of the United States, and for Other Purposes." Among the protections of the Voting Rights Act are the bans on literacy tests, English language comprehension (and provision of non-English ballots), and onerous (and superfluous) identification documents.

14. Americans with Disabilities Act, Public Law 101–325, 101st Congress (July 26, 1990), www.ada.gov/pubs/adastatute08.htm: "An act to establish a clear and comprehensive prohibition of discrimination on the basis of disability." This legislation and subsequent amendments offer (moderately) comprehensive rights to employment, services of human commerce, and participation in the *polis*. Among the protections of the Americans with Disabilities Act are prohibitions of firing or refusing to hire, segregation, harassment, and denial of reasonable accommodation(s) or access on the basis of a disability(ies).

15. In a nation where veterans of world wars and military conflicts worked alongside soldiers of different races, consider the visceral impact of media coverage on, for example, Brown v. the Board of Education of Topeka (1954), the Montgomery Bus Boycott (1955–56), Freedom Riders (1961), the Birmingham Campaign (April–May 1963), and the March on Washington (August 1963). Consider too that through the efforts of Martin Luther King, Jr., the Southern Christian Leadership Conference, the Student Nonviolent Coordinating Committee, and their allies, the nation's hypocrisy was exposed and evidenced particularly in violent civilian, military, and police aggression against deliberately non-violent protesters.

16. A good deal of my questioning and challenge to the dominant way of proceeding was inspired by anti-racism work with Pax Christi USA and critical theory à la Foucault. Among others, see Michel Foucault, *The Archaeology of Knowledge and the Discovery of Language* (New York: Pantheon Books, 1972).

17. A good deal of discriminatory practices have been and continue to rely on dualist presumptions that place some people (those exemplifying a

favored norm) over the mass of people who "fail" the norm. See Iozzio, "Norms Matter: A Hermeneutic of Disability/a Theological Anthropology of Radical Dependence," *ET-Studies* 4, no. 1 (2013): 89–106.

18. See US Equal Employment Opportunity Commission, "Prohibited Employment Policies/Practices" (2009), www.eeoc.gov/laws/practices/.

19. The category disability was added in 1990 to the EEOC bases covered by the Civil Rights Act.

20. See Code of Federal Regulations (ADA Title II) 28 CFR §35.104 Definitions and (ADA Title III) 28 CFR §36.104 Definitions.

21. On who qualifies, see Robert D. Dinerstein, "The Americans with Disabilities Act of 1990: Progeny of the Civil Rights Act of 1964," *Human Rights* 31, no. 3 (2004): www.americanbar.org/publications/human_rights_magazine_home/human_rights_vol31_2004/summer2004/irr_hr_summer04_disable.html. On reasonable accommodations, see Bonnie Poitras Tucker, "The ADA's Revolving Door: Inherent Flaws in the Civil Rights Paradigm," *Ohio State Law Journal* 62 (2001): 335–90.

22. See US Department of Justice, *Americans with Disabilities Act Title III Regulations: Nondiscrimination on the Basis of Disability by Public Accommodations and in Commercial Facilities*, "Supplementary Information" (Washington, DC: DOJ, 2010), www.ada.gov/regs2010/titleIII_2010/titleIII_2010_regulations.pdf.

23. Rosemarie Garland Thomson has coined the term *normate*. For her definition, see Garland Thomson, *Extraordinary Bodies: Figuring Physical Disability in American Culture and Literature* (New York: Columbia University Press, 1996), 8: "the veiled subject position of cultural self, the figure outlined by the array of deviant others whose marked bodies shore up the normate's boundaries. The term normate usefully designates the social figure through which people can represent themselves as definitive human beings. Normate, then, is the constructed identity of those who, by way of the bodily configurations and cultural capital they assume, can step into a position of authority and wield the power it grants them."

24. In reference to these capabilities, I recognize that each of us/all of us develop them with the help of many others through the infrastructures provided in greater or lesser degrees by our local, national, and international villages.

25. The coverage mandates have been challenged and, as recently as 2013, the US Supreme Court struck down as unconstitutional the requirement of certain jurisdictions, known for voter suppression, to preclear any voting changes with the federal government before implementing those changes. See Oluma Kas-Osoka, "A New Preclearance Coverage Formula: Renewing the Promise of the Voting Rights Act," *Washington University Journal of Law and Policy* 47, no. 1 (2015): 151–74.

26. The vote leading up to the November 2016 presidential election was the first to test the effect of the 2013 Supreme Court ruling. Without the Department of Justice approval to change rules and practices, "people are turned away from the polls, or purged from the rolls, or refused ID," early voting is curtailed, and something likened to a "hassle tax"—waiting in long lines to cast a ballot—imposed. See Emily Bazelon, "The Supreme Court Ruled That Voting Restrictions Were a Bygone Problem. Early Voting Results Suggest Otherwise," *The New York Times*, Nov. 7, 2016, www.nytimes.com/2016/11/07/magazine/the-supreme-court-ruled-that-voting-restrictions-were-a-bygone-problem-early-voting-results-suggest-otherwise.html?_r=0.

27. See Brennan Center for Justice, "New Voting Restrictions in Place for 2016 Presidential Election," New York University School of Law, www.brennancenter.org/voting-restrictions-first-time-2016.

28. See the United States Department of Justice, "About Section 5 of the Voting Rights Act," *Shelby County* Decision, www.justice.gov/crt/about-section-5-voting-rights-act; and Dana Liebelson, "The Supreme Court Gutted the Voting Rights Act. What Happened in These 8 States Will Not Shock You," *Mother Jones*, April 8, 2014, www.motherjones.com/politics/2014/04/republican-voting-rights-supreme-court-id.

29. See Julian Cardillo, "The Americans with Disabilities Act: 25 Years Later," *BrandeisNOW*, www.brandeis.edu/now/2015/july/parish-ada-qanda.html. Cardillo interviews Susan Parish, Professor and Dean, Heller School for Social Policy and Management, Brandeis University, who opines that injunctive relief yields small rewards to complainants to dis-incentivize legal recourse, and further even if defendant/employer loses the cost is low, and "Employers would be more likely to follow the law, and hire and promote people with disabilities, if the incentives were stronger."

30. On the systemic vulnerability of black lives in the US, particularly in vulnerability to law enforcement, see Richard Baudouin, ed., *Ku Klux Klan: A History of Racism and Violence* (Montgomery, AL: The Southern Poverty Law Center, 2011); Tom McKay, "One Troubling Statistic Shows Just How Racist America's Police Brutality Problem Is," *News.Mic*, https://www.mic.com/articles/96452/one-troubling-statistic-shows-just-how-racist-america-s-police-brutality-problem-is; The Editorial Board, "The Truth of 'Black Lives Matter,'" *The New York Times*, September 3, 2015, www.nytimes.com/2015/09/04/opinion/the-truth-of-black-lives-matter.html?_r=0. People with disabilities are at substantially greater risk for violence, 4 to 10 times more likely, than the general dominant population, see Karen Hughes, et al., "Prevalence and Risk of Violence against Adults with Disabilities: A Systematic Review and Meta-analysis of Observational Studies," *The Lancet* 379 (2012): 1621–29; Lisa Jones, et al., "Prevalence and Risk of Violence Against Children with Disabilities: A

Systematic Review and Meta-analysis of Observational Studies," *The Lancet* 380 (2012): 899–907.

31. See Kenya Downs, "When Black Death Goes Viral, It Can Trigger PTSD-Like Trauma," *PBS NewsHour*, www.pbs.org/newshour/rundown/black-pain-gone-viral-racism-graphic-videos-can-create-ptsd-like-trauma/. On exposure of systemic, institutionalized racism, see Julian Zelizer, "Is America Repeating the Mistakes of 1968?," *The Atlantic*, July 8, 2016, www.theatlantic.com/politics/archive/2016/07/is-america-repeating-the-mistakes-of-1968/490568/.

32. See also Kaveny, *Law's Virtues*, "Part I: Law as Moral Teacher."

33. Among others, see Gayatri Chakravorty Spivak, "Can the Subaltern Speak?" in *Marxism and the Interpretation of Culture*, ed. Cary Nelson and Lawrence Grossberg (Champaign: University of Illinois Press, 1988), 271–313; and Edward W. Said, *Orientalism* (New York: Random House, Inc/Vintage Books, 1979, 1978).

34. On being an ally and in solidarity with individuals and communities who have been (and often remain) oppressed by the colonialism that protects systemic racism, ableism, and heterosexism, see "Allyship and Solidarity Guidelines," Unsettling America: Decolonization in Theory and Practice, unsettlingamerica.wordpress.com/about/.

35. See, e.g., Michelle Alexander, *The New Jim Crow: Mass Incarceration in the Age of Colorblindness* (New York: The New Press, 2012); and Erving Goffman, *Asylums: Essays on the Social Situation of Mental Patients and Other Inmates* (New York: Anchor Books, 1961).

36. See APA Presidential Task Force on Preventing Discrimination and Promoting Diversity, *Dual Pathways to a Better America* (Washington, DC: American Psychological Association, 2010), 19.

37. Among others, see Vatican Council II, *Gaudium et Spes*; John Paul II, *Sollicitudo rei Socialis*; Benedict XVI, *Caritas in Veritate*; Francis, *Evangelii Gaudium*; see also Christine Firer Hinze, "The Drama of Social Sin and the (Im) Possibility of Solidarity: Reinhold Niebuhr and Modern Catholic Social Teaching," *Studies in Christian Ethics* 22, no. 4 (2009): 442–60.

38. See Iozzio, "Solidarity: Restoring Communion with Those Who Are Disabled," *Journal of Religion, Disability, and Health* 15, no. 2 (2011): 139–52.

39. I often wonder if I am asking too much of the law or if my expectations are too high. Then again, many individuals—parents, teachers, clergy, communities of common faith or purpose, and institutions of an ecclesial, professional, governmental kind—could *and should* hold themselves to do more than the minimums that these laws require.

40. The American Academy of Religion has been proactive in facilitating conversations on these intersections, particularly in the collaborative work and subsequent panel presentations and concurrent sessions sponsored by the

AAR's four Standing Committees on the Status of (1) Women, (2) Racial and Ethnic Minorities, (3) Lesbian, Gay, Bisexual, Transgender, Intersex, and Queer Persons, and (4) People with Disabilities in the Profession (the order here follows the committees' inceptions from first to most recent). For disciplines noting intersectionality, see, e.g., Jennifer C. James and Cynthia Wu, "Race, Ethnicity, Disability, and Literature: Intersections and Interventions," *MELUS* 31, no. 3 (2006): 3–13; and Beth Ferri, "A Dialogue We've Yet to Have: Race and Disability Studies," in *The Myth of the Normal Curve*, ed. Curt Dudley-Marling and Alex Gurn (New York: Peter Lang Publishing, Inc., 2010), 139–50.

41. Among my colleagues in disability studies, those deliberately engaging ethics include Kecia Ali, Julia Watts Belser, Amy Laura Hall, Heike Peckruhn, Hans Reinders, Darla Schumm, and Jon Swinton.

42. The history is scandalous. Among others, see Henri Jacques Stiker, *A History of Disability* (Ann Arbor: University of Michigan Press, 2002); Bruce G. Link and Jo C. Phelan, "Conceptualizing Stigma," *Annual Review of Sociology* 27 (2001): 363–85; Erving Goffman, *Stigma: Notes on the Management of Spoiled Identity* (Upper Saddle River, NJ: Prentice Hall, 1963).

43. Iris Marion Young, "Five Faces of Oppression," in *Justice and the Politics of Difference* (Princeton, NJ: Princeton University Press, 2011), 41.

44. Among others, see Sharon V. Betcher, *Politics and the Spirit of Disablement* (Minneapolis: Augsburg Fortress Press, 2007).

45. On normal, see Rosemary Garland Thomson, *Extraordinary Bodies: Figuring Physical Disability in American Culture and Literature* (New York: Columbia University Press, 1997); on power, see Michel Foucault, *Power*, ed. James D. Faubion, trans. Robert Hurley, et al. (New York: The New Press, 2000).

46. Goffman, *Stigma*, 3.

47. See especially Catherine Mowry LaCugna, *God for Us: The Trinity and Christian Life* (New York: HarperCollins Publishers, 1991).

48. Louis J. Puhl, *The Spiritual Exercises of St. Ignatius: Based on Studies in the Language of the Autograph* (Chicago: Loyola University Press, 1951), 50.

49. Although not immediately related to the point, the tradition of Ancient Near East and Roman crucifixion included, frequently enough, impalement. See David Tombs, "Crucifixion, State Terror, and Sexual Abuse," *Union Seminary Quarterly Review* 53, nos. 1–2 (1999): 89–109.

50. Among others, on war, see Theresa S. Betancourt, Jessica Agnew-Blais, Stephen E. Gilmar, David R. Williams, and B. Heidi Ellis, "Past Horrors, Present Struggles: The Role of Stigma in the Association between War Experiences and Psychosocial Adjustment among Former Child Soldiers in Sierra Leone," *Social Science and Medicine* 70, no. 1 (2010): 17–26; on refugees, see Pavan Joseph and Nasir Warfa, "Suicide and Self-Harm among Refugees and Asylum Seekers," in *Suicidal Behavior of Immigrants and Ethnic Minorities in*

Europe, ed. Diana D. van Bergen, Amanda Heredia Montesinos, and Meryam Schouler-Ocak (Boston: Hogrefe Publishing, 2015); on incarceration, see Alexander Mikulich, Laurie Cassidy, and Margie Pfeil, *The Scandal of White Complicity in US Hyper-incarceration: A Nonviolent Spirituality of White Resistance* (New York: Palgrave Macmillan, 2013); on urban violence, see Javier Auyero, Philippe Bourgois, and Nancy Scheper-Hughes, eds., *Violence at the Urban Margins* (New York: Oxford University Press, 2015); on the environment, see Alexandre Berthe and Luc Elie, "Mechanisms Explaining the Impact of Economic Inequality on Environmental Deterioration," *Ecological Economics* 116 (2015): 191–200.

51. See Yiu Sing Lúcás Chan, *The Ten Commandments and the Beatitudes: Biblical Studies and Ethics for Real Life* (Lanham, MD: Rowman & Littlefield Publishers, 2012).

52. So conclude Venerable Bede, William Spohn, James Keenan, and Pope Francis, among others.

53. James F. Keenan, *The Works of Mercy: The Heart of Catholicism* (Lanham, MD: Rowman & Littlefield Publishers, 2008), 4. See also Keenan, "The Scandal of Mercy Excludes No One," *Thinking Faith, Jesuit Media Initiatives*, December 2, 2015, www.thinkingfaith.org/articles/scandal-mercy-excludes-no-one.

Part Three

IMMIGRATION

3. Radical Solidarity
Migration as Challenge for Contemporary Christian Ethics

Kristin E. Heyer

This chapter first appeared in *Journal of Catholic Social Thought* 14 (2017): 87–104.

My own reflections on how the Christian narrative both disrupts dominant scripts regarding immigration flows and how migrants' experiences challenge theological ethics have been shaped by experiences at the United States-Mexico border.[1] Many have referred to the Arizona desert as the Lampedusa of North America. During my last visit to the binational Kino Border Initiative in Ambos Nogales (Arizona/Mexican border), I spoke with recently deported migrants at their aid center. One gentleman had spent twenty-six of his twenty-seven years in central California, brought there as a one-year-old by his uncle. He had worked harvesting pistachios and almonds to support his wife and four U.S. citizen children without trouble, even on the occasions he could not produce a driver's license for a routine stop. In the past two years, each such stop landed him in jail—with the third resulting in deportation to Nogales, Sonora. He expressed dread at starting over in a country foreign to him. Up the road at Casa Nazaret, we sat with deported women planning to reattempt the journey north in spite of the considerable dangers it posed. The women at the shelter were simply desperate to be reunited with their families in the U.S. One had worked at a hotel chain in Arizona for many years, supporting her two citizen children on her own after her husband left them; describing her initial reason for migrating from Mexico, she said, resigned, "At home you either eat or send your children to school." The Nazareth House residents repeatedly broke into tears as they shared the pain of being separated from their children and their experiences in detention.

Desert walks on the Arizona side have brought home the reality of a border fortification strategy that maximizes the risk of death. Whereas the rule of law rightly occupies a privileged place in the United States, I was struck during my visit to an Operation Streamline (deportation) hearing there by the sharp contrast between our nation's law-and-order rhetoric on the one hand, and the lack of accountability or transparency in Border Patrol procedures on the other—or the lack of due process afforded immigrant detainees. We watched young men and women shackled at the wrist, midsection, and ankles collectively herded through the legal process, lacking sufficient time with an attorney to comprehend what was happening and several lacking adequate translation. Closer to home I have met with undocumented university students facing impossible choices (for example, between disclosing their parents' whereabouts to immigration and customs enforcement or facing deportation, family separation, and the loss of university scholarships).

Encounters wherein questions of citizenship and enforcement tactics take on flesh and blood have shaped my reflections about the Christian narrative in light of migration. Despite significantly beefed up fortification—the United States continues to spend more on immigration enforcement than all other enforcement activities of the federal government combined—the recent increase in arrivals of unaccompanied minors and families from Honduras, El Salvador, and Guatemala rekindled fears of a "border out of control." The humanitarian outflow continues, driven increasingly by the fear of violence at the hands of organized crime in these northern triangle countries, with nearly 40,000 unaccompanied children and an equal number of mothers with children having arrived in the United States in Fiscal Year 2015.[2] Migrants from Honduras flee a home with the world's highest number of homicides per capita where gang members murder with impunity—the threat driving many such migrants is precisely the breakdown of the rule of law at home.

Whereas my own immigrant nation's celebratory narrative underscores ideas like hospitality, liberty, and democracy (reflecting Emma Lazarus' welcome to "huddled masses yearning to breathe free" at the Statue of Liberty's base), its legislative debates about immigration have historically centered on issues of national security, economic instrumentalism, and social costs rather than human rights. These operative lenses shaping its immigration debate can mask realities and become surrogates for other cultural and political concerns. Actual encounters with reluctant or desperate migrants alert us to significant dissonance between dominant political assumptions and the inhumane impact of many policies and practices. Christian ethics provides resources for scrutinizing dominant rhetoric to uncover the interests and values that principally drive immigration policy. If fear and profit largely hold sway, dehumanizing newcomers according to dominant scripts of "lawbreakers" or "takers," Christian commitments shape a (counter)narrative of our common humanity, and such solidarity has crucial implications for a just immigration ethic.

Prophetic and gospel imperatives of justice and compassion for the vulnerable together with scriptural texts enjoining hospitality to strangers ground a Christian immigration ethic. Just as the Good Samaritan promises additional recompense to the innkeeper, Christians are called to enter the world of the neighbor and "leave it in such a way that the neighbor is given freedom along with the very help that is offered."[3] The lack of freedom enjoyed by present and would-be migrants pointedly illustrates the urgency of this responsibility. The radical hospitality that tutors Christians' vision does not reduce our immigration response to charity or largesse, but requires justice. Immigrants encounter legion forms of injustice: the standard treatment of day laborers marked by rampant wage theft violates fundamental fairness in exchange. The regional juxtaposition of relative luxury and misery while basic needs go unmet challenges basic notions of distributive justice. The nearly 2,000-mile U.S.-Mexico border bisects the sharpest divide in average income on the planet. The impact of free trade agreements and utterly outmoded visa policies impede persons' active participation in social life. Becoming neighbor to the migrant demands meeting basic responsibilities in justice, particularly given the role a receiving nation has played in shaping conditions that directly contribute to irregular migration.[4]

Too often "the locus of responsibility remains solely with the migrant, excluding the global and transnational context in which migration occurs."[5] Writing from Qatar, Ian Almond recently proposed an "instability tax" be levied upon "any capital-possessing entity, private or governmental, which has contributed to the destabilizing of refugee-producing regions"—whether hedge funds profiting off commodity-trading in African minerals or weapons manufacturers profiting from selling arms to the Middle East, or any multinational who has profited "from the systemic degradation or destabilization of a poorer country."[6] The inability of small family farmers in Mexico to compete with agricultural subsidies implicates taxpayers to their north. Frameworks of structural and restorative justice bid policymakers to address root causes of displacement and hold stakeholders accountable for its consequences, rather than engage in amnesic scapegoating or enforcement-only approaches. Theological ethics invites us away from "crisis management" and toward honest, contextual assessments of what enduring patterns the crises reveal.

Hence whereas significant theological and migration scholarship considers how contributions from Scripture, Catholic social thought, ecclesiology, and economic ethics reorient the immigration debate, xenophobic and shortsighted responses prevail. Christian ethics must better attend, it seems, to the forces that inhibit solidarity with migrants and abet human rights violations. In light of non-rational influences on moral agency, formulating the best moral and political arguments is necessary but not sufficient. Hence I wish to focus on several challenges to Christian ethics these dynamics pose: first, the need to take seriously the depth and complexity of sin when fostering a just immigration ethic (attending to nonvoluntary factors alongside important human rights protections or negotiating the limits of national sovereignty); and second, the invitation to reconsider the impact of certain idealized norms and emphases in light of the experiences of migrant women.

Dynamics of Resistance: Sin, Inhospitality, and Injustice

A moral anthropology marked not only by relational agency but also by the complexities of sin—pride, insecurity, ignorance, group egotism—should ground our analysis of the interlocking forces at play amid pervasive commodification of migrant women and men. Whereas a Christian anthropology yields substantive claim rights that transcend citizenship status, challenging the legitimacy of many exclusionary political and economic policies, persistent resistance to a human rights paradigm endures. On Lampedusa, Pope Francis signaled how we must not only encounter migrants with compassion and justice but also heal global indifference and idolatry. Twentieth-century Christian elaborations of collective egotism and social sin can help unmask operative disvalues that harden resistance to a Christian immigration ethic.

Reinhold Niebuhr's insights on individual sin that becomes magnified in groups shed light on trends that harm immigrants, whether via government policies or nativist narratives. On his view, when we resolve our anxiety over the paradox of finitude and self-transcendence in sin, our pride and will-to-power inevitably wreak injustice.[7] For Niebuhr the universal human experience entails the sin of "seeking security at the expense of another life."[8] In his elaboration of the way collective pride multiplies injustice and conflict, Niebuhr singles out the nation state, as "most able to make absolute claims for itself, to enforce those claims by power and to give them credibility by the majesty and panoply of its apparatus."[9] Not only do state repression and national exceptionalism bear out this analysis, but also efforts to overcome insecurity that directly contribute to migration flows: whether through opportunistic capital investment, material extraction in developing countries, or active recruitment of racialized and gendered immigrant labor.[10]

Niebuhrian group egotism is evident in exclusionary construals of national identity and in strategies that obscure such endeavors alike. Nativist elements of U.S. culture have historically served to manufacture an imagined sense of community.[11] Representations of the outsider as a social menace have been continually reinvented in moments of national crisis, with the general pattern evidencing xenophobia's productive function in the national imagination. "The project of imagining a homogeneous nation is never complete. It requires the continual presence of the immigrant as other, through whom citizenship and belonging are rearticulated."[12] Subhuman rhetoric that results from this politics of difference remains strikingly similar (and racialized) across diverse global contexts. (In the European context, we have recently heard commentators refer to refugees as "swarms and invasions of cockroaches" in some quarters). In the United States, anti-immigrant sentiment rooted in this construal of a fixed national identity over and against an "outsider" has led to the demonization of populations of color through increasingly mainstream outlets—we see this in a recent 40% increase in anti-Hispanic hate crimes.[13] The politics of exclusion continue to play out in the evolving refugee crisis here in Europe and on the presidential campaign trail in the United States. Hence Niebuhrian "group pride" of national, economic, and ethnic elites eclipses immigrants' full humanity from consideration with violent and unjust consequences.

Such cultural forces that consistently elevate national or societal security concerns above moral ones wield significant influence. Probing the relationship between such structural injustices and legitimating ideologies can illuminate these modes of resistance to a Christian immigration ethic. Expanding beyond the narrow construal of social sin in Catholic encyclicals to incorporate insights from liberation theology allows us to more comprehensively unmask the ideologies that facilitate pervasive rights violations and callous indifference. Certainly, the structures of injustice identified by Pope John Paul II as he elaborated the scope and meaning of social sin over his corpus connect to contemporary patterns of irregular migration: lawmakers and industry lobbyists make concrete decisions that shape visa caps and commodity subsidies with harmful effects. Yet his theological circumscription of the category to underscore individual responsibility constrains its value for uncovering the subtle social dynamics that impact personal agency.[14]

The Medellín and Puebla analyses are more sensitive to the unconscious dimension of social sin and the impact unjust structures have on personal agency.[15] The blindness produced by absolutizing human attitudes holds relevance for an adequate understanding of the scope and responsibility for sin;[16] such blindness can prevent recognition, since exploitative institutions both are sustained by the appearance of legitimacy and "tend to create a culture of conformity and passivity."[17] Employing the category of social sin to connect the structural injustices with liberationists' more nonvoluntary influences that abet and result from communal actions elucidates more of a dialectical relationship between personal and social sin: structures are both consequential and causal in nature, and persons are subjectively responsible for sinful situations yet remain subject to external influences. This understanding has significant bearing on the topic of receptivity to an ethic of justice: that is, socioeconomic and political structures that lead to undocumented immigration are connected to the ideological blinders that obstruct hospitality to immigrants.

On this view distinct yet related elements of social sin shape complex dynamics at play in such resistance. For example, the primacy of deterrence has institutionalized security concerns rather than concerns for human rights or family unity in U.S. immigration laws; the nation's economic interests have been institutionalized in uneven free trade agreements.[18] When concerns about our identity get distorted by xenophobia and fear, anti-immigrant sentiment and ethnic-based hate crimes surge. At a more subtle level, a consumerist ideology shapes citizens' willingness to underpay or mistreat migrant laborers either directly or through indirect demand for inexpensive goods and services. These interconnected attitudes and institutions then produce the blindness that lulls residents into equating "law-abiding" with "just" or into apathetic indifference.

Writing about the European context, Marianne Heimbach-Steins links analogous colonial legacies. She suggests colonial structures shaped not only long-term international political and economic relationships that have inhibited equal participation but also "culturalist patterns, ideologies of domination and subordination which continue to influence the way international migrants are treated in legal systems…and economic and social practices of their [origin or destination] societies."[19] Hence despite dismantled political structures of traditional colonialism, strategies of political and social exclusion and power asymmetries persist.[20]

Such intersections with respect to the global economy have been of particular concern to Pope Francis. In *Evangelii Gaudium* he warns that our "economy of exclusion and inequality kills." He rightly challenges not only the reductive market ethos dominating trade and migration policies that casts migrants as "pawns on a chessboard," but also its desensitizing effects: "The culture of prosperity deadens us; we are thrilled if the market offers us something new to purchase; and in the meantime all those lives stunted for lack of opportunity seem a mere spectacle; they fail to move us."[21] Idolatries focused on having over being can impede solidarity with immigrants as much as nationalistic ones: they shape loyalties, frame questions, inform votes.

Some ideological currents of neoliberal globalization—fatalistic understandings of the "price of progress" or "Market Fundamentalism"—

configure our coordinates for what becomes normal or conceivable.[22] The tendency within and beyond U.S. culture to understand the freedom of the markets as a categorical imperative rather than instrumental good can blind us to the gospel's demands.[23] These ideologies reinforce international structures that impede accountability to a global common good. By contrast, the idea that the economy should serve the person raises serious concerns not only about the freedom of markets compared to people, but also about the significant financial stakes in broken immigration systems—detained immigrants fill beds, deportations fill private buses. Indeed, elements of the "immigration industrial complex," have become a transnational, multibillion dollar affair.[24] Share prices for GEO group and Corrections Corporation of America spiked in the summer of 2014—with the influx of migrant children crossing the border—in light of improved occupancy across their federal "real estate portfolios."[25] As Anna Rowlands has argued, such practices also "distance the state from direct responsibility for the moral conduct of [outsourced detention] processes."[26] Various commitments to economic growth at all costs can become authentic bondage that contributes to scotosis.

Converting from Entrenched Social Sin: Radical Solidarity

These intertwined patterns of social sin require repentance from idolatries that disempower those beyond our immediate spheres of concern and borders. From repentance and conscientization we are called to conversion toward interdependence in solidarity. In contrast to a narrative of the self-made person, a Christian understanding of ourselves as freely "gifted" can motivate actions that enact gratuity in response. Such metanoia can occur through personal encounters and relationships that provoke new perspectives and receptivity. Given the non-voluntary dimensions of social sin, Christian ethics must be challenged not only to call for the defense of human dignity or hospitality to strangers, but to attend to these complex structures and ideologies that abet complicity, preventing justice for migrants. Viewing immigration through the lens of individual culpability alone—whether reducing irregular migration to the actions of willful lawbreakers or blaming inhospitality on militant nationalists—obscures the multileveled, subtle dynamics at play. Migration exists not only within but because of complex global structures that benefit some at the expense of others.[27] Given the reach of exclusionary global dynamics, and the consequent inadequacy of both state-centered responses and migrant-focused enforcement, radical solidarity can help (re)frame migration as a shared international responsibility and cultivate conversion from pervasive idolatries. I employ the term "radical" here in terms of its etymological meaning related to "the roots." Tapping into root causes not only of migration but also of dehumanizing apathy or over resistance calls forth institutional solidarity as well as an incarnational solidarity that profoundly retrains attitudes, fostering a culture of encounter that shapes decisions and policies. It also demands conflictual solidarity, where warranted, rather than unduly optimistic approaches that ignore power dynamics shaping pervasive harm and injustice.

Pope John Paul II forwarded solidarity as the key virtue demanded in a globalized era of de facto interdependence: "the social face of Christian love."[28] David Hollenbach has proposed *institutional solidarity* as a necessary means of moving patterns of global interdependence from ones marked by domination and oppression to ones marked by equality and reciprocity. Institutional solidarity demands the development of structures that offer marginalized persons a genuine voice in the decisions and policies that impact their lives.[29] It requires the inclusion of comprehensive sets of stakes at the decision-making table, structures of institutional accountability and transparency, and empowered participation (subsidiarity).[30]

As unwilling migrants become dislodged from traditional livelihoods, cultures, and homelands by globalized economic forces, conflicts, or climate change, they confront political boundaries in likewise transitional conditions. The "deterritorialization of basic economic, social and cultural practices from their traditional moorings in the nation state"[31] has led nation states to respond in paradoxical ways: what Marcelo Suàrez-Orozco characterizes as "hyper-absence" regarding the flows of capital across national borders and "hyper-presence" in terms of militarizing borders and regulating membership.[32] Understanding immigration as "individual actions of emigrants" wherein individuals are the primary site for enforcement and responsibility has become increasingly incompatible with transnational politics and economies.[33] On the one hand, the displacement of government functions onto nongovernmental institutions and the need to enforce human rights protections indicate a change in the exclusivity and competence of state authority;[34] on the other hand, despite these institutional and philosophical shifts, the state continues to guarantee and distribute rights.[35]

Understanding human rights as transcendent of citizenship and immigration dynamics as related to unjust international political and economic divides makes the cultivation of such solidarity with "near and distant neighbors" ever urgent.[36] In contrast to focusing on the symptoms of immigration alone, the concept of institutional solidarity helps (re)frame migration as an international issue linked to trade and geopolitics. The virtue of solidarity can help convert inadequate structures and distorted visions in the face of our de facto interdependence. This institutional solidarity will require nations to share accountability in the wake of the Westphalian model's "partial eclipse" and to convert from opportunistic patterns of interdependence. Migrant deaths in the Arizona desert and Mediterranean alike make poignantly clear the stakes of nations failing to understand themselves as collectively responsible for these shared challenges.

In light of the depth and lure of sinful resistance to the steep challenge global solidarity imparts, two additional dimensions of solidarity are required: incarnational and conflictual solidarities. Given the grip of egotism in our "soap bubbles" of indifference, some observers have described the reception of recent Catholic teaching on solidarity as superficial or nonexistent. Incarnational solidarity departs from valuable intellectual and institutional dimensions of solidarity to immerse our bodies and expend precious energy in practices of concrete accompaniment in the real world. Christine Firer Hinze's evocative metaphors for the reach of consumerism reflect the dynamics of social sin: a culture whose "kudzu-like values and practices so crowd the landscape of daily lives that solidarity finds precious little ground in which to take root."[37] She highlights consumerist culture's use of seduction and misdirection to "lay a soothing, obfuscating mantle over systemic injustices that solidarity would expose, [as] its participants are…fed a stream of distractions and novelties, and situated in a 24/7 schedule of work-spend-consume that virtually ensures they will 'pay no attention' to the suffering multitudes behind the curtain."[38] Given the interconnection between unjust international structures in need of reform and these pervasive ideologies, an "incarnational" solidarity like Hinze has proposed complements the institutional solidarity advanced above. In his 2015 Message for World Day of Migrants and Refugees, Pope Francis framed his calls for protecting migrants' dignity and excavating root causes in a gospel response of mercy that leads to solidarity with others and cultivating a culture of encounter.[39]

At the same time, promoting solidarity among institutions and persons cannot bypass conflict and loss. Liberation theologians and social ethicists have noted magisterial Catholicism's tendency to prioritize unity, harmony, and synthesis in ways that circumvent necessary conflict. Without confronting issues of economic and political power and engaging grassroots mobilization, work toward and implementation of changes to the status quo will remain stunted; so contesting inequalities also requires a tolerance for disagreement, may entail lament or righteous anger—in short the recalcitrance of the privileged may demand a more "conflictual solidarity" as well. In a world where luxury and misery rub shoulders,[40] economic idolatry serves to avert our gaze from Lazarus; moreover, amid such skewed access to power, genuine solidarity may demand conflict.[41] The Australian bishops have noted that righteous anger in the face of injustice is a Christian and necessary response of love. They also promote proactive engagement of the poor and the oppressed as the engine of such change, given that "God has chosen the little and excluded ones to play the key role in the drama of humanity and to act as the central agents of the Kingdom."[42] Niebuhr's realism mentioned above helps hone a sense of conflictual solidarity. His consideration of group egotism purifies an overly irenic approach to structural and ideological change alike,[43] emphasizing groups' distortion by "the effects of members' inattention and ignorance due to finitude, their culpable flights from understanding and responsibility, and their selfish grasping after power, possessions and profit."[44]

An awareness of power dynamics and the entrenched temptations of sin at personal, social, and structural levels prompts Christians to hopeful and shrewd resistance to the economic idolatries and structural injustices neoliberal globalization inflicts.

Whereas Christian insights into sin and solidarity significantly reorient reigning approaches marked by crisis management or economic functionalism, migrants' experiences and insights also suggest additional challenges to Christian ethics, "growing edges" where Christian moral frameworks may be critiqued and nourished by attention to the constraints they face along with the courage and resilience they exhibit. I would like to turn briefly to the way in which gender-neutral analyses of migration and the typical purview of family ethics can miss critical dimensions of migrants' experiences and moral responses alike as one example.

Gendering Migration Analyses: Challenges for Catholic Family Ethics

The operative market logic that fosters push and pull factors and exploitation also obscures immigrants' full humanity as mothers, fathers, and children. Recent patterns of migration across the Americas reflect global feminization trends: Latin American immigrant women have increasingly joined the U.S. labor force after a history of disproportionately male migration north. Heightened U.S. border enforcement since the mid-1990s has contributed to this trend; as it became more difficult to cross without documents or travel back and forth seasonally, male migrants extended their stays and arranged for their families to join them. Significantly more women are migrating on their own, as well. With stagnating male wages in the lower sector and the growth of female-headed households, migrant women's employment wields increasing significance in determining families' economic well-being.[45] Women on the move face particular threats, from sexual assault by smugglers to abuse on the job. Less likely to qualify for employment-based immigration than men, most migrant women work in the informal sector. Domestic work, for example, regularly leaves migrant women victim to exploitation through long hours, isolation, and low wages. In fields and factories, undocumented women are often perceived by predators as "perfect victims" of sexual assault: they remain isolated, uninformed about their rights, and are presumed to lack credibility.[46] Beyond well-founded fears that reporting abuses will risk job loss and family separation via deportation, women lack access to legal resources and face language barriers and cultural pressures.[47] These threats to migrant women's well-being frequently impact families on both sides of the border. In light of a Catholic understanding of the family's social mission, conditions that perpetuate family separation undermine the common good. The integral family humanism highlighted in Catholic family ethics reorients immigration stakes away from economic or political calculations. Families comprise our most intimate relationships such that protracted separation threatens our very human subjectivity.

Yet it is not only neoliberal capitalism or callous attitudes that harm immigrant families. Particular understandings regarding the nature of women and the value of caregiving labor also contribute to these patterns. Assumptions about the complementarity of the sexes that often lurk below Catholic family ethics bolster unequal burdens for the work of social reproduction with religious sanction. Even with his praise for women's "immense contributions to the church" (at the Philadelphia cathedral) Pope Francis continues recent papal emphases on women's "feminine genius," which he notes "finds a particular, even if not exclusive, expression in motherhood." The language he uses suggests a "deeper theology of women" need not meaningfully contest the "equal but different" status that hinders women's flourishing in "public" and "private" venues alike. These conceptions mask aspects of women's labor, legitimize a "second shift"—felt most poignantly by women at the bottom economic rungs struggling for their own families' survival—and increasingly pit women against one another in shouldering the work of social production.

A lack of shared responsibility for the daunting demands facing mothers in the low-wage workforce is frequently camouflaged by lip service given to a narrow construal of family values in U.S. political and ecclesial settings. As upper- and middle-class women have been liberated from some domestic tasks, in many cases this is accomplished by relying upon low-wage workers (frequently undocumented migrants), thereby duplicating gendered labor or reinforcing traditional divisions of labor. Whereas one class of women may gain liberation from such tasks in the service of external workplace participation (or leisure), this dynamic ensures that the work remains women's work. Anthropologist Jennifer Hirsch describes this "outsourcing of caring" in the developed world in vivid terms: "Now the changing of diapers of both the very young and the very old—as well as the cleaning of the toilets of those who are, however temporarily, between Huggies and Depends (infant and elder diapers)—is done largely by darker-skinned hands." The nanny from Manila who raises the children of working parents in Manhattan is propelled not only by a global capitalist order to which commoditized love belongs, but also by assumptions about caregiving work.

Just as a narrow focus on marital and sexual norms obscures social factors harming families, dominant portrayals of marriage and family can issue inadequate ideals. The iconic Christian symbol of motherhood of "the Virgin Mary peacefully cradling a newborn baby" does not fully speak to the experiences of many mothers who "must tirelessly labor to feed and protect their children."[48] Attending to the concrete pressures facing transnational families may help the church better appreciate the violence, fragility, and cultural forces—beyond relativism or sexual libertarianism—that directly impact families' lives. A Christian family ethic under-attentive to the transnational family dynamics neglects significant factors that complicate strict ideals. Supporting families demands cultural norms that equitably share and value caregiving work, economic and political policies that unite families, and enforcement strategies that do not hinder family and community well-being. Rather than uncritically denigrating or glorifying migrants' survival strategies or family networks, it is important to bear in mind ways in which they are shaped by the challenges of economic insecurity; this dynamic suggests that ethics and social policies alike must not focus on changing family behaviors alone, but also improving economic conditions and supporting a range of existing family arrangements.

Attending to women and children on the move and families in limbo across the Americas exposes patterns at odds with Christian commitments to human rights and the sanctity of family life. In turn, idealized family and gender norms risk reifying particular virtues or cultural models in isolation and can overlook significant barriers to familial flourishing. These caveats prompt contemporary Christian family ethics' important emphases on families' inherently sacred and social dimensions toward more inclusive and reality-based norms for families and communities. Even as dominant lenses in immigration debates conceal via partial or false narratives (e.g., distortions of security, rule of law, or economic concerns), it is urgent to also interrogate ways in which dominant ethical frameworks similarly mask complex realities and genuine values when they overlook the experiences of vulnerable agents. Familial patterns of distributive injustice across the double (or triple) "shift," the trials of separated family members, and migrant women's courage in the face of formidable barriers highlight shortcomings of ethical methods that assume agency without constraint. Cross-border encounters remind us that migration decisions are rarely personal choices alone. Such experiences underscore the inadequacy of approaches that flatly criminalize irregular migrants (as in, "what part of illegal don't you understand?" sound bites). Criminal justice systems and Christian churches alike too seldom focus on enduring structures and ideologies that abet crime and sin. The experiences of migrant women can help alert both spheres to these inadequate notions of agency. Gender-neutral analyses of migration in ecclesial and political settings miss critical dimensions of migrants' experiences and diminish an adequate moral response. Radical solidarity with migrant women demands confronting "the roots" of their vulnerability and exploitation in all quarters.

Conclusion

Border encounters highlight mutual dynamics—whether those necessary for integration of newcomers in the spirit of intercultural *convivencia* or considering how Christian ethics' own methodologies must continually be informed by new voices. Even as fundamental Christian categories expose and squarely condemn pervasive threats to migrants' well-being, they remain inadequate to the fullness of their experience. Keeping the three-dimensionality of the immigrant in our range of vision—at once constrained and courageous, compromised and competent—remains essential for the work of Catholic ethics and the work of social change alike. Justice demands the protection and empowerment of immigrants amid the thicket of barriers they confront. In the end, while important research focuses more on crafting theological and moral arguments for just immigration policy, I remain convinced the task of Christian ethics must extend to shaping imagination for receptivity. Whereas fear of the other is easily mass-marketed, mutual understanding across difference can be harder to come by and engender.

In his historic address to the U.S. Congress last month, Pope Francis summoned listeners to something seemingly far less radical than solidarity or subversive hospitality or kinship: The Golden Rule. Identifying as a fellow descendant of immigrants from a shared continent of foreigners, he asked the American people through their representatives to identify with the needs and dreams propelling the immigrants traveling north in search of a better life for themselves and for their loved ones, asking, "Is this not what we want for our own children?" He pleaded with us not to give into a temptation to discard them as troublesome or fear and dehumanize them due to their numbers. Citing Matthew 7:12, he transformed what might seem a lower bar for ethics than those proposing a radical solidarity would promote into the ground of mutual understanding across difference. With characteristic directness and clarity he concluded, "In a word, if we want security, let us give security; if we want life, let us give life; if we want opportunities, let us provide opportunities. The yardstick we use for others will be the yardstick which time will use for us."[49] Pope Francis's prophetic solidarity with immigrants throughout his papacy and his unwavering attention to ideologies that inhibit such kinship offer us a way forward. We who are "settled" must remember that even remaining adrift in a sea of indifference is a privilege. May the church cultivate radical solidarities that "heal the wounds" of social sin that threaten our common good and our common home.

Notes

1. Portions of this essay are adapted from arguments I advance in *Kinship across Borders: A Christian Ethic of Immigration* (Washington, DC: Georgetown University Press, 2012) and "The Politics of Immigration and a Catholic Counternarrative: A Perspective from the United States," *Asian Horizons* 8, no. 4 (December 2014): 719–37.

2. Testimony of Most Reverend Mark J. Seitz, bishop of El Paso, TX, before the Senate Committee on Homeland Security and Governmental Affairs on Ongoing Migration from Central America: An Examination of FY 2015 Apprehensions, available at http://www.usccb.org//about/migration-policy/congressional-testimony/upload/seitz-ongoing-migration.pdf.

3. John R. Donahue, *The Gospel in Parable* (Philadelphia: Fortress Press, 1988), 133.

4. John J. Hoeffner and Michele R. Pistone, "But the Laborers Are… Many? Catholic Social Teaching on Business, Labor and Economic Migration," in *And You Welcomed Me: Migration and Catholic Social Teaching*, ed. Donald

Kerwin and Jill Marie Gerschutz (Lanham, MD: Lexington, 2009), 74. For an excellent discussion of such connections, see William R. O'Neill, SJ, "Anamnestic Solidarity: Immigration from the Perspective of Restorative Justice," paper delivered at the 2009 Catholic Theological Society of America Halifax, Nova Scotia (June 5, 2009). See also Kristin Heyer, "A Response to 'Restorative Justice as a Prophetic Path to Peace?'" Plenary Address by Stephen J. Pope," *Catholic Theological Society of America Annual Proceedings* 65 (2010).

5. Silas W. Allard, "Who Am I? Who Are You? Who Are We? Law, Religion, and Approaches to an Ethic of Migration," *Journal of Law and Religion* 30, no. 2 (June 2015): 323.

6. Ian Almond, "The Migrant Crisis: Time for an Instability Tax?" *Political Theology Today* (September 22, 2015) available at http://www.politicaltheology.com/blog/the-migrant-crisis-time-for-an-instability-tax/.

7. Reinhold Niebuhr, *The Nature and Destiny of Man*, vol. 1, *Human Nature* (Louisville, KY: Westminster/John Knox Press, 1996; orig. Charles Scribner's Sons, 1941), 179.

8. Niebuhr, *Nature and Destiny*, 182. Consequently guilt "represents the objective and historical consequences of sin," for which the sinner is held responsible; guilt represents "the actual corruption of the plan of creation and providence in the historical world," 222.

9. Niebuhr, *Nature and Destiny*, 209. Niebuhr describes group egotism in terms of the egotism of racial, national, and socioeconomic groups.

10. Yen Le Espiritu, *Home Bound: Filipino American Lives across Cultures, Communities and Countries* (Berkeley: University of California Press, 2003), 207 as cited in Gioacchino Campese, "*¿Cuantos Más?*: The Crucified Peoples at the U.S./Mexican Border," in *A Promised Land, A Perilous Journey: Theological Perspectives on Migration* (Notre Dame: University of Notre Dame, 2008), 279.

11. As reflected in the short-lived Alien and Sedition Act of 1798, imposed by the Federalist administration of John Adams, the representation of the foreigner as a political and social menace has been a fundamental element of American nationalism since the founding. Ali Behdad, *A Forgetful Nation: On Immigration and Cultural Identity in the United States* (Durham, NC: Duke University Press, 2005), 10.

12. Behdad, *A Forgetful Nation*, 11–12.

13. T. Brader, N. A. Valentino, and E. Suhay, "What Triggers Public Opposition to Immigration? Anxiety, Group Cues, and Immigration Threat," *American Journal of Political Science* 52 (2008): 959–78.

14. I analyze John Paul II's and Latin American theologians' approaches to social sin in "Social Sin and Immigration: Good Fences Make Bad Neighbors," *Theological Studies* 71, no. 2 (June 2010): 410–36. Whereas social sin

may not directly cause personal sin, it "creates an environment in which it becomes more difficult to make good choices," heightening the tendency "present because of original sin to turn away from God." Mark O'Keefe, OSB, "Social Sin and Fundamental Option," in *Christian Freedom: Essays by the Faculty of the Saint Meinrad School of Theology*, ed. Clayton N. Jefford (New York: Peter Lang, 1993), 142.

15. The adoption of the language of social sin in liberation theology emerged with the 1968 Medellín, Colombia, conference where the Latin American bishops explicitly identified their reality as a sinful situation of institutionalized violence rooted in "the oppressive structures that come from the abuse of ownership and of power and from exploitation of workers or from unjust transactions." Consejo Episcopal Latinoamericano (CELAM), "The Church in the Present-Day Transformation of Latin America in Light of the Council" (Washington, DC: U.S. Catholic Conference, 1973), 78, 49. The 1979 gathering of CELAM at Puebla, Mexico, underscored the Medellín assessment, while attending more to the relationship between personal and structural sin. CELAM, "Evangelization at Present and in the Future of Latin America" (Washington, DC: National Conference of Catholic Bishops, 1979).

16. In *Sollicitudo rei socialis* and *Evangelium vitae* Pope John Paul II identifies non-voluntary elements that remain in tension with his significant emphasis on personal responsibility but hold potential for expanding beyond a derivative notion of social sin: the "all-consuming desire for profit" and "the thirst for power, with the intention of imposing one's will upon others" to which nations and blocs are prone, imperialistic ideologies and "the almost automatic operation of economic and political institutions;" the "eclipse of the sense of God and of man [that] inevitably leads to a practical materialism, individualism, utilitarianism, and hedonism," and the "darkening of the human conscience both individually and in society—a confusion about good and evil that encourages the culture of death and consolidates structures of sin." See *Sollicitudo rei socialis* 37 and *Evangelium vitae* 23–24.

17. Gregory Baum, "Structures of Sin," in *The Logic of Solidarity: Commentaries on Pope John Paul II's Encyclical "On Social Concern,"* ed. Gregory Baum and Robert Ellsberg (Maryknoll, NY: Orbis, 1989), 113–14.

18. Whereas the aggregate impact of NAFTA or CAFTA is complex, most agree they have taken a negative toll on the most vulnerable populations in Latin America, who rely more than ever on remittances sent home by family members who migrate to the United States. In 2008, the bishops of Mexico directly linked the recent surge in immigration to the United States to the effects of NAFTA on small rural communities whose farmers are unable to compete with heavily subsidized producers north of their border. Chapter 4 of my *Kinship across Borders* considers this issue in further detail.

19. Marianne Heimbach-Steins, "Migration in a Post-colonial World," in *Religious and Ethical Perspectives on Global Migration*, ed. Elizabeth W. Collier and Charles R. Strain (Lanham, MD: Lexington Books, 2014), 93.

20. Heimbach-Steins, "Migration," 87.

21. Pope Francis, *Evangelii Gaudium* 54.

22. Timothy Jarvis Gorringe, "Invoking: Globalization and Power," in *The Blackwell Companion to Christian Ethics*, ed. Stanley Hauerwas and Samuel Wells (Malden, MA: Blackwell Publishing Ltd., 2004), 353.

23. Robert W. McElroy, "Market Assumptions: Pope Francis' Challenge to Income Inequality," *America*, November 3, 2014.

24. See Tanya Golash-Boza, "The Immigration Industrial Complex: Why We Enforce Immigration Policies Destined to Fail," *Sociology Compass* 3, no. 2 (Feb 2009): 295–309 for a genealogy of this idea, which alludes to the conflation of national security with immigration law enforcement and "the confluence of public and private sector interests in the criminalization of undocumented migration, immigration law enforcement, and the promotion of 'anti-illegal' rhetoric" (295).

25. Nicole Flatow, "Private Prison Profits Soar as Companies Cash In on Incarcerated Immigrants," *Think Progress*, September 2, 2014, available at https://thinkprogress.org/private-prison-stocks-soar-as-companies-cash-in-on-incarcerated-immigrants-8a1ffd83041e/.

26. Anna Frances Rowlands, "On the Temptations of Sovereignty: The Task of Catholic Social Teaching and the Challenge of UK Asylum Seeking," *Political Theology* 12 (2011): 843–69.

27. Allard, "Who Am I?," 324.

28. John Paul II, *Solicitudo rei socialis* 40.

29. David Hollenbach, SJ, "The Life of the Human Community," *America*, November 4, 2002, 7.

30. David Hollenbach, SJ, *Common Good & Christian Ethics* (New York: Cambridge University Press, 2002), 225.

31. Marcelo M. Suarez-Orozco, "Right Moves? Immigration, Globalization, Utopia and Dystopia?" in *American Arrivals: Anthropology Engages the New Immigration*, ed. Nancy Foner (Santa Fe, NM: School of American Research Press, 2003), 50.

32. Suarez-Orozco, "Right Moves?," 51.

33. Saskia Sassen, *Globalization and Its Discontents: Essays on the New Mobility of People and Money* (New York: The New Press, 1998), 6–8.

34. Sassen, *Globalization and Its Discontents*, 24–26.

35. Seyla Benhabib, *Another Cosmopolitanism* (New York: Oxford University Press, 2008), 175. Seyla Benhabib identifies a concomitant development as the "disaggregation of citizenship." She notes that as institutional developments unbundle three constitutive dimensions of citizenship—collectively identity, the

privileges of political membership, and the entitlements of social rights and benefits—an increasing number of people worldwide "find themselves not sharing in the collective identity of their host countries while enjoying certain rights and benefits as guest workers or permanent residents" (45).

36. William O'Neill, SJ, "Rights of Passage: Ethics of Forced Displacement," *The Journal of the Society of Christian Ethics* 27, no. 1 (Summer 2007): 123.

37. Christine Firer Hinze, "Straining toward Solidarity in a Suffering World: *Gaudium et spes* 'After Forty Years,'" in *Vatican II: Forty Years Later, College Theology Society Annual Volume 51*, ed. William Madges (Maryknoll, NY: Orbis, 2005), 180.

38. Hinze, "Straining toward Solidarity," 181–82.

39. Holy Father's Message for World Day of Migrants and Refugees, October 1, 2015, available at https://w2.vatican.va/content/francesco/en/messages/migration/documents/papa-francesco_20140903_world-migrants-day-2015.html .

40. Second Vatican Council, *Gaudium et spes* 63.

41. Denis Goulet, *The Cruel Choice: A New Concept in the Theory of Development* (New York: Atheneum, 1971), 170 as cited in Sniegocki, *Catholic Social Teaching and Economic Globalization: The Quest for Alternatives* (Milwaukee: Marquette University Press, 2009), 314.

42. Australian Catholic Bishops Conference, "A New Beginning: Eradicating Poverty in our World," (1996), 68 as cited in Sniegocki, *Catholic Social Teaching and Economic Globalization*, 320.

43. Niebuhr's distinct approach better attunes us to the profound challenges facing structural conversion as he "tracks the way sinful self-interest clouds awareness of structural sin, confounds efforts to understand it, and removes the motivation to combat it." See Christine Firer Hinze, "The Drama of Social Sin and the (Im)possibility of Solidarity: Reinhold Niebuhr and Modern Catholic Social Teaching," *Studies in Christian Ethics* 22, no. 4 (2009): 457.

44. Hinze, "The Drama of Social Sin," 457.

45. Chenoa A. Flippen, "Intersectionality at Work: Determinants of Labor Supply among Immigrant Latinas," *Gender & Society* 28, no. 3 (June 2014): 404–5.

46. See Southern Poverty Law Center, "Injustice on Our Plates: Immigrant Women in the U.S. Food Industry," 42.

47. Southern Poverty Law Center, "Injustice on Our Plates," 42.

48. Cathleen Kaveny, "Defining Feminism: Can the Church and World Agree on the Role of Women?" *America*, February 28, 2011.

49. Address of Pope Francis to the Joint Session of the U.S. Congress, September 25, 2015.

Part Four

LGBTQ

4. Catholic Lesbian Feminist Theology

Mary E. Hunt

This chapter first appeared in *Sexual Diversity and Catholicism: Toward the Development of Moral Theology*. Edited by Patricia Beattie Jung with Joseph Andrew Coray. Collegeville, MN: Michael Glazier, 2001.

Catholic lesbian feminist theology is no longer an oxymoron. Like the gay Catholic work of John McNeill and the queer Catholic work of Robert Goss, it simply reflects another perspective within a wide tradition that is always getting wider.[1] Catholic feminist theology is well established.[2] But the lesbian dimension is only now surfacing as part of a larger debate.

One reason for this lacuna is the mistaken but widespread notion in a patriarchal culture that homosexuality is really a male experience. Or, if women are involved, we are involved in a way that is derivative of men. Androcentric readings of scriptures and the erasure of lesbian experiences as such have allowed theologians and ethicists (both male and female) to ignore the specificity of lesbian women. For example, it is not clear that Catholic moral theology on homosexuality is based on any knowledge of lesbians' lives. We are understood, if at all, as some dim reflection of gay men, or some odd permutation of heterosexuality. Happily, this is not the case in real life. Our experience needs to be reflected in theology. And, just as important, we need to "do theology" out of our particularity if the Christian community is to be whole and its reflections on questions of ultimate meaning and value are to be valid.

The Vatican intensified the contradiction by silencing Sr. Jeannine Gramick, SSND, and Fr. Robert Nugent, SDS, in 1999 because of their pioneering work to build bridges between lesbian/gay and other Catholics. At that time Joseph Cardinal Ratzinger reiterated the kyriarchal position that homosexual orientation is "disordered" and that homosexual acts are "intrinsically evil."[3] But many Catholics who love a lesbian daughter or a gay son, who live next door to a lesbian couple, or who work with a gay man have come to realize that this is simply wrong. They add their common sense to the range of psychological, philosophical, sociological, and theological arguments marshaled in opposition to the institutional Catholic Church's view.

In this climate I offer with caution a Catholic lesbian feminist starting point for theological reflection. First, the dangers of essentialist thinking lurk. Just as there is a wide spectrum encompassing what we call "Catholic," so too is "lesbian" disputed territory in the sexual arena. Is one born a lesbian? Does one become a lesbian? If so, how and why? Likewise, "feminist" has grown from its gender-based origins to encompass analyses and strategies aimed at overcoming many inequalities, including racism, economic deprivation, and other forms of structured/interstructured injustice. Nonetheless, I believe that a well-defined Catholic lesbian feminist perspective can contribute clarity and, with luck, insight to the discussion.

I begin this sketch for a portrait—as surely more extensive treatment is required in the future—in three steps. First, I note that the kyriarchal view of homosexuality is based on male experience in a patriarchal church and that it ignores women's experiences. I do so not to claim the moral superiority of lesbians, but to suggest that our rejection of the male-defined policy goes well beyond feeling excluded. It is symptomatic of structures of exclusion and of sex-specific kyriarchal policies promulgated without women's input, such as the non-ordination of women, that affect the whole church. Second, I outline five theological/theoretical sources offered by feminist/womanist/*mujerista* theologians and writers that help to shape a Catholic lesbian feminist theological starting point in an increasingly pluralistic religious context. Third, I suggest what a Catholic lesbian feminist theology might look like in such a setting as we expand the horizons of contemporary spirituality.

My approach is speculative, relying on analysis and imagination as well as on data and history. It is fundamentally theo-ethical, aimed at taking seriously the experiences of women that have yet to inform kyriarchal Catholicism. From a feminist liberation theological perspective, I am concerned with how theology emerges from human experiences and how theological teachings influence the faith lives of adherents. Such a theology is rooted in Catholic social justice teachings and culture, coheres with the reality on which it is based, and fosters the faith of those for whom it is intended. In this case I have a "preferential option" for lesbian voices that have been silenced. I join the other authors in this anthology in renewing Catholic moral theology through tradition-conscious and community-respecting work.

Kyriarchal Catholicism, the Ban on Male Homoerotic Activity, and the Telling Absence of Women

Feminist critiques of kyriarchal Catholicism began with language and imagery, as Mary Daly so nimbly pointed out more than thirty years ago.[4] Among the well-known sticky wickets of contemporary Catholicism are male names for the Divine, symbols and images such as Father, Lord, Ruler, King; the right to test a vocation to the priesthood reserved to males only, coupled with most significant decision-making left in the hands of ordained men; and male-centered sexual ethics, especially the ban on women's reproductive choice.

There is substantive disagreement between the teachings of the kyriarchal Church and the theological practices and teachings of many Catholic feminists. For example, female language for the Divine, including pronouns and images like the name Sophia, is used commonly in feminist liturgical base communities, those places where so many Catholic feminists worship. Priesthood is redefined in feminist theological terms, and its duties, including celebrating the Eucharist, are shared in feminist Catholic groups. These are serious disagreements that admit of no easy resolution, but Catholic life goes on despite them. Of course there are penalties. A case in point is the Massachusetts Women-Church group being banned from church property by Bernard Cardinal Law. Likewise, privileges are conferred on those who conform, as in the extension of a mandatum to teach in Catholic higher education according to the specifications of *Ex Corde Ecclesiae* only to those whose theology matches that of the kyriarchal Church.

While the substance of such theological disagreements is not trivial, and the price is often high, even more problematic is the fact that structures of power have not evolved to foster new ideas based on the diversity of human experience. Despite decades of feminist work, the androcentric bias remains firmly in place because there is literally no opening for women at the highest levels of church life where policy is decided. Nor is there any move toward renewed institutional structures that would include more and varied people in the process. I believe that this failure to bring about structural changes is, in the long run, far more serious than any of the gender-specific matters at hand. A more participatory process would allow other information to surface because respected members of a mature community would bring those experiences to the table.

The non-ordination of women is a case in point.[5] Whether women are eventually ordained is for many feminist theologians less important than whether decision-making structures are changed to reflect a more inclusive, participatory model. In fact, we are skeptical whether the ordination of women to the priesthood as presently conceived will ever achieve that goal. Even if a few conforming women are ordained and placed in positions of decision-making, the fundamental model will not be altered. This exclusive dynamic is clear in the institutional Church's position on homosexuality, formulated by clerics in the absence of a range of lesbian/gay/bisexual and transgendered peoples' experiences. Anecdotal and some survey research on the high percentage of male priests who are gay adds the pathetic dimension of self-hatred to this scene.

Pre–Vatican II Catholic theology relied relatively little on Scripture. But in this case, texts that condemn male homosexual behavior were part of the weight of evidence: Genesis 19:1–29, the misinterpreted story of inhospitality from which the dreaded word *sodomy* was born; Genesis 38:1–11, the spilling of seed that is seen as a violation of procreative laws; Leviticus 18:22, men who lie with men commit an abomination; Leviticus 20:13, men who commit this sin are to be killed.[6] Nary a mention of lesbian women, who certainly were not spilling seeds, much less treating strangers inhospitably! I think rather of Ruth and Naomi who, if anything, were a suggestive prototype of committed women's friendship, whether lovers or not. But they are oddly missing from the discussion.

Nonetheless, when it comes to policy, lesbian women are equally enjoined from same-sex sexual practices. Why? Because the general

Catholic theological approach before feminist correctives, and still today in those unreconstructed Catholic approaches, was to assume, however falsely, that women's experiences were included in male experiences. It is only with Romans 1:26 that women merit a mention on their own terms: "Their women exchanged natural intercourse for unnatural...." But even this portion of the text is left aside in most interpretive arguments, which end with sweeping condemnations based on male experience.

Bernadette Brooten, in her impressive study on female homoeroticism in the early Christian period, claims that Paul "used the word 'exchanged' to indicate that people knew the natural sexual order of the universe and left it behind."[7] In her view, the Pauline idea of female sexuality was based on presumed gender differences and a hierarchically dualistic way of thinking about sex, with men in charge and women in a receiving mode. This model was foisted onto same-sex couples such that one homosexual partner was thought to act as a male and the other as a female.[8] She observes that in the Pauline world, gay men gave up status by allegedly adopting a passive role in homosexual conduct, while lesbian women theoretically gained status by giving up a passive role.[9] Some critics argue that Dr. Brooten's reading gives far more credit for nuance to Paul than he deserved. In any case, the differences between women and men in same-sex relations seem to have gotten lost when it comes to the use of Scripture to inform policy.

Far more weight in Catholic theology was placed on philosophical teachings, especially natural law, where the hetero-bias is strong. Still, no one seems to have probed the obvious, namely, what women thought was natural, how women experienced their love for one another, what women felt about making love with each other without fear of pregnancy or the need for an abortion. But now we know better, and it is time to formulate Catholic lesbian feminist theology accordingly.

It is hard to imagine a contemporary discussion, one that might have been part of the Gramick/Nugent case, for example, in which Church officials would make a blanket argument against homosexuality in the face of the abundant data on lesbian lives. First, they would have to discuss the matter *with* lesbian women, not talk *about* people who are fully capable of representing their own position. This would be a breakthrough, signaling the willingness of kyriarchal Catholic theological policy makers to engage in dialogue, not rule by fiat.

Then they would have to reject, or at least counter, the abundant psychological evidence that finds most lesbian women healthy and well adjusted despite social pressures, as Isaiah Crawford and Brian D. Zamboni have shown.[10] They would need to bypass the thousands of lesbian-led families in which children are being raised to be productive citizens. They would be forced to ignore the testimony of Catholic lesbian women who find that root values of love and justice from our religious tradition inform our lives and relationships.[11] Such a conversation would be evidence of a historic methodological shift, as well as, presumably, one that reflects new content.

Church officials would have to deal with the fact that lesbian women, like gay men, are more than the sum of our genitalia. As such, we expect to be treated like all other persons who make up the Catholic community, not pigeonholed and denounced with terms that have no bearing on our being. We expect to be agents in the formation of, and not passive recipients of, the theo-ethical teachings of our tradition. This requires changes in structures that are finally far more profound than changes in teachings on homosexuality, however revolutionary such positive teachings would be. These changes require a democratic, participatory approach to being Church that has thus far been roundly rejected by those who make decisions, and vigorously endorsed by those who engage in Church reform.

Up to now I have passed over the matter of lesbian sexuality as such. I do so not because it is irrelevant. To the contrary, it is important as part of the data of revelation that go into theological reflections. But part of the patriarchal trap in Catholic theology is the presumption that what is at stake is primarily sex and not also, and perhaps in fact more foundationally, power. I see the structural power issues as critical to renewed theo-ethical work. While it might make life slightly easier to accomplish a repeal of the "disordered," "intrinsically evil" language, I consider it even more important that we challenge the way in which such policy is made and the notion that there is one Catholic position on the question. Learning to live with and value a diversity of opinions among Catholics will, in my judgment, stand us in better stead in an increasingly pluralistic context.

Further, the "sex" in question as the parameters of debate are set within Catholicism is normatively heterosexual and open to procreation.

Any other kind of sex is automatically defined as "objectively immoral." On those terms there can be no fruitful discussion that does not put lesbian women in a defensive position with regard to our own lives and in an oppositional posture with regard to gay men. I refuse to start there.

Rather, I insist that what is in play is precisely who decides, and how we decide, what is important in the moral arena, what will be prioritized for discussion and how issues will be couched. From a lesbian feminist perspective, the most important issue is not sex as such, however defined, but how we learn to live respectfully as a Christian community of people who share a diversity of lifestyles. Privileging one, in this case heterosexuality, is patriarchy's trick to which feminists are now wise. Its widespread implications in employment, inheritance, and family law are too devastating to be ignored.

Part of the patriarchal furor over homosexuality is caused by undue emphasis on the genital sexual component to the detriment of any careful analysis of the "homo," or social, dimension of same-sex love, much less any analysis of the love component. Let's start there. Two women or two men who fall in love, just like their hetero counterparts, experience feelings that not even the most competent poet can capture on a page. They are attracted to each other, an attraction they live out physically as well as emotionally. They enjoy life together—meals, sex, movies, sports—and do not want that time to end, ever. So they commit to each other, work out the parameters of their relationship, figure out finances, children, aging parents, and all the other aspects of daily life that shared love involves. With luck, Catholics might say with grace, they enjoy a long life together in the company of friends and family. Same-sex love is, after all, first and foremost love.

I am not naive about the fact that many people—heterosexual and homosexual, bisexual and transgendered (though those terms are now problematic and contested)—have no such storybook experiences. Nor am I unaware that the lack of support systems for same-sex love propels some people, especially some gay men, toward anonymous sex and a bar/bath scene that leave much to be desired. But those realities have as little to do with homosexuality as such as brothels and wife abuse have to do with heterosexuality as such. They need to be looked at critically, of course, but not on the basis only of sexuality. They need to be evaluated as potential health risks, just as sexual abuse is evaluated not primarily in terms of sex but of violence. To do otherwise is to miss the obvious, and/or to actualize an anti-homosexual agenda.

Moreover, lesbian women and gay men have less in common than is sometimes thought. I say this not to disconnect us in the struggle for justice, and not to imply any moral superiority of women, whose opportunities for casual sex are generally fewer. To the contrary, I want to clarify our respective starting points to highlight the "lesbian" on its own terms, something rarely done in discussions where the gendered aspects of homosexual experience are conflated.

For example, economic resources are different when two men form a bond versus when two women come together. Two white male incomes usually outweigh two female incomes, with all of the accompanying privilege, access, and entitlement of white men in a patriarchal society. Racial and class differences affect this dynamic, but the general trend toward male hegemony is clear and not trivial in Catholic circles where such privilege is codified. Differences in the power to ensure their own safety accrue variously to men and women. Two men can be mutual protection, much needed as hate crimes mount. But as Adrienne Rich wrote, "Two women sleeping together have more than their sleep to defend."[12] These differences point to deep issues that require ethical problematizing so as to approximate justice for all.

Add sex-role socialization, access to work and legal protections, and we find extremely varied experiences for lesbian women and gay men.[13] This is not to mention the complexities for bisexual and transgendered people, whose situations are beyond the scope of this essay. All of this raises ethical work to do and still not a mention of lesbian genital sex. In short, there is much more at stake than who sleeps with whom. Yet kyriarchal Catholic theologians persist in offering a blanket condemnation of that about which they know so little. They seem to have no regard for the many complexities of same-sex love in a heterosexist context. There must be a better way that does not play lesbian women and gay men off against one another and us against our heterosexual, bisexual and transgendered friends, a way that serves to make the world safer for people of all lifestyle choices.

Feminist Theological/Theoretical Sources and Strategies That Pave the Way for Lesbian Claims

Feminist theologians/theorists have been in the vanguard of those promoting social justice through careful consideration of the interlocking structures of kyriarchy. What began as a gender analysis is now, thanks to womanist, *mujerista*, and other women's challenges, a full-scale social change project encompassing racial and economic issues, attention to nationality and ability, age and gender, and including attention to the earth and all its inhabitants. It is from this rich resource that I cite five insights that help to situate a Catholic lesbian feminist theological starting point.

Women's Moral Agency and Bodily Integrity

Feminist Christian ethicist Beverly Wildung Harrison, in her landmark book on abortion *Our Right to Choose*, makes the case for women's moral agency.[14] She cites the history of philosophy as full of impediments to women's decision-making, from women barred from giving testimony to pregnant women kept from deciding whether to continue or terminate their pregnancies. Human history is proof that women can and do make good decisions on reproductive health as in other matters.

Coupled with this ability to be a moral agent is what she calls "women's bodily integrity," the extent to which women have responsibility for our bodies. Pregnancy makes this obvious, but so, too, I believe, does lesbian life wherein the female body is also central. Against the tide of patriarchal logic, women who love women are moral agents fully capable of making good decisions to love others whose bodies are similar. This does not mean that all lesbian relationships are good. Indeed, just like some heterosexual relationships, some lesbian relationships are morally dubious, as when they contain violence or otherwise inhibit the growth of the partners. But in principle, lesbian relationships are rooted in the bodily integrity of women who choose women for their intimate companions, respecting their bodies as bodies.

Community Focus

A second insight comes from *mujerista* Catholic theologian Ada María Isasi-Díaz, whose insistence on community helps to mitigate what might be the privatizing aspects of an individual focus.[15] She argues for this in light of the Hispanic women with whom she lives and works, contending that it is not her view as a theologian but the community's considered judgment that counts. In so doing she reverses the Anglo tendency to tout the rugged individual.

The tendency toward privatized analysis that might emerge from a lesbian starting point needs to be countered by understanding how wider communities of women, including heterosexual and bisexual women, understand issues. It is often the case, for example in the ordination of Catholic women, that what excludes one excludes all, albeit for lesbian women on more virulent terms. Such solidarity is key to avoiding co-optation, and such communal thinking is a check against privatization.

Erotic Power

A third useful idea comes from the brilliant work of poet and essayist Audre Lorde, who wrote about "the erotic as power."[16] Here the insight comes specifically from a lesbian woman's experience of just how powerful erotic attractions and attachments can be. She saw this as a force for social change, "a well of replenishing and provocative force."[17]

For Catholic lesbian feminist theological work, it is this positive possibility that sets the stage for discussion of lesbian sexuality. Far from denying or degrading women's sexual pleasure, far from minimizing or magnifying its importance, Audre Lorde names all women's sexuality, using that of lesbian women as a prototype, as "creative energy empowered."[18] She explains why those who would contain it so often relegate it to the bedroom, when in fact erotic energy "becomes a lens through which we scrutinize all aspects of our existence…[causing us] not to settle for the convenient, the shoddy, the conventionally expected, nor the merely safe."[19] It is on these terms that I would begin a conversation with Vatican officials on the "ordered" nature of same-sex love and the "intrinsically good" nature of same-sex acts.

Justice Connections

Episcopal priest Carter Heyward contributes "our passion for justice" to the theological mix.[20] She insists that issues of sexuality are intimately connected to other justice struggles, beginning with racism and economic inequalities. Likewise, she implies that working on one issue propels one to see these connections because they are embodied in real people who suffer. From the experience of oppression comes a perhaps heightened sense of the need for solidarity. This lesbian feminist analysis is a major strategic offering. It is what allows those of us who are white lesbian women to relativize our struggle alongside that of people who are discriminated against on account of their race or ethnicity. It compels those of us who are economically affluent lesbians to put our energies into social change for economic justice. It helps to redirect our focus from sex to power so that we avoid the traps of arguing the wrong question.

Feminist Friendship

A fifth feminist insight comes from my own work on friendship as the normative adult relationship.[21] I believe that friendship, unlike marriage, is available to everyone, and that it has the potential to level the ethical playing field when it comes to evaluating relationships in communities. Far from being a privatized, romantic notion, friendships have political, practical implications. Building social structures on the basis of friends and not family allows everyone to benefit; everyone can be a friend, while not everyone can be married. Major legal and social changes would follow. For example, the case for universal health coverage would be made on the basis of our being/having bodies rather than on the current thinking that links coverage to having a job that provides coverage or being married to someone who does. Wholesale new ways of thinking come from a friend-based model rather than a family-based model.

The priority on friendship comes from a lesbian feminist perspective, but it does not stay there. Widely applied, it heads off the potentially atomizing aspects of postmodern life. It helps to counter the temptation to repeat the heterosexual model of marriage in an effort to be inclusive.

Instead, it offers to heterosexual, bisexual, transgendered, and homosexual people alike (however helpful/unhelpful those categories may turn out to be) the chance to think and act anew. A number of scholars have taken up this theme as a normative model of adult relating, both in theology and biblical studies, from a range of perspectives.[22]

Taken together, these five insights—women's moral agency and bodily integrity, a community focus, erotic power, the justice connections, and friendship as the normative adult relationship—form a solid feminist basis on which to critique patriarchal ways of thinking about homosexuality. It is the larger dimension of women's well-being and justice, not simply the lesbian dimension, that is crucial. These form a starting point from which to construct a Catholic lesbian feminist theology.

A Catholic Lesbian Feminist Theology

It is relatively easy to deconstruct patriarchal theology, especially when it is so clearly rooted in assumptions and practices that postmodern life has replaced, such as the assumed connection between sex and reproduction. It is more difficult to propose a constructive Catholic approach, since there is so little practice at offering new models that take women's experiences seriously. But before talking about the divine, it is important to clarify some of the more accessible human dimensions. I begin the theological and ethical conversation from this Catholic lesbian feminist starting point in the interest of moving the discussion forward on a fresh footing. I choose three issues central to contemporary lesbian life as the foci in the hope that they reveal contours of a larger whole.

Lesbian Sexual Expression

Lesbian sexual expression is, I daresay, as far from the experience of kyriarchal churchmen as possible. I shudder to think what they imagine lesbian women do in bed, in the shower or on the beach, at the grocery store or on vacation, at the movies or in a car, at work, or wherever else human beings express affection, care, and love for one another in genital and non-genital ways. What is it about how we play tennis or feed our children, volunteer in the community or take naps that makes us "disordered"? What is the difference between these ordinary things done by homosexual women (making them, strictly speaking, homosexual acts) and homosexual *sexual* acts? Are they all "intrinsically evil"? The real issue this question raises, of course, is how sexual expression is part of a larger relational constellation, and how that relationship is conducive of community. The rest, as the rabbis say, is commentary.

Lesbian women, like all human beings, seek to get and give love, enjoy expressing that love in physical ways, including genital contact when appropriate, and integrate our affective lives into complex and differentiated wholes. What we do in bed need not be objectified and labeled any more than any other sexual expression as long as it is safe and consensual. Survey evidence and my several dozen years of practice make me confident in saying that pleasure is pleasure, even more so when one's partner is beloved and trusted.

What does call for moral scrutiny is the extent to which we act safely, responsibly, mutually, and with care in our sexual dealings, the same criteria I would apply to all sexual behavior, no more, no less to lesbian women. With the HIV/AIDS pandemic full blown, the moral compass points toward prevention, even for lesbian women, who are among those at lowest risk. Then the intimate link between spirituality and sexuality can be nurtured in a Catholic lesbian feminist way and its fruits shared abundantly.

Shared Motherhood

One of the delights of the contemporary lesbian/gay life is the so-called baby boom, with thousands of lesbian and gay people having and/or adopting children. What could be more pleasing music to Catholic ears? From the Virgin Mary on, motherhood has always been valued. Now, in some happy cases, it is doubled! "Be fruitful and multiply" seems newly to apply to us! At least it is easier than it used to be for lesbians to have children, a substantive change in the thirty years since the Stonewall riots launched a wholesale lesbian/gay movement.

Reliable statistics do not exist because of the catch-22 of custody and the continued stigma in some circles about same-sex parenting. But anecdotal evidence abounds for the fact that new families are springing up where couples used to dwell. In the case of lesbians, there are now families with two mothers, whether both adopt a child, or one bears and the other adopts.

Such a boom has its pluses and minuses. Like the move toward same-sex marriage, it can lead to a certain pressure to have children, subtly reinforcing the heterosexist notion that to live responsibly without children of one's own is somehow a lesser life choice. I reject that, knowing many people who nurture and care in ways other than child-rearing. But the delights (not to mention the challenges) of forming a family and bringing up children are now experienced by a growing number of lesbian women and gay men.

I see this as evidence of the goodness of same-sex relationships, requiring the same degree of commitment, stability, and intention, and perhaps a little more, than for heterosexual couples. In fact, I see parenting as a more productive starting point than same-sex marriage for leveling the ethical playing field when it comes to some social benefits.

Some stable lesbian families have much to teach some unstable heterosexual couples about providing for the needs of children, balancing the demands of work and home life, keeping a relationship fresh amid diapers and homework. But it is precisely in such an everyday situation that religious faith is helpful for orienting decision-making, setting priorities, and coping with the inevitable problems. More so, faith communities, especially active parishes or small base communities like women-church groups, are the logical places for Catholic lesbian-led families to worship and expect support.

A Lesbian Call to Holiness

All theological projects are finally larger than any theo-political goals, any structural changes or dogmatic differences. They are aimed at fostering the spiritual well-being of faithful people, nurturing the divine-human love in its myriad forms. That is why, at base, the Vatican's claims about "disordered" and "intrinsically evil" dimensions of homosexuality are so destructive. People who hear such rhetoric rightly question the wisdom of everything else that comes from the same dubious source.

Catholic lesbian feminist spirituality is set in an increasingly pluralistic religious context. With more Muslims than Presbyterians, and spiritual options growing by leaps and bounds, the U.S. religious landscape is changing, dotted with opportunities for those who leave their traditions of origin in search of a closer fit with their current beliefs. I respect this and realize why it is the preferred mode of so many Catholic lesbians. But for those who wish to remain part of the tradition into which they were born or which they chose at an earlier time in life, it seems unjust to have a Vatican-promulgated anti-lesbian/gay policy act as a barrier. Hence my effort to develop a theology that is fully consistent with the best of Catholic social teaching and sacramental life: the call to holiness for all Catholics emphasized by Vatican II and the invitation to break bread and do justice.

Conclusion

The development of a systematic Catholic lesbian feminist theology is a larger project than one essay and a task for more than one person. But I hope that the groundwork laid here will serve as a foundation for others who seek to move beyond the parameters of a heretofore-unproductive debate. At least a Catholic lesbian feminist starting point signals another community at the table, another group bringing abundant resources to share, and an eagerness to do so. At most, such a theological perspective signals that the Catholic tradition is worthy of its name, universal, when those who have been marginalized join the community. Then the hard work of learning to live fruitfully with difference will start in earnest.

Notes

1. John McNeill's trilogy is foundational to Catholic gay theology: *The Church and the Homosexual* (Boston: Beacon, 1976); *Taking a Chance on God* (Boston: Beacon, 1988); *Freedom, Glorious Freedom* (Boston: Beacon, 1995). Robert Goss's *Jesus Acted Up: A Gay and Lesbian Manifesto* (San Francisco: HarperSanFrancisco, 1993) is the basic text in queer Catholic work. There is simply no Catholic lesbian equivalent yet.

2. Catholic feminist theology in the United States is grounded in the foundational work of Mary Daly, Rosemary Radford Ruether, and Elisabeth Schüssler Fiorenza, among others. It includes such scholars as Sandra Schneiders, Shawn Copeland, Elizabeth Johnson, and Margaret Farley, to name just a few of the dozens whose work is changing the face of the field.

3. *Kyriarchal* is a word coined by biblical scholar Elisabeth Schüssler Fiorenza to describe the interlocking forms of oppression such as racism, gender discrimination, economic injustice, and the like that combine in patriarchy to oppress people. See her *But She Said: Feminist Practices of Biblical Interpretation* (Boston: Beacon, 1992), 117, 123.

4. Mary Daly included a savvy treatment of lesbian issues in *Beyond God the Father* ([Boston: Beacon, 1973], 124–27), arguing that being a lesbian does not make one a feminist any more than being heterosexual excludes one from being involved in social change.

5. The issue is framed helpfully in *The Non-ordination of Women and the Politics of Power*, *Concilium* 1999/3, ed. Elisabeth Schüssler Fiorenza and Hermann Häring (Maryknoll, NY: Orbis, 1999).

6. Walter Wink distinguishes between these "unequivocal condemnations" and several other more ambiguous ones, e.g., 1 Cor 6:9 and 1 Tim 1:10. See his "Homosexuality and the Bible" in *Homosexuality and the Christian Faith: Question of Conscience for the Churches*, ed. Walter Wink (Minneapolis: Fortress, 1999), 33–49.

7. Bernadette J. Brooten, *Love between Women: Early Christian Responses to Female Homoeroticism* (Chicago: The University of Chicago Press, 1996), 244.

8. Brooten, *Love between Women*, 303.

9. Brooten, *Love between Women*, 266.

10. Isaiah Crawford and Brian D. Zamboni, "Informing the Debate on Homosexuality: The Behavioral Sciences and the Church," in *Sexual Diversity and Catholicism: Toward the Development of Moral Theology*, ed. Patricia Beattie Jung and Joseph Andrew Coray (Collegeville, MN: Liturgical Press, 2001), 216–50.

11. An early Catholic collection is Barbara Zanotti, ed., *A Faith of One's Own: Explorations by Catholic Lesbians* (Trumansburg, NY: Crossing Press, 1986).

12. Adrienne Rich, "The Images," in *A Wild Patience Has Taken Me This Far* (New York: Norton, 1981), 3.

13. Bisexual people's religious experiences are only now being taken seriously on their own terms. See Debra R. Kolodny, ed., *Blessed Bi Spirit: Bisexual People of Faith* (New York: Continuum, 2000). Transgendered peoples' faith perspectives remain to be published.

14. Beverly Wildung Harrison, *Our Right to Choose* (Boston: Beacon, 1983).

15. Ada María Isasi-Díaz, *En La Lucha/In the Struggle: A Hispanic Women's Liberation Theology* (Minneapolis: Augsburg Fortress, 1993).

16. Audre Lorde, "Uses of the Erotic: The Erotic as Power," in *Sister Outsider* (Trumansburg, NY: Crossing Press, 1984), 53–59.

17. Lorde, "Uses of the Erotic," 54.

18. Lorde, "Uses of the Erotic," 57.

19. Lorde, "Uses of the Erotic," 57.

20. Carter Heyward, *Our Passion for Justice: Images of Power, Sexuality, and Liberation* (New York: Pilgrim Press, 1984).

21. Mary E. Hunt, *Fierce Tenderness: A Feminist Theology of Friendship* (New York: Continuum, 1991).

22. See, e.g., Janice Raymond, *A Passion for Friends* (Boston: Beacon, 1986); Sharon H. Ringe, *Wisdom's Friends: Community and Christology in the Fourth Gospel* (Louisville, KY: Westminster John Knox, 1999).

5. Theology of Whose Body?

Sexual Complementarity, Intersex Conditions, and La Virgen de Guadalupe

Katie M. Grimes

This chapter first appeared in the *Journal of Feminist Studies in Religion* 32, no. 1 (2016): 75–93.

John Paul II's theology of the sexually complementary body props up existing Catholic magisterial teaching on marriage and the ordination of women.[1] It does so largely by presenting the obedient receptivity displayed by Mary at the annunciation as an icon of femininity and the active personality of Jesus and his Divine Father as icons of masculinity.[2] In this reigning magisterial sexual schema, the sexed body reveals a sexed soul: sexual difference pervades the psychological, spiritual, and ontological realms.[3]

John Paul II's theory of sexual truth, I argue, crumbles in the face of scientific and experiential challenges. Rather than reflecting upon human sexual experience as a truly inductive argument would, John Paul II dismissed experientially based challenges to his theory as lamentable distortions of the "truth" about masculinity and femininity. Rather than deriving "ought" from "is," John Paul II asserted "is" from "must."[4] John Paul II's theology of the body fails even on its own terms. In particular, I contend, the Virgin Mary herself does not fulfill John Paul II's criteria of femininity. Both during the annunciation and afterward, she acts quite queerly.

In order to make this argument, I first provide a brief overview of John Paul II's definitions of femininity and masculinity. Second, I argue that recent developments in the field of fertilization science call John Paul II's theory of the sexual person into question. Third, I demonstrate the ways in which the irruption of the intersex person into history further undermines John Paul II's understanding of the human body. Fourth, I discuss the ways in which Mary does not conform to the rules of womanhood that John Paul II supplied. Fifth, I explain why the "dangerous memory" of the Virgin Mary recorded in Luke's account of the annunciation and unwittingly offered in Virgilio Elizondo's reading of the Nican Mopohua reveals John Paul II's gender essentialism as not just inaccurate but one-sided: despite insisting that ontological gender must always match anatomical sex, John Paul II created a symbolism of sex and gender in which men can be feminine but women must never be masculine.[5]

Despite my non-Hispanic whiteness, I focus on Guadalupe for two main reasons. First, beloved by Mexican and Mexican American Catholics, she plays an increasingly formative role in shaping the theological and social imagination of my North American context. Second, John Paul II elevated her to patron of the Americas, despite the fact that she undermined core tenets of his anthropological theory. Guadalupe draws attention to the instabilities and contradictions within his sexual theology in ways few other figures could.

John Paul's Theology of Femininity and Masculinity

John Paul II described sexual complementarity as stipulating that "man and woman are called from the beginning not only to exist 'side by side' or 'together,' but they are also called to exist mutually 'one for the other.'"[6] For John Paul II, "man and woman" exist for each other not just in the macro level of society but also in the micro level of a heterosexual marriage, which provides the telos of the human person.[7]

This complementarity of sexual difference bespeaks more than mere generalities.[8] According to John Paul II, sexual identity holds constant regardless of social or historical context and exists more or less uniformly within each human person.[9] As John Paul II explained, "The personal resources of femininity…are…different" than the personal resources of masculinity.[10] Individuality transpires within the boundaries of an essential masculinity and femininity.[11] This universal sexual difference in turn reinforces a universally prescriptive and conjugal heterosexuality. Because every man is masculine and every woman feminine, every woman is oriented toward spousal union with a man just as every man is oriented toward spousal union with a woman. John Paul II conceived of a system without exceptions.[12]

For John Paul II, femininity and masculinity exist deep within the human person and not just at the level of anatomical difference.[13] In his view, the body, specifically the genitals and reproductive organs, "manifests the spirit."[14] As he explained on another occasion, "Body expresses person."[15] Sexual anatomy symbolizes and reveals one's interpersonal gifts and inclinations.[16] For example, women's anatomical capacity for motherhood renders women "more capable than men of paying attention to another person." For John Paul II, "motherhood concerns the whole person, not just the body, nor even just human 'nature.'"[17] Women are feminine all the way down.

John Paul II founded his prescriptive understanding of femininity on a Marian typology. In "becoming Theotokos," *Mary* "signifies the fullness of the perfection of what is characteristic of woman." For John Paul II, Mary's yes to Divine insemination provided "the culminating point, the archetype, of the personal dignity of women."[18] Women's loving receptivity characterizes their personality as not just mothers but also sexual lovers. According to John Paul II, "The gift of interior readiness to accept the child and bring it into the world is linked to the marriage union."[19] Woman possesses the capacity to make space in her body for a child because she has first made space in her body for her husband.

As the complement to woman's passive receptivity, man plays the role of active initiator of human love. While "the mystery of woman is revealed in motherhood," John Paul II located "the mystery of man's masculinity" in "the generative and fatherly meaning of his body."[20] Like woman's body, the meaning of man's body is revealed typologically. Just as women take their cues from Mary's receptive and maternal acceptance of God's masculine will, so men follow in the footsteps of a quintessentially masculine Christ. In this way, John Paul II contended, "Because Christ's divine love is the love of a Bridegroom, it is the model and pattern of all human love and men's love in particular." Specifically, John Paul II continued, "The bridegroom is the one who loves, the Bride is loved: it is she who receives love, in order to love in return."[21] Mary is not just the mother of Jesus; she is also his bride. Jesus is not just the son of Mary; he is also her bridegroom.

In deploying this gendered iconography of divinity and humanity, John Paul II *made* what Elizabeth Johnson has termed "'a necessary ontological connection' between the male human being Jesus and a male God."[22] John Paul II stated this relation explicitly. While the essentially maternal character of femininity makes women like Mary, the essentially paternal character of masculinity makes men God-like: according to John Paul, men "reveal and relive on earth the very fatherhood of God."[23] Jesus reveals the masculine meaning of man's body by acting as bridegroom both on the cross and in his relationship to the church. For John Paul II, Jesus's passion was not passive. Jesus was not killed; he chivalrously "[gave] himself up for her," heroically dying for his feminine mother-bride.[24]

As the example of Jesus's spousal love for the church demonstrates, for John Paul II, human beings were not male or female because they have certain types of bodies or use them in certain types of ways; rather, they have certain types of bodies and ought to use them in certain types of ways because they are male or female at the level of ontology. For this reason, despite the fact that John Paul II figured motherhood as "the fruit of the marriage union of a man and woman," even consecrated female virgins embody the essentially maternal spirit of femininity.[25] Interpreting Mary's virginal maternity as not an exception but the rule, John Paul II identified virginity and motherhood as the "two dimensions" or "paths in the vocation of women as persons."[26] According to John Paul II, women can be either virgins, consecrated as brides of Christ, or mothers, vowed in marriage to a male spouse. And both types of women "realize the personal value of their own femininity by becoming a 'sincere gift,'" either to God in the case of virginal religious sisters or to their husband in the case of sexually active women. In both cases, the woman loves her spouse receptively. Just as a married woman receives the prior love of her husband by returning it, so virgin women respond to Christ's prior gift of love by loving in return.[27] In so doing, married women and virginal ones imitate Mary's essentially feminine and receptively self-giving form of love and personhood.

In addition to affirming the sexual complementarity of "man" and "woman," the procreative compatibility of male and female body parts during vaginal intercourse also evidences both the essentially receptive character of femininity as well as the essentially active character of masculinity.[28] As John Paul II argued, "In sex husband and wife reveal and know each other."[29] In this way, "the marriage act" contains a "fundamental structure [that] constitutes the necessary basis for an adequate reading and discovery" of what he termed the "language of the body."[30] The full meaning of masculinity and femininity is known only through sexual intercourse.[31] For John Paul II, sexual intercourse alone enables the "definitive discovery of the meaning of the human body in its masculinity and femininity."[32]

And what language does the body engaged in sexual intercourse speak? Although John Paul II did not explicitly refer to genitalia, they implicitly informed his conclusions about sexual complementarity.[33] As John Paul II argued, "In Genesis, nakedness constitutes the immediate context of the doctrine about the unity of the human being as male and female."[34] "Man" and "woman" not only bear equally human bodies but these bodies also can fit together and become "one flesh" during sexual intercourse.[35] The implications of John Paul II's sexual theology appear clear. As "the one who loves," man initiates sexual activity. His desire comes first.[36] As the one who "receives love, in order to love in return," woman responds favorably to man's desire.[37] Sexual intercourse both ratifies and reveals the active character of masculinity and the passively receptive character of femininity. The man penetrates. The woman's vagina does not act on its own; it responds. These automated, anatomical characteristics symbolize the gendered person as a whole. Every aspect of a woman's body is figured as geared toward making room for a man's body. Every distinctly masculine aspect of a man's body is figured as geared toward gaining access to and entry in a woman's body.[38]

Just as the penis penetrates the vagina, so sperm penetrate the ovum. Just as the vagina responds to the penis's prior activity by receiving it, so the ovum responds to the prior activity of the sperm by receiving it.[39] In creating woman and therefore marriage, God "provides the visible world of creatures with particular conditions so that 'the love of God may be poured into the hearts' of the beings created in his image." Woman, as bride, is the one into whom God's love is poured first.[40] Man must love woman first because God loves humanity first. Just as woman responds to masculine love by returning it, so ought human beings to respond to God's love in kind.[41] Here, John Paul II seemed to imbue God's love with a seminal quality. This analogy, perhaps unintentionally, compares the symbolically heterosexual love of a masculine God for a femininely receptive humanity to the pouring of seminal fluid into the woman's vessel of a body.

Understood in this way, masculinity and femininity possess a heterosexual complementarity. Just as activity exists for the sake of receptive passivity, so receptive passivity operates only upon active initiation. Just as sperm finds procreative completion in the ovum, so the ovum is brought to procreative completion by the sperm. What the penis/sperm is, so is man; what the vagina/ovum is, so is woman.[42] The magisterium does not intend to reduce the human person to a sex act. In their view, these body parts reveal the sexual personality.

Inductive Counterarguments to John Paul's "Theology of the Body"

John Paul II touted the coherences between his sexual theology and the findings of the scientific field of sexology.[43] But John Paul II's attention to sexual science proved selective. Concrete marital experience demonstrates that sometimes the wife initiates sex and activates male desire. Sometimes, her desire precedes her husband's.[44] And sometimes, the wife controls the flow of sexual activity while the husband passively receives it.[45] More than just the conductor of sexual activity, women sometimes take the dominant spatial position during sexual intercourse, placing themselves "on top." In some cases, a wife possesses a higher sex drive than her husband. In practice, any heterosexual relationship will unfold as a cycle of giving and receiving in which neither partner qualifies as the "first mover." Rather than handing out unfiltered truth, John Paul II thus offered a subjective interpretation of sex.

Nor did John Paul II's implied description of the semiotics of sperm and ovum qualify as objective or self-evident. As anthropologist Emily Martin has demonstrated, in the case of fertilization science at least, scientific data has been filtered through the prism of preexisting ideology. In this way, she explains, predominantly male scientists have fabricated what she terms a "scientific fairy tale" in which the passive egg "must depend on the sperm for rescue." In this tale of masculine heroism, the sperm embark upon an uncertain and treacherous "mission" dedicated to "moving through the female genital tract in quest of the ovum."[46] In these accounts, she summarizes, "Sperm are described as penetrating the egg, and specific substances on a sperm's head are described as binding to the egg." As Martin's work demonstrates, John Paul II has not been the only one to "construct a romance based on stereotypical male and female roles."[47]

Martin does more than merely point out interpretive bias. She also calls our attention to new data. Recent research reverses fairy tales both magisterial and scientific. In fact, sperm do not actively swim toward a passively waiting ovum. Nor do they penetrate the ovum. They are instead "attracted by the egg and activated by it."[48] Overturning the myth of the heroic sperm, bio-physicists at the Johns Hopkins University have discovered that, rather than swimming toward the egg, sperm are pulled toward the ovum in a process called chemotaxis. The ovum shoots out chemicals that tow the stranded sperm toward it.[49] As Martin summarizes, "The forward thrust of sperm is extremely weak." They do not act as "forceful penetrators."[50] The sperm spend most of their energy swimming sideways, not forward; they attempt to escape any surface they encounter.[51] Rather than penetrating the egg, they are captured by it. If anything, sperm act more cowardly than valiantly. Further undermining gender conventions, in human beings, chemotaxis does not simply direct sperm; it selects them.[52]

While sperm and ovum certainly act as complementary partners in the process of conception, they do not conform to the gender roles that the magisterium has assigned them. If we deign to assign inanimate tissues a sexual personality, then the ovum seems to embody John Paul II's understanding of the masculine personality much more than the sperm does. In fact, the sperm does not seem masculine at all; it instead acts as John Paul II claimed woman does. The ovum does the heavy lifting, acting as actively, if not more so, than the sperm. The sperm serves as the lady-in-waiting. The ovum certainly is not passive. Nor is the ovum receptive. Yes, a sperm eventually is made to come inside the ovum. But the ovum acts much more like a pillaging thief than a lovingly receptive mother. The ovum takes the sperm; the ovum does not wait to be asked;

the ovum does not even wait for an answer. The ovum takes the sperm inside more akin to the way a predator consumes its prey.

These findings bring John Paul IIs theory of sexual complementarity into question. For John Paul II, body symbolizes being. The person is what the body can do. According to John Paul II's theory, if the ovum acts aggressively, then women contain a body at least partially masculine. Even more troubling for John Paul II, these masculine body parts contribute to women's "capacity for motherhood." If women become mothers only by an act of anatomical aggression, then motherhood cannot be depicted as the revelation of woman's fundamental receptive openness to the other in the way that John Paul II claims. Drawing upon John Paul II's definition of femininity and masculinity, we would have to conclude that women become mothers only by acting in masculine fashion. John Paul II's theory further stipulates that, even at his most anatomically masculine, the moment of ejaculation, man sends forth sperm that act like damsels in distress. In truth, sperm and ovum do not reverse roles. While Mary, in her revelation of the feminine personality, may have said yes to God's offer of salvific insemination, the sperm do not acquiesce to the ovum's inquest on their own accord. They must be taken.

But the queer comportment of ovum and sperm are not the only aspects of human embodiment that this magisterial "theology of the body" ignores.[53] As Susannah Cornwall points out, while magisterial authors insist that the human person can only exist as "male or female," the existence of intersexed persons disputes this.[54] Identifying as "a liminal or 'third' gender," some intersex people occupy an identity neither male nor female.[55] Not even the genitals are always either male or female: as Patricia Beattie Jung and Joan Roughgarden highlight, "about one in ten thousand [people] are born without functioning gonads and/or with gonads possessing both testicular and ovarian tissue."[56] No mere binary, sex instead exists as a spectrum.[57]

The existence of human beings with intersex conditions also undermines John Paul II's understanding of what a woman's body looks like. As Cornwall points out, while "many intersex people...identify as women...this does not necessarily mean that their bodily experiences are the same as those shared by a majority of women." For example, "most women with intersex conditions will not be able to menstruate, become pregnant and give birth to children."[58] While God created human beings "male and female," the existence of intersex human beings demonstrates that God did not create human beings only male and female. John Paul's sexual anthropology does not account for all the human beings God created.[59]

And given that intersex human beings are also created in God's image, they suggest a God who is not just "male and female" but intersex as well. For this reason, we can no longer accept John Paul II's depiction of heterosexual marriage as a uniquely clear "mirror…of the communion of love that is in God, through which the Three Persons love each other in the intimate mystery of the one divine life." The spousal unity of male and female does not express a singular "likeness to the divine communion." John Paul II's own theology requires this interpretation. Indeed, as John Paul II affirmed, "Every individual is made in the image of God," and "being a person in the image and likeness of God thus also involves existing in a relationship, in relation to the other 'I.'"[60] By depicting heterosexual relationships as quintessentially God-like, John Paul II provided intersex human beings no way to image God. Those intersex people who bear bodies neither male nor female possess no way to participate in a heterosexual relationship; John Paul II precluded them from fully imaging God from the start. The spousal unity of male and female therefore does not express a singular "likeness to the divine communion" as John Paul II claimed.[61] Interpersonal relationships in which intersex human beings participate also must qualify as icons of God's Trinitarian communion.

The Un-Feminine Mary

Science and human experience notwithstanding, I contend that John Paul II's system of sexual symbolism contradicts itself. Magisterial notions of sexual complementarity fail not just on inductive grounds but also on deductive ones. Indeed, gender trouble abounds even in the pages of scripture. While Mary may have passively accepted the active and initiatory love of the Holy Spirit, the Gospels portray her on other occasions as one who loves with masculine activity. In the Magnificat, a staple of Catholic devotional piety, Mary cries out to the God who fills the hungry with good things, and sends the rich away empty (Luke 1:53

NRSV). Well versed in the history of her Jewish people, Mary invokes the "promise [God] made to [her] ancestors" (Luke 1:55 NRSV). In so doing, she reveals herself an active participant in God's covenant with the Israelites.[62]

The Gospel of Luke's account of Mary's impregnation also carries latent queer tendencies. In Luke's account, God sends to Mary a male angel, Gabriel, as messenger. But the agent of Mary's impregnation, the Holy Spirit, does not carry an explicitly defined gender identity. In fact, as scholars like Johnson and Elisabeth Schüssler Fiorenza have demonstrated, for much of history, Christians "construed the divine Spirit in female terms."[63] Early Christians likely imagined the Holy Spirit as feminine largely because they "attributed to the Spirit the motherly character which certain parts of the Scriptures had already found in Israel's God."[64] As Johnson explains, "While Scripture considers the Spirit more of an impersonal than personal power, the resonances of some ancient language and symbols indicate that it is appropriate to speak of Spirit in metaphors of female resonance."[65] Jurgen Moltmann echoes Johnson and Schüssler Fiorenza, affirming their claims about the familiarity of maternal imagery for the Holy Spirit to early Christians, especially in Syria. This historical precedent makes pneumatological sense: "If believers are 'born' of the Holy Spirit," Moltmann contends, "then we have to think of the Spirit as the 'mother' of believers." For this reason, we ought to conceive of the Holy Spirit as feminine.[66]

While Luke almost certainly did not intend the interpretation I suggest, the scholarship of thinkers like Johnson, Schüssler Fiorenza, and Moltmann, along with the example set by early Christians, allows us to recast Mary's insemination not as an encounter between masculine activity and feminine receptivity but as a display of double feminine sexual complementarity. While Mary's feminine body might have made the First Person of the Trinity a Father, she is inseminated by a Divine Person commonly figured as feminine.

In addition to being impregnated by a feminine Holy Spirit, Mary also said yes to a God who is truly, but not exclusively, feminine. Johnson provides an important, but increasingly unheeded word of caution here. We ought not to "ontologize sex in God." Sexuality, she explains, does not comprise "a dimension of divine being." In speaking Divine sex and gender, we reflect not the nature of God but "the symbolic nature of religious language."[67] But this does not make the femininity of God less real. As Johnson asserts, "Images and names of God do not aim to identify merely 'part' of the divine mystery…they [instead] intend to evoke the whole."[68] God-talk operates symbolically while describing God in God's totality. John Paul I testified to this when he proclaimed, "God is our father; even more God is our mother."[69] John Paul I was able not just to describe God as like a mother or father, but to call God a mother and father. Both are true of God simultaneously.[70] But as Johnson reminds us, God qualifies as both mother and father simultaneously not because God can be spliced into different dimensions or parts but because God truly is a mother and a father, albeit symbolically.

With the rules of theological speech fresh in our minds, Mary's impregnation appears even queerer. More than simply "overshadowed" by a Mother Spirit, Mary also exhibited receptivity to a Mother God. The Virgin Mary does what John Paul II deemed both impossible and perverse: she displays sexual and maternal receptivity to feminine and not masculine activity. This would suggest that, contrary to John Paul's heterosexual anthropology, feminine receptivity does not necessarily need a masculine complement. Femininity can fulfill femininity. An interaction between feminine beings enabled Jesus Christ to become flesh. Mary's impregnation by a feminine Holy Spirit further unsettles John Paul II's heterosexual anthropology in that she never received her husband's body into her own. Mary displayed openness to overshadowing by a feminine Holy Spirit but closed to penetration by a human man. While religious sisters who remain virgins may display a characteristically feminine receptivity to God, this God is truly feminine.

Our Lady of Guadalupe Causes Gender Trouble?[71]

Mary continues to act unladylike—even outside the pages of Holy Scripture. Although he declared her "Empress of Latin America," La Virgen de Guadalupe overturns not affirms John Paul II's theory of sexual complementarity. Drawing upon the work of Virgilio Elizondo, a founder of US Latino theology, I argue that Guadalupe interrupts the history of not only white supremacist imperial domination but also femininity's patriarchal captivity.[72] Rather than providing a model of passively receptive femininity, Guadalupe epitomizes the so-called masculinization of women, which John Paul II bemoaned.[73]

In order to prove this, I analyze Elizondo's reading of the Nican Mopohua, the masterful mid-seventeenth-century Nahuatl poem that recorded the memory of Guadalupe's interaction with "the poor, dignified *campesino*," Juan Diego, a century earlier.[74] Elizondo affirms the theological importance of this text primarily because, in "providing the indigenous account of the real new beginnings of the Americas," the Nican Mopohua serves as a liberating corrective to the origin stories the Spanish and their descendants recounted.[75] During the Guadalupe event, Mary plays the active role—she inseminates Juan Diego with her salvific word and he receives and says yes to her command. Like Mary, he obediently receives a mission and brings it into physical being.[76] Like God, Guadalupe makes Juan Diego's body an instrument of her will.

But I also critique Elizondo. Interpreting the Nican Mopohua through the lens of both liberation theology and his experience as a colonized *mestizo* of Mexican descent living in a white supremacist settler state, Elizondo rightly perceives parallels between Mary and Juan Diego as they relate to God's preferential love for the crucified peoples of history. But, I contend, he fails to appreciate the way these similarities contest prevailing magisterial understandings of sex and gender. In order to make this argument, I enumerate parallels between the Nican Mopohua and Luke's account of the annunciation in order to uncover Guadalupe as an icon of masculine divinity and Juan Diego as an icon of feminine humanity. I then contend that, as such, Guadalupe reveals a maternity that is both masculine and priestly. In this article, I analyze texts more than I speculate about historical events; my interest lies primarily, though not exclusively, in the ways we interpret the written memories of these two events as recorded in the Nican Mopohua and the Gospel of Luke, respectively.

As Elizondo points out, the Nican Mopohua presents Our Lady of Guadalupe's visit with Juan Diego as a type of second annunciation.[77] Both occasions qualify as the dawn of "something new," a type of "cosmic event [that] will be completed through the cooperation of a historical human being." Like Mary, "Juan Diego is drawn to the divinely chosen center of creation to be invited to collaborate in this new divine-human encounter." The Nican Mopohua's memory of the apparition of

Guadalupe resembles Luke's account of the annunciation in other ways as well. Like the angel Gabriel who greets the Virgin Mary by calling, "Hail Mary," Guadalupe hails Diego by calling, "Dignified Juan, dignified Juan Diego."[78] Like biblical Mary, Juan encounters the Divine emissary aurally in the Nican Mopohua. To him, she says,

> I very much want and ardently desire that my hermitage be erected in this place. In it I will show and give to all people all my love, my compassion, my help, and my protection. And for this merciful wish of mine to be realized, go there to the palace of the bishop of Mexico…so that you may make known to him how I very much desire that he build me a home right here, that he may erect my temple on the plain.[79]

Notice how this mirrors the angel's words to Mary in Luke: Gabriel tells Mary God's plans for her and then recites the work God will do in the world through Mary. The Lord desires that Mary give birth to his son; Guadalupe desires that Juan Diego bring her hermitage into being. This son "will be great and will be called Son of the Most High, and the Lord God will give him the throne of David his father"; Guadalupe's hermitage will mediate her love, compassion, help, and protection to all people.[80]

The similarities extend beyond the moment of initial contact. In both cases, Mary and Juan Diego's receptive acceptance of the Divine will place them in great danger. Accepting Divine insemination makes Mary an unwed mother. Accepting Divine commission makes Juan Diego a haughty and insubordinate Indian. Both types of deviant behavior are ordinarily punished with grave violence. Unwed mothers, like haughty Indians, threaten and disobey the prevailing socio-religious order; they are typically punished through violence and even death. Neither possesses sufficient social standing to provide credible testimony of his or her own goodness. The bishop refuses to believe Juan Diego's testimony without a sign; Joseph does not believe Mary's virtue without Divine assurance. Both texts portray Mary and Juan Diego evading expected punishment not through their own power but through the protection of God/Guadalupe. Just as the Lord visits Joseph in a dream and convinces him to abandon his plans for a quiet divorce, Guadalupe hides Juan Diego from the view of episcopal agents planning to kill him.[81]

Their missions also make them exceptional. Just as the biblical Mary's receptivity allows her to bear new life while remaining a virgin, Juan's receptivity allows him to exercise authority over white bishops despite his status as a subordinate Indian. And both Juan Diego and Mary are figured as uniquely capable of carrying out this Divine mission. Just as the angel tells Mary that she has "found favor with God," Guadalupe explains to Juan that "it is absolutely necessary that you personally go and speak about [my desire that a hermitage be built] and that precisely through your mediation and help, my wish and my desire be realized."[82]

In echoing the annunciation, the Nican Mopohua's account of the Guadalupe event paradoxically reverses the gender dynamics the annunciation has been used to authorize. I contend that at Tepeyac, the hill on which Guadalupe appeared to Juan Diego, Guadalupe plays the masculine role of inseminating bridegroom while Juan Diego plays the role of femininely receptive bride. At Tepeyac, Guadalupe initiates the encounter with Juan; like the "aggressive egg," she "calls him [up the hill] to come closer to her side."[83] Refuting John Paul II's claim that man "initiates love," the Nican Mopohua depicts Guadalupe's words as "producing love" in Juan Diego. Indeed, her "alluring" words draw love out of him.[84] While John Paul II portrayed Mary as fundamentally receptive in her all-encompassing love and willingness to accept God's will, the Nican Mopohua depicts her as loving with masculine assertiveness. Acting like a bridegroom, she loves first. Following John Paul II's spousal schema, I conclude that, in so doing, she takes Juan Diego as her bride.

Guadalupe further acts in masculine fashion by asserting her will not in response to prior male action but as a prompt to it. Catholic orthodoxy notwithstanding, Guadalupe does not present herself as acting on behalf of either her masculine Father-God or her male Son-God. In her appearance at Tepeyac, she claims authority over both Juan Diego and white male bishops.[85] And, in coming as a voice and not as a body, Guadalupe subverts "the typical stereotypes" that link masculinity to "creative transcendence and knowledge of the truth" and femininity to "bodylines and the earth."[86] In this way, I contend, Guadalupe acts as an inseminating agent. She brings new life into being through her instigating word and not inside her passively receptive body.

Conversely, Juan Diego serves as a type of second Mary, performing the link between receptivity and submission to the Divine will.[87] Just as Mary declares, "May it be done to me according to your word," Juan Diego "bows [again] before her," and says, "My Owner and my Queen, I am already on the way to make your statement and your word a reality." While Mary professes herself the "handmaid of the Lord," Juan Diego declares himself "your poor servant."[88] Like the earthly Mary who allowed God to dwell among God's people, Juan Diego provides Guadalupe a way to make herself physically present on earth.

As interpreted by Elizondo, Juan Diego qualifies as a "new Mary" in a second way. For John Paul II, Mary serves as a "new Eve," who "assumes in herself and embraces the mystery of the 'woman' whose beginning is Eve." In so doing, Mary presents a "return to the 'beginning' in which one finds the 'woman' as she was intended to be in creation."[89] Elizondo similarly calls Juan Diego "the prototype of the new human being of the Americas" due to his "collaborating in [a] new divine-human endeavor."[90] And like Mary, Juan Diego submits to this collaboration by lending Guadalupe/God his body. Just as God could not bring God's Son into the material world without the cooperation of Mary's body, Guadalupe needs Juan Diego's body to give her maternal love material expression in the form of a hermitage.[91] In both cases, Guadalupe/God yearns to intensify the physicality and fleshliness of their parental love for human beings: God the Father desires a human Son while Guadalupe aches to make her maternal love physically present among her people.[92]

In addition to frustrating John Paul II's typology of Marian femininity, Elizondo also unravels his own implicit gender assumptions. While Elizondo calls Guadalupe "mother," he unwittingly describes her procreative activity in masculine terms. According to Elizondo, the "Mother God regenerates life."[93] Her creative energies bring new life into existence outside of her body. When Elizondo calls Mount Tepeyac "the womb," which Guadalupe uses to bring a new creation into being, he figures her as a mother without a womb.[94] She generates new life not inside of her body but by the power of her word and will. In this, she displays an inseminating masculinity; she creates life by generating it in someone else's womb rather than receiving it inside of her own body. Elizondo's theological interpretation of the events at Tepeyac can also be used, I argue, to identify Juan Diego as a type of womb-bearer. Rather than simply standing "in the very womb of human life" as Elizondo asserts, he actually provides it.[95] Like Mary, he has made the "new creation" by bringing it about. Further resembling Mary, he collaborates in this accomplishment by using his body to bring God's presence into material being.

Elizondo unintentionally misinterprets the Guadalupe event as a confirmation of gender stereotypes. Rightly wishing to condemn the Catholic Church's racist exclusion of indigenous and African-descended peoples from the priesthood, Elizondo identifies Juan Diego as a priest. At Tepeyac, Elizondo contends, "Juan Diego functions as the priest" because he "responds to the divine call and climbs the hill to be the mediator between the Mother of God and the bishop."[96] Even Diego's receptivity is recast as a display of masculine activity; he responds by taking action. Elizondo in turn portrays Guadalupe not as priestly mediator but as God, sometimes identifying her as "the feminine face of God."[97] On other occasions, however, Elizondo describes Guadalupe not as God but as a mediator between God and God's people.[98] If Juan Diego qualifies as a priest, then so must Mary; and if Guadalupe is not God but a mediator of this God, then so must she express a priestly personality. Either way, Elizondo's reading implies that Mary, the revelation of true femininity, bears the powers of a priest.

Especially as read by Elizondo, the Guadalupe event affirms the good news of the annunciation by reversing the gender dynamics it has been used to justify. The God who "has scattered the proud...brought down the mighty from their thrones, exalted those of humble estate, and has filled the hungry of good things," also sends a masculine mother to comfort God's people.[99] Declining to perform magisterial femininity, Guadalupe injects gender trouble straight to the heart of John Paul II's theological symbolism of sex and gender.[100] Guadalupe comes as a mother, but she does not act in feminine fashion. Revealing the masculine maternal, she instead acts as a mother who procreates by inseminating a womb that is not her own; she displays not passive receptivity but active initiation. She plays the role of bridegroom and takes a human man as her bride. She exercises the powers of a priest. If Mary provides the model for all humanity but especially for all women, as John Paul claimed she does, then she sets for them a very queer example.

THE GUADALUPE EVENT AND MAGISTERIAL TEACHING

The Guadalupe event therefore presents us with one of two options: we must either revise our definitions of masculinity and femininity so that Guadalupe qualifies as feminine or we must unhinge gender from anatomical sex so that Guadalupe does not betray her womanhood by acting in masculine fashion. In truth, magisterial teaching has already selected this second option. Despite insisting that all women must be feminine, and all men must be masculine, John Paul II's theology of the body already has severed gender from anatomical sex, albeit unintentionally, but only in the case of men. In his view, all human beings, men as well as women, he believed, "are called through the Church, to be the 'Bride' of Christ." "Being the bride," which he deemed "the feminine element, becomes a symbol of all that is 'human.'"[101] In the sexually complementary cosmos that John Paul II imagined, if humanity is feminine in its relation to God, then so is God masculine.

John Paul II further deployed this otherwise subversively queer symbolism not to overturn conventional norms but to reinforce them. Turning the Eucharist into "the sacrament of the bridegroom and the bride," John Paul II concluded that, since the church is feminine, the priests who confect the Eucharist must be masculine. For this reason, he argued, ordination must remain for men only. Rather than the queering of the so-called sacrament of the bridegroom and the bride, the all-male Last Supper evidences the necessary masculinity of the priesthood.[102] John Paul II did not find it odd that Christ would decide to institute a sacrament that epitomized sexual love between man and woman at an all-male meal. The all-male Last Supper makes the Eucharist wedding feast not gay but patriarchal. But male priests are not only masculine. According to John Paul II, when men vow virginity, they also adopt an essentially feminine relation to Christ.[103]

For these reasons, Guadalupe undermines John Paul II's theology of the body not just by acting unladylike but also by claiming for herself what John Paul II believed belongs only to men: the right to play more than just one gender role. Current magisterial arguments against the ordination of women paradoxically rest not on a bilateral gender essentialism but on an asymmetrical system of sexual expression in which men possess the freedom to act feminine but women are denied the freedom to act masculine. While John Paul II explicitly warned against what he terms "the masculinization of women," he prescribed and celebrated the feminization of men before God. Rather than prohibiting male femininity, he wished simply that men not act feminine before women.[104]

John Paul II's asymmetrical anxiety about gender expression casts doubt on his attempt to portray sexual complementarity as sexually egalitarian and lends credence to feminist critiques that John Paul II's description of femininity reinforces sexual hierarchy.[105] He does not mind when men play the feminine role in their relation to a masculine God; he in fact celebrates it. While men can be feminine before God and among each other, they can never be feminine in their dealings with human women. Why? If men can relate to women as God relates to humanity but women can only relate to men as human beings respond to God, then perhaps feminine receptivity and masculine activity are not so equal after all. More than John Paul II wished that men remain masculine, I contend, he believed that masculinity ought never to be subordinate to femininity.

According to the terms of John Paul II's Marian typology of femininity, if Guadalupe claims masculinity for herself in her interactions with the man, Juan Diego, then so can human women. His symbolism of sexual complementarity also stipulates that, if the earthly Mary receives into her body the overshadowing power of a feminine Holy Spirit, then so can earthly women receive feminine power into their bodies. Indeed, if Mary is not consistently feminine, then John Paul II's logic provides no reason why other women must be. Whether assessed inductively or deductively, the foundations of John Paul II's theology of the body appear profoundly unstable. The human body does not look like he said it does, and the Virgin Mary will not act as he believed she must.

Notes

1. Lisa Sowle Cahill, *Family: A Christian Social Perspective* (Minneapolis: Fortress Press, 2000), 92; and Todd A. Salzman and Michael G. Lawler, *The Sexual Person: Toward a Renewed Catholic Anthropology* (Washington, DC: Georgetown University Press, 2008), 86–87.

2. John Paul II, *Mulieris Dignitatem*, 1988, pars. 5, 11, http://w2.vatican.va/content/john-paul-ii/en/apost_letters/1988/documents/hf_jp-ii_apl_19880815_mulieris-dignitatem.html.

3. John Paul II, General Audiences: "Theology of the Body," 19:4, https://www.ewtn.com/library/PAPALDOC/JP2TBIND.HTM.

4. Katie Grimes, "Butler Interprets Aquinas," *Journal of Religious Ethics* 42, no. 2 (June 1, 2014): 202. Written by a Nahuatl scholar, the Nican Mopohua tells the story of La Virgen de Guadalupe in Nahuatl.

5. Elizabeth A. Johnson, *Truly Our Sister: A Theology of Mary in the Communion of Saints* (New York: A&C Black, 2006), 209; and Johann Baptist Metz, *Faith in History and Society: Toward a Practical Fundamental Theology* (New York: Crossroad, 2007), 110.

6. John Paul II, *Mulieris Dignitatem*, par. 7.

7. John Paul II, "Theology of the Body," 19:4; and John Paul II, *Familiaris Consortio* (On the Family), 1981, par. 11, http://w2.vatican.va/content/john-paul-ii/en/apost_exhortations/documents/hf_jp-ii_exh_19811122_familiaris-consortio.html.

8. John Paul II, *Familiaris Consortio*, 8:1.

9. John Paul II, *Mulieris Dignitatem*, par. 29.

10. John Paul II, *Mulieris Dignitatem*, par. 10.

11. John Paul II, "Theology of the Body," 20:5.

12. Note how John Paul's essentialist understanding of sex and gender differs from that proposed by Elizabeth Johnson, who conceives of "one human nature celebrated in an interdependence of multiple differences. Not a binary view of two forever predetermined male and female natures, nor abbreviation to a single ideal, but a diversity of ways of being human: a multipolar set of combinations of essential human elements, of which sexuality is but one." This view allows us to extend respect to "all persons in their endless combinations of anthropological constants, boundlessly concrete" (*She Who Is: The Mystery of God in Feminist Theological Discourse* [New York: Crossroad, 2002], 155–56).

13. John Paul II, "Theology of the Body," 9:4.

14. John Paul II, "Theology of the Body," 45:2.

15. John Paul II, "Theology of the Body," 14:1.

16. John Paul II, "Theology of the Body," 8:1.

17. John Paul I, *Mulieris Dignitatem*, par. 4.

18. John Paul I, *Mulieris Dignitatem*, par. 5.

19. John Paul I, *Mulieris Dignitatem*, par. 18.

20. John Paul II, "Theology of the Body," 21:2.

21. See Hans Urs von Balthasar, *Love Alone Is Credible* (San Francisco: Ignatius Press, 2005), esp. chap. 5.

22. Elizabeth Johnson, *Abounding in Kindness: Writings for the People of God* (Maryknoll, NY: Orbis Books, 2015), 200.

23. John Paul II, *Familiaris Consortio*, par. 25.

24. John Paul II, *Mulieris Dignitatem*, par. 23.

25. John Paul II, *Mulieris Dignitatem*, par. 18.

26. John Paul II, *Mulieris Dignitatem*, par. 17.

27. John Paul II, *Mulieris Dignitatem*, par. 20.

28. John Paul II, "Theology of the Body," 11:3.

29. John Paul II, "Theology of the Body," 20:4.

30. John Paul II, "Theology of the Body," 114:6.

31. Balthasar's influence again shines through. In Hans Urs von Balthasar, *New Elucidations* (San Francisco: Ignatius Press, 1986), he argues, "It always remains true that in sexual intercourse it is the man who is the initiator, the leader, the shaper, while the woman's love—even if it is not passive, but just as active in its own way—is still essentially receptive" (196).

32. John Paul II, "Theology of the Body," 20:5.

33. John Paul II, "Theology of the Body," 10:2.

34. John Paul II, "Theology of the Body," 11:6.

35. John Paul II, "Theology of the Body," 13:2.

36. John Paul II, *Mulieris Dignitatem*, par. 25.

37. John Paul II, *Mulieris Dignitatem*, par. 29.

38. John Paul II, *Mulieris Dignitatem*, par. 26.

39. Thomas Aquinas explicitly attributes passivity to woman's sex organs and activity to man's sex organs (*ST* I.92.1; *ST* II-II.154.1). Aquinas argues that the various species of lust ought to be "differentiated on the part of the woman rather than the man, because in the venereal act, the woman is passive and is by way of matter, whereas the man is by way of agent" (*ST* II-II.154.1).

40. John Paul II, *Mulieris Dignitatem*, par. 29.

41. John Paul II sounds very much like Balthasar here. See Hans Urs von Balthasar, *TheoDrama: Theological Dramatic Theory*, vol. 1, *Prologomena* (San Francisco: Ignatius Press, 1988), 286.

42. This thinking has deep roots in Catholic moral theology. See Aquinas, *ST* I.92.1.

43. Karol Wojtyla, *Love and Responsibility*, rev. ed. (San Francisco: Ignatius Press, 1993), 47.

44. Andrea Sachs, "Help for Sex-Starved Wives," *Time*, April 7, 2008, http://content.time.com/time/health/article/0,8599,1728520,00.html; and Hugo Schwyzer, "Turns Out Women Have Really, Really Strong Sex Drives: Can Men Handle It?," *The Atlantic*, June 6, 2013, https://www.theatlantic.com/sexes/archive/2013/06/turns-out-women-have-really-really-strong-sex-drives-can-men-handle-it/276598/.

45. Admittedly, some sexologists, like Marta Meana, do seem to confirm John Paul II's assessment of women's sexuality when they claim that, for women, "being desired is the orgasm." But even this coherence disputes John Paul's larger sexual conclusions. For Meana, "Women's desire is not relational,

it's narcissistic" as "women may be far less relational than men" (quoted in Daniel Bergner, "What Do Women Want? Discovering What Ignites Female Desire," *New York Times*, January 22, 2009, https://www.nytimes.com/2009/01/25/magazine/25desire-t.html).

46. Emily Martin, "The Egg and the Sperm: How Science Has Constructed a Romance Based on Stereotypical Male-Female Roles," *Signs* 16, no. 3 (April 1, 1991): 490.

47. Martin, "The Egg and the Sperm," 492.

48. David H. Freedman, "New Theory on How the Aggressive Egg Attracts Sperm," *Discover Magazine*, June 1, 1992, http://discovermagazine.com/1992/jun/theaggressiveegg55.

49. A. Cohen-Dayag, I. Tur-Kaspa, J. Dor, S. Mashiach, and M. Eisenbach, "Sperm Capacitation in Humans Is Transient and Correlates with Chemotactic Responsiveness to Follicular Factors," *Proceedings of the National Academy of Sciences* 92, no. 24 (November 21, 1995): 11039–43, http://www.ncbi.nlm.nih.gov/pmc/articles/PMC40566/.

50. Martin, "The Egg and the Sperm," 492–93.

51. For an overview of the more recent research into chemotaxis, see Aduén Andres Morales García, "The Response of Human Spermatozoa to Chemoattractants" (PhD diss., University of Birmingham, England, 2009), http://etheses.bham.ac.uk/630/1/MoralesGarcia1OPhD.pdf. For recent research into the related phenomenon known as thermotaxis, see Anat Bahat and Michael Eisenbach, "Sperm Thermotaxis," *Molecular and Cellular Endocrinology, Signal Transduction in Health and Disease: Highlighting Pineal Biology and Biological Clocks* 252, nos. 1–2 (June 27, 2006): 115–19.

52. Cohen-Dayag et al., "Sperm Capacitation."

53. Susannah Cornwall, "Telling Stories about Intersex and Christianity: Saying Too Much or Not Saying Enough?" *Theology* 117, no. 1 (2014): 26, https://journals.sagepub.com/doi/abs/10.1177/0040571X13510228.

54. Cornwall, "Telling Stories about Intersex and Christianity," 24.

55. Cornwall, "Recognizing the Full Spectrum of Gender?" 239.

56. Patricia Beattie Jung and Joan Roughgarden, "Gender in Heaven: The Story of the Ethiopian Eunuch in Light of Evolutionary Theory," in *God, Science, Sex, Gender: An Interdisciplinary Approach to Christian Ethics*, ed. Patricia Beattie Jung, Aana Marie Vigen, and John Anderson (Urbana: University of Illinois Press, 2010), 226.

57. Susannah Cornwall, "Recognizing the Full Spectrum of Gender? Transgender, Intersex, and the Futures of Feminist Theology," *Feminist Theology* 20, no. 3 (2012): 236–41, esp. 237.

58. Cornwall, "Recognizing the Full Spectrum of Gender?" 239.

59. Cornwall. "Telling Stories about Intersex and Christianity," 29.

60. John Paul II, *Mulieris Dignitatem*, par. 7.

61. John Paul II, *Mulieris Dignitatem*, par. 7.

62. John Paul's Marian typology also ignores the role Mary claims for herself at the Wedding of Cana. Here, Mary again acts as the initiator. She is the asker; it is Jesus who says yes to her. Mary leads; her son follows. On at least one occasion in scripture, therefore, Mary and Jesus themselves defy the gender roles that John Paul has assigned him.

63. Elisabeth Schüssler Fiorenza, *Jesus: Miriam's Child, Sophia's Prophet; Critical Issues in Feminist Christology* (New York: Bloomsbury Academic, 1994), 176; and Johnson, *She Who Is*, 50.

64. Johnson, *She Who Is*, 50.

65. Johnson, *She Who Is*, 130.

66. Jurgen Moltmann, *The Source of Life* (Minneapolis: Fortress, 1997), 35.

67. Johnson, *She Who Is*, 54.

68. Moltmann, *Source of Life*, 35.

69. Richard R. Gaillardetz, *When the Magisterium Intervenes: The Magisterium and Theologians in Today's Church; Includes a Case Study on the Doctrinal investigation of Elizabeth Johnson* (Collegeville, MN: Liturgical Press, 2012), 236.

70. Johnson, *She Who Is*, 172.

71. Judith Butler, *Gender Trouble: Feminism and the Subversion of Identity* (New York: Routledge, 2006), xxxi.

72. Virgilio Elizondo, *Guadalupe: Mother of the New Creation* (Maryknoll, NY: Orbis, 2013), 112.

73. John Paul II, *Mulieris Dignitatem*, par. 10. See also Balthasar, "Women Priests? A Marian Church in a Fatherless and Motherless Culture" (*Communio* 22 [Spring 1995]: 165–70), in which he scoffs at "an unnatural masculinization of woman" (quotation on 165).

74. Elizondo, *Guadalupe*, 3–4, 6.

75. Elizondo, *Guadalupe*, xvii.

76. Elizondo, *Guadalupe*, 8.

77. Timothy Matovina, Virgil Elizondo, and Allan Figueroa Deck, *The Treasure of Guadalupe* (Lanham, MD: Rowman & Littlefield, 2006), 31.

78. Matovina, Elizondo, and Deck, *The Treasure of Guadalupe*, 37.

79. Matovina, Elizondo, and Deck, *The Treasure of Guadalupe*, 7.

80. Matovina, Elizondo, and Deck, *The Treasure of Guadalupe*, 8.

81. Elizondo, *Guadalupe*, 12–13.

82. Elizondo, *Guadalupe*, 10.

83. Freedman, "New Theory on How the Aggressive Egg Attracts Sperm"; and Elizondo, *Guadalupe*, 7.

84. Elizondo, *Guadalupe*, 7.
85. Elizondo, *Guadalupe*, 8.
86. Elizondo, *Guadalupe*, 61; and Johnson, *She Who Is*, 165.
87. Elizondo, *Guadalupe*, xi.
88. John Paul II, *Mulieris Dignitatem*, par. 5; and Elizondo, *Guadalupe*, 8.
89. Elizondo, *Guadalupe*, 11.
90. Elizondo, *Guadalupe*, xi, 37.
91. Elizondo, *Guadalupe*, 111.
92. Elizondo, *Guadalupe*, 72.
93. Elizondo, *Guadalupe*, 43.
94. Elizondo, *Guadalupe*, 38.
95. Elizondo, *Guadalupe*, 37.
96. Elizondo, *Guadalupe*, 46.
97. Matovina, Elizondo, and Deck, *The Treasure of Guadalupe*, 51.
98. Elizondo, *Guadalupe*, 47.
99. Elizondo, *Guadalupe*, 59.
100. Here, I allude to Judith Butler's "theory of the performativity of gender" as articulated and deployed by Stefanie Knauss in "Exploring Orthodox Jewish Masculinities with Eyes Wide Open," *Journal of Religion and Film* 17, no. 2 (2013): 2–4, https://digitalcommons.unomaha.edu/jrf/vol17/iss2/7/; and Butler, *Gender Trouble*, 173.
101. John Paul II, *Mulieris Dignitatem*, par. 25.
102. John Paul II, *Mulieris Dignitatem*, par. 26.
103. John Paul II, *Mulieris Dignitatem*, par. 20; and Balthasar, *New Elucidations*, 194.
104. John Paul II, *Mulieris Dignitatem*, par. 10.
105. Cahill, *Family*, 92.

Part Five

POVERTY AND ECONOMIC INEQUALITY

6. Social Conscience and Politics in the United States of America
Reflections

Mary Jo Bane

This chapter originally appeared as Mary Jo Bane. "Social Conscience and Politics in the United States of America: Reflections." *International Journal of Public Theology* 5 (2011): 352–65.

Europeans might be forgiven for thinking that since the United States seems not to have a social conscience, reflections from North America are likely to be less than helpful. But I would like to think that reflections from America have more to offer than an opportunity for Europeans to feel self-satisfied, or for some Americans to regret that their country is not more European.[1]

My argument is as follows: America is quite different from other countries in the Organization for Economic Co-operation and Development (OECD), in terms of its religiosity and the prevalence of both religious affiliation and religious practice—America is much more religious. It is also different from other OECD countries in its provision of public safety nets, which are considerably less generous and comprehensive than those in Europe. If one focused only on Christian theology, one might expect a different pattern. Theology notwithstanding, however, I will argue that there are some institutional and ideological patterns in American religion that perhaps underlie both these tendencies.

If the association between religiosity and public safety nets in America is consistent both with the empirical data and a plausible explanation, then the patterns of religious life and practice in America may be part of the "problem" in American responses to poverty. They may also, however, be part of the solution, and not simply because of gospel teaching. America is also distinctive in the breadth, diversity, and vitality of voluntary associations and charities, including houses of worship and other religiously based voluntary organizations. The voluntary sector cannot replace the public sector, but it can, perhaps, provide the organizational foundation for the development of social conscience and civic dialogue, and a counter to the increasingly toxic political sphere. This may be the best hope for the emergence of an American social conscience and may also provide an interesting framework for others to think about.

American Religiosity

Americans are much more likely than Europeans to identify with a religious denomination and much more likely to report regular church attendance. The differences, in whichever survey one looks, are quite striking, and impossible to explain away by reporting or statistical errors. A Gallup International poll on religion in the world at the end of the last millennium, for example, found that forty-nine percent of Western European respondents reported that God was important in their lives, compared to eighty-three percent of North Americans. Twenty percent of Western European respondents reported that they had attended church at least once in the previous week, compared to forty-seven percent of North Americans.[2] Only sixteen percent of Americans reported themselves to be religiously unaffiliated, a percentage that has risen in recent years but that is still quite low.[3]

In a more recent poll (2010), sixty-five percent of Americans responded that religion is important in their daily lives. The average for all rich countries (per capita annual income of $25,000 or more) was a forty-seven percent interest in religion; for Sweden this is seventeen percent, in the UK the interest in religion is twenty-seven percent, and in France it is thirty percent.[4]

Americans are very diverse in their religious affiliations. Catholicism is the largest single denomination, encompassing about a quarter of the American population, but the varieties of evangelical Protestantism taken together have a roughly equal number of adherents. Much of America worships in Christian churches that are not affiliated with any denomination; the large megachurches, for example, are independent and distinct.[5]

The vibrancy and diversity of American religious life means that most Americans can find a congenial church home that meets their individual needs among the diversity of denominations and congregations. The absence of an established church and the presence of what might be called a free market for religion makes this possible. Denominations, sects, and independent churches have developed, grown, competed for members, diminished, and died; they continue to do so. Americans change churches and religions quite freely. A recent poll found that forty-four percent of Americans reported that they did not now belong to the religious denomination in which they were raised.[6] Of that group, a third were now unaffiliated to a religious denomination, but two-thirds had changed denominations. Americans seem to search out and find the churches that meet their needs. When asked why they had changed churches, most of these respondents reported that their former church was not meeting their spiritual needs and that they had found a religion and religious services that they liked better.[7]

The historian Mark Noll characterizes American religious life as voluntary, self-directed, and rooted in individual choice.[8] Opposition to religious establishment, like religious toleration, was at first a pragmatic response to diversity—no denomination wanted to be the one that was not established or tolerated—but later became a principled stance, enshrined in the Bill of Rights along with other individual freedoms.

I will look next at the needs that religious affiliation meets for Americans. From a sociological perspective rather than a theological one, at many points in our history such needs seem to have been for stability, order, and community in a turbulent world. The American economy has long been competitive and entrepreneurial, with high mobility and a relatively high tolerance for risk taking. As a nation of immigrants, most of the population came from abroad, more or less recently. Churches on the frontier became the places that brought people together. Both today and historically, churches have served as havens for the immigrant community, helping to provide not only community for new immigrants but also supports for moving into the larger society. Similarly, churches have always been a stabilizing institution in poor and ethnic minority communities; for example, the black church has been and remains very important to that community. It is clearly the case that, whatever variety of roles they play in the lives of Americans, religious communities are very important institutions in the US.

American Support (or Lack Thereof) for the Poor

America is also distinct from Europe in its relatively high poverty rates and comparatively ungenerous public safety nets. An analysis of data from the Luxembourg Income Study by Tim Smeeding, using comparable relative poverty measures from 2000, showed the US with the highest poverty rates among eleven rich countries.[9] According to this analysis, the US poverty rate was seventeen percent, compared with, for example, eight percent for Germany and five percent for Finland. These differences in poverty rates can be attributed largely to differences in tax and transfer policies, particularly the generosity of public assistance programs like unemployment insurance and family allowances. The same researchers found that twenty-six percent of the pre-transfer poor in the US were lifted out of poverty by tax and transfer policy, compared with an average of sixty percent in the other ten rich countries in the survey.[10] Families whose earnings place them below the poverty line get considerably more public help in most European countries than they do in America, and are therefore much less likely to be poor overall.[11]

Economists Alberto Alesina and Ed Glaeser studied poverty in the US and Europe, and report on their analyses in a book with the subtitle *A World of Difference*.[12] They note that the US spends about eleven percent of Gross Domestic Product (GDP) on social benefits and other transfers (social insurance for the elderly and the disabled, unemployment insurance and other labor market benefits, family benefits, health benefits), while the countries of continental Europe spend about eighteen percent and the UK spends sixteen percent GDP on social welfare.

These differences cannot, according to Alesina and Glaeser, be explained by patterns of income, inequality, or mobility. Instead, their econometric study suggests the importance of institutions, ideology, racial and ethnic tensions, and geography. The institutional factors they identify as important include voting systems with single-member winner-take-all constituencies rather than proportional representation, a constitution "crafted by men of property, determined to stop the state from expropriating their wealth,"[13] and a system of checks and balances that makes it difficult for government to legislate and regulate. They also note the absence historically of a socialist left. These institutional structures are at least partly responsible for the relative inability of the US federal government to enact bold policies—most notably, in recent times, health care reform—and especially to enact generous benefit programs for the poor.

Ideology is also part of the pattern they identify. The ideological difference is not that Americans do not care about the poor, or do not believe that government should help those in need; they do care, as public opinion polling consistently reveals. In the Pew Religious Landscape Study, for example, sixty-two percent of respondents agreed with the statement: "Government should do more to help needy Americans, even if it means going deeper into debt."[14] Yet they also strongly believe (contrary to the facts, in truth) that America is a land of mobility and opportunity, and that everyone can get ahead if they are disciplined and hard working. (Sixty-seven percent agreed with the statement: "Most people who want to get ahead can make it if they're willing to work hard.")[15] Poll results consistently show that Americans, in contrast to Europeans, believe that the poor could escape poverty if they worked harder.

Ethnic and racial diversity can contribute to both beliefs and political institutions that work against public generosity to the poor. Alesina and Glaeser note that racial and ethnic segregation and conflicts have historically precluded working-class solidarity and have instead led to political mobilization based on ethnic conflicts. Geography—the low density and vast spaces of much of America—has provided a safety valve for the discontented and made it more difficult to organize. The nation's frontier and immigrant history generated beliefs that America was different from class-bound Europe and that it was indeed a land of mobility and opportunity.

In addition to the explanations explored by Alesina and Glaeser, there are two other features of American politics and society that may affect the fate of the poor. One is the increasing inequality in wealth and income, accompanied by increasing polarization in lifestyle and in politics. This polarization is part of the reason that it is so difficult to get anything done in American politics, with its institutions requiring rather large majorities for the enactment of laws. Recent new works on inequality, by Jacob Hacker and Paul Pierson and by Larry Bartels, make powerful arguments that rising income and wealth inequalities are reflected in political inequality and in policy actions that benefit the rich and hurt the poor.[16] Bartels shows that members of Congress are much more responsive to their upper-income constituents than to their poor and middle-class constituents.[17] Hacker and Pierson argue that the very wealthy, the top one percent, largely control politics through both campaign contributions and shared ideology, and that policies have disproportionately benefited them at the expense of the poor.[18]

Ethnic and racial divisions (explored to some extent by Alesina and Glaeser) and political polarization (explored by Hacker, Pierson, and Bartels) are reinforced by residential sorting, which has become quite pronounced in the US. Americans in general have sorted themselves into communities that are relatively homogeneous both demographically and politically. Nearly half of all Americans in 2004 lived in what Bill Bishop calls "landslide counties," where the margin of victory for the winning candidate is at least twenty percentage points.[19] This political sorting reflects location decisions made on the basis of lifestyle as well as income, with households choosing to live near others who are similar to themselves. The effects of the sorting are amplified by political strategies of both parties that polarize the electorate. Patterns of social interaction and of information gathering seem to exacerbate ideological and political polarization. Thus, income inequality and residential sorting influence ideology, by separating the rich from regular interaction with the poor. These features increase polarization, by encouraging interaction chiefly among people who share political viewpoints. In the US, moreover, they contribute to the political institutions and policies that short-change the poor.

Are Religiosity and Lack of Generosity Connected?

One might think that a more religious country, primarily Christian, would be more generous toward the poor than a less religious country, given the powerful teachings of the Christian gospel and other religious traditions about duties toward the poor and the vulnerable. Yet the relationship is in the opposite direction when Europe and America are compared. We should ask whether this is mere coincidence, or whether America might therefore be even less generous if it were less religious, and Europe even more generous if it were more religious; or whether we should reach some other conclusion.

There are, I think, some similarities between the explanations for American patterns of religious life and for American politics around public safety nets—or, more accurately, the lack thereof. Possible explanations for the differences in public generosity between the US and Europe, as discussed above, are political institutions built on individualism, choice, and distrust of government; an ideology of mobility and opportunity; racial and ethnic divisions; political influence dramatically skewed toward the rich; geographical sorting.

Religious communities as they have developed in America reflect and to some extent reinforce these background features of American political life. An open, fluid, very diverse society led to both a vibrant religious sector and a set of institutions that check government power. An ideology of individualism and choice characterizes attitudes toward both religious affiliation and governmental power. This ideology encompasses distrust of hierarchy and too powerful institutions, in both government and religion.

Religious communities as they have developed in America are largely independent and tolerant; they recognize the validity of different religious traditions and celebrate diversity in religious beliefs and practices. The Pew Religious Landscape Survey found, for example, that seventy percent of survey respondents (including seventy-nine percent of Catholic respondents) expressed agreement with the statement: "Many religions can lead to eternal life."[20] In a survey reported by Putnam and Campbell, eighty-four percent of respondents agreed that: "Religious diversity has been good for America."[21]

They are also largely accepting or even celebratory of the American ideology of mobility and opportunity. Protestantism is aptly Protestant in its ethics, praising or at least not disapproving the material success of its adherents and, in some evangelical and Pentecostal churches, explicitly promoting religion as a road to worldly success as well as to heaven.[22]

Catholicism in America cannot be divorced from its immigrant history, with many Catholic communities now proud of their ascension to the middle and upper classes, and other Catholic communities providing support for new immigrants eager to replicate that success.

The social conscience in American religion, even in Catholicism, is rooted much more in private charity than in public distributive justice, consistent with these ideological tendencies. Church communities believe in, and to some extent practice, taking care of each other; many of them give generously to victims of natural disaster and to others whose poverty or misfortune seems to be beyond their control. However, churchgoing Americans are not particularly supportive of government actions to address poverty. Church-going Americans, including Catholics, are more likely to vote Republican than are non-churchgoers, and they are just as likely to distrust government. In addition, while more than sixty percent of Americans say that government should do more to help the needy, they are dubious both about the capacity of government to make things better and about the neediness of many of the poor. The churches' emphasis on private charity and voluntarism may reinforce this outlook.

The most important way in which church communities may contribute to American attitudes and policies toward the poor is through residential and lifestyle sorting. This is strengthened rather than countered by patterns of religious practice, which, as noted above, are very diverse and allow people to sort themselves into like-minded religious congregations that mirror other aspects of the sorting; not only geographical residence but also lifestyle and aesthetic preferences. Putnam and Campbell emphasize this connection between religion and political attitudes, which occurs, they argue, not because of explicit politics in sermons or church activities but because of patterns of interaction with co-religionists.[23] They contend that religious congregations serve as "echo chambers" for politics because "religious social networks influence the ways in which individuals piece together their politics and their religion."[24]

In short, I do not believe that Americans' lack of commitment to government support for the poor is in contradiction to their religiosity. American patterns of religious practice have their roots in institutions and ideologies that also endorse an individualistic attitude toward government and toward the poor, a distrust of large authoritarian institutions, and an emphasis on private charity. The segregation and polarization of American society and politics, reinforced by the way religion is organized and practiced, further contribute to the difficulty in coming together politically to support the poor. There may also be a tendency for religious social networks to affirm the sense of entitlement of the wealthy who come together in sorted congregations; these social interactions are likely to be more powerful than explicit teachings to the contrary.

If such reinforcing tendencies have contributed, even in part, to America's dismal record on poverty and poverty alleviation, they may have implications for a possible renewal of social conscience in America. More specifically, understanding these tendencies may help us understand the Catholic social conscience and provide some foundation for its renewal.

Social Conscience and Politics in American Catholicism

Catholic parishes in America share some of the characteristics of American religion described above. They developed as immigrant churches, communities that afforded protection against the insults dealt out by the larger society, but also organizations that laid the foundation for entry into that society.[25] Today the Catholic Church is once again a haven for immigrants—now from Mexico, Latin America, and Asian countries like Vietnam and the Philippines. It does not discourage immigrants from adopting the ethos of their new home; indeed, it encourages them to work hard, educate their children, and strive to get ahead. At the same time, it provides some services and supports to people as they do so.

American Catholicism is characterized by some of the same patterns and tendencies that are seen in American religion more generally. The history and institutional structures of American Catholicism, especially geographically based parishes, underline sorting and polarization. American Catholicism has accommodated to the individualistic ideology of the larger society. Moreover, questions of values and social conscience have become conflated with politics and have led to polarization within the church as in society at large, and an accompanying difficulty in the development of an inclusive Catholic social conscience.

The ideology of tolerance and individual choice, mobility and opportunity, and distrust of government was accepted if not fully embraced in the history of American Catholicism, rooted in its immigrant origins. The Catholic immigrants of the nineteenth and early twentieth centuries came into a country that was prosperous and open relative to the countries they had emigrated from but was also Protestant in public life—implicitly if not explicitly. Catholics wanted to be accepted or at least tolerated by their new home country, which in the early years they surely were not.

Mostly, however, they wanted to make better lives for themselves and their children in a new world of opportunity. The parishes that were established to serve the immigrants recognized that Catholicism was a minority religion. Some among the Catholic hierarchy worked for religious tolerance, blunting the then received doctrine of the church that the best church was an established church. Catholic parishes encouraged their members to work hard, build strong families, and educate their children, the better both to serve God and to get ahead in a partly meritocratic country that did no favors to Catholics. The parishes also provided community for their members: a safe and supportive haven from the sometimes-hostile Protestant world of the larger society, which was in many ways reflected in public life—for example, in the rituals and curricula of the public schools.

Over the century or so following the large Catholic migrations from Europe, Catholics did in fact work hard, go to school (to a large extent, their own Catholic schools), and get ahead. By the end of the twentieth century, the descendants of the early immigrants were at least equal to and by most measures ahead of the country as a whole in educational level, social status, and income. For example, a recent survey showed that thirty-three percent of Catholics had family incomes of $75,000 or greater, compared with thirty-one percent of the national sample. Twenty-six percent of Catholics had college or post-graduate degrees, compared with twenty-seven percent of the national sample.[26] The basic story of mobility and opportunity, for these Catholics, seems to have been realized. New immigrants are to some extent replicating the patterns of the earlier immigrants, with the now Spanish and Asian immigrant parishes upholding the ideology and providing the same safety and support.

Catholic parishes also, I believe, reinforce or at least reflect the economic inequalities and the polarizing tendencies that are bringing

American politics to a rancorous halt. Catholic parishes are, for the most part, geographically defined and thus mirror the residential patterns found more widely. These patterns are increasingly segregated, most clearly by income and ethnicity but also by lifestyle and politics.

We know from research on networks and attitudes that social interaction and dialogue tends as often to polarize as to bring together. People interact with others who endorse, or at least do not challenge, their beliefs and political attitudes; these interactions seem to increase polarization rather than diminish it. It is hard to imagine that this does not happen also within Catholic parishes. Between parishes, some will be richer and more ideologically and politically conservative, others more ideologically and politically liberal. Some will emphasize pro-life activities; others will emphasize social justice.[27] Members within those parishes will interact with each other and bolster each other's beliefs; they will seldom interact with members of very different parishes. Even if the pastor and staff of the parish would like to counter these tendencies, they are unlikely to do so, both because pastors need to please—or at least not offend—people to keep them coming back, and because it is questionable, in my view, whether sermons make much difference in people's lives anyway.

What I am suggesting is that the structure and life of Catholic parishes—not by design but simply through the practice of sorting, by lifestyle as well as geographically—reinforce both the ideology of mobility and opportunity and the political polarization that seems to make it impossible for Americans to agree on public action of any type. The lack of dialogue across the divide makes it difficult for society, and therefore for politics, to approach issues as problems to be solved rather than as ideological positions to be shouted about.

These tendencies show themselves in political and values differences among Catholics. About a third of Americans who identify themselves as Catholic also identify as Republicans (with another third identifying as Democrat and the rest as independent). About a third (overlapping, no doubt) identify as politically conservative. There is an almost even split between Catholics who believe that government should be larger and those who believe it should be smaller. American Catholics are split over theological issues, such as the Bible. They are also split over what have come to be called values issues in American politics.[28]

An illustration of the polarization among Catholics that is also a polarization in America more generally is the debate over abortion. There is an almost even split between Catholics who believe that abortion should be legal all or most of the time and those who believe it should be illegal all or most of the time. These patterns hardly differ from those of the population as a whole.[29] On both ends of the spectrum, these opinions are strongly held; they influence the way American Catholics think about the poor, because the political debate is often phrased around the question of which issues ought to be most important, even non-negotiable.

This raises the question of whether life issues, for example, are non-negotiable in politics for Catholics or whether social justice issues are just as, or more, important. Catholics ought to be able to be both pro-life and pro-poor; they ought to be able to have civil discussions over what it means to be pro-life and pro-poor and which public policies are best suited to address both protection of life and support for the poor. Yet such discussions seem impossible, in practice. Support for a constitutional amendment to outlaw abortion is a litmus test for one side; support for large government entitlements is a litmus test for the other side. Neither of these measures is going to come about in America. The US is much more likely to address these issues, if it ever does, in more nuanced and complicated ways that rely on civil society and on government nudges more than on sweeping programs or draconian laws. It is difficult, however, to explore the approaches that might prove to be workable solutions to either set of problems, because of the polarization of positions that has taken place on both sides.

A New Approach to a Catholic Social Conscience

This analysis leads me to focus less on explicit teaching about social justice and obligations to the poor and the vulnerable, and more on the structures, interactions, and activities of Catholic parishes. Clarification of Catholic social teaching may be helpful—I look forward, for example, to a readable English translation of *Caritas in Veritate*. I believe, however, that attention to practices and structures may be even more helpful, if this might lead to a questioning of ideology and to a less polarized politics. (Such an approach may also be helpful in places other than America, although obviously the history and the structures will be different.)

One aspect of this attention has to do with voluntarism and service, a ubiquitous feature of American civic life but, interestingly, less a feature of Catholic parish life.[30] Church-run food pantries, shelters, and tutoring programs cannot solve the social ills of America. Yet they can help and, perhaps more importantly, they can provide a setting within which more fortunate Catholics encounter those who are less fortunate. Insight gained, at a personal level, into the lives of those who are working hard and not getting ahead may be a more effective goad to a questioning of the ideology of mobility and opportunity than are statistics, however compelling they may seem.

A second aspect has to do with the encouragement and structuring of opportunities for dialogue around social issues. The most catholic (with both a capital and a lower-case "c") approach would be both pro-life and pro-poor, and would recognize the fact that people of good will, including Catholics, can reasonably disagree about the most effective and appropriate ways, private and public, to pursue a pro-life and a pro-poor agenda. If at least some parts of the American citizenry, perhaps Catholic, could explore public issues without shouting at each other, it might be possible to make some progress toward an American approach to poverty that was more consistent with the facts about mobility and opportunity, and more open to a combination of public and voluntary action. I would like to think that Catholicism provides not only the intellectual resources for such dialogue, in the richness of its tradition of social teaching, but also the sociological resources, through its parishes, to help overcome the barriers that prevent a social conscience in America from maturing into practical action.

In conclusion, it is probably somewhat idiosyncratic to come at the issue of social conscience through history and sociology, and it no doubt reflects my personal and my American bias for fact-based and pragmatic solutions to problems rather than theoretical or even theological approaches. I hope, nonetheless, that this might provide an alternative way of thinking both about the problems associated with poverty and social conscience, and about possible solutions, in America and elsewhere.

Notes

1. For the purposes of this article, "America" and "American" refer to the United States of America and its citizens.

2. Gallup International, "Gallup International Millennium Survey," *Gallup International Association* (2000), http://www.gallup-international.com/ContentFiles/millennium15.asp.

3. The Pew Forum on Religion & Public Life, "U.S. Religious Landscape Survey," *The Pew Forum on Religion & Public Life* (2007), https://www.pewforum.org/2008/06/01/u-s-religious-landscape-survey-religious-beliefs-and-practices/. This report contains detailed information about religious affiliation and the fluidity of religious identification and practice in the US.

4. Steve Crabtree, "Religiosity Highest in World's Poorest Nations: United States Is among the Rich Countries That Buck the Trend," *Gallup, Inc.* (August 31, 2010), http://www.gallup.com/poll/142727/Religiosity-Highest-World-Poorest-Nations.aspx.

5. Pew Forum, "U.S. Religious Landscape Survey." See also Robert D. Putnam and David E. Campbell, *American Grace: How Religion Divides and Unites Us* (New York: Simon and Schuster, 2010), for a detailed discussion of the 2006 "Faith Matters" survey.

6. The Pew Forum on Religion & Public Life, "Faith in Flux: Changes in Religious Affiliation in the U.S.," *The Pew Forum on Religion & Public Life* (April 27, 2009), https://www.pewforum.org/2009/04/27/faith-in-flux/.

7. Pew Forum, "Faith in Flux."

8. Mark Noll, *The New Shape of World Christianity: How American Experience Reflects Global Faith* (Downers Grove, IL: InterVarsity Press, 2009).

9. Timothy Smeeding, "Poor People in Rich Nations: The United States in Comparative Perspective," *Journal of Economic Perspectives* 20, no. 1 (2006): 69–90, as cited by Daniel R. Meyer and Geoffrey L. Wallace, "Poverty Levels and Trends in Comparative Perspective" in *Changing Poverty, Changing Policies*, ed. Maria Cancian and Sheldon Danziger (New York: Russell Sage Foundation, 2009), 54–55.

10. Meyer and Wallace, "Poverty Levels and Trends in Comparative Perspective." The authors also cite as a source for their data Janet C. Gornik and Markus Jäntti, "Child Poverty in Upper-Income Countries: Lessons from the Luxembourg Income Study," in *From Child Welfare to Child Well-Being: An International Perspective on Knowledge in the Service of Making Policy*, ed. Sheila B. Kamerman, Shelley Phipps, and Asher Ben-Arieh (New York: Springer, 2010), 339–68.

11. These data predate the global recession of 2007–9 and the round of deficit reduction occurring in many European countries, most recently and dramatically in Britain. Recent poverty data for the US show record high poverty rates in 2009; European poverty rates have also almost certainly gone up. However, I anticipate that the differences between the US and Europe are likely to remain even with these changes.

12. Alberto Alesina and Edward L. Glaeser, *Fighting Poverty in the US and Europe: A World of Difference*, The Rodolfo De Benedetti Lecture Series (New York: Oxford University Press, 2004).

13. Alesina and Glaeser, *Fighting Poverty in the US and Europe*, 217.

14. The Pew Forum on Religion & Public Life, "Social and Political Views," ch. 2 in "U.S. Religious Landscape Survey," 101.

15. Pew Forum, "U.S. Religious Landscape Survey," 101.

16. Jacob S. Hacker and Paul Pierson, *Winner-Take-All Politics: How Washington Made the Rich Richer—and Turned Its Back on the Middle Class* (New York: Simon and Schuster, 2010); Larry M. Bartels, *Unequal Democracy: The Political Economy of the New Gilded Age* (Princeton, NJ: Princeton University Press, 2010).

17. Bartels, *Unequal Democracy*.

18. Hacker and Pierson, *Winner-Take-All Politics*.

19. Bill Bishop, *The Big Sort: Why the Clustering of Like-Minded Americans Is Tearing Us Apart* (New York: Mariner Books, 2009).

20. Pew Forum, "U.S. Religious Landscape Survey."

21. Putnam and Campbell, *American Grace*, 520.

22. See, e.g., "prosperity" in S. Brouwer, P. Gifford, and S. D. Rose, *Exporting the American Gospel: Global Christian Fundamentalism* (New York: Routledge, 1996).

23. Putnam and Campbell, *American Grace*.

24. Putnam and Campbell, *American Grace*, 436.

25. See Jay P. Dolan, *In Search of American Catholicism: A History of Religion and Culture in Tension* (New York: Oxford University Press, 2003), and John T. McGreevy, *Catholicism and American Freedom: A History* (New York: W. W. Norton, 2004).

26. Pew Forum, "U.S. Religious Landscape Survey."

27. E.g., my worship community, the Paulist Center of Boston, emphasizes social justice in its description of its mission and identity; see the Paulist Center, http://www.paulistboston.com. The *Weekly Standard* does not approve, see Jonathan V. Last, "A Curious Kind of Catholic," *The Weekly Standard*

LLC—a Weekly Conservative Magazine & Blog (July 25, 2004), https://www.weeklystandard.com/jonathan-v-last/a-curious-kind-of-catholic.

28. See Pew Forum, "U.S. Religious Landscape Survey," for coverage of all these trends.

29. Pew Forum, "U.S. Religious Landscape Survey."

30. See Mary Jo Bane, "The Catholic Puzzle: Parishes and Civic Life," in *Taking Faith Seriously*, ed. Mary Jo Bane, Brent Coffin, and Richard Higgins (Cambridge, MA: Harvard University Press, 2005), 63–93.

7. Pope Francis, Women, and the Church for the Poor

Lisa A. Fullam

This chapter first appeared in *Pope Francis and the Future of Catholicism in the United States: The Challenge of Becoming a Church for the Poor*. Edited by Erin Brigham, David E. DeCosse, and Michael Duffy. San Francisco: University of San Francisco Press, 2015.

Pope Francis has called for a fundamental shift in the pastoral emphasis of the church, calling leaders and laity alike to embrace Jesus's priority of welcoming the poor and the outcast. At the same time, Francis has spoken about women and women's roles in church and society in a way that is, at best, confusing. He calls for an increase of women's voice and authority, yet he undercuts that message when he addresses how that might work.

Here is the problem: the poor are disproportionately women and their dependent children. The Church of the Poor is a church in which women's voices must be heard and women's issues addressed—and the status quo is not working.

A Poor Church on the Side of the Poor

The urgency with which Francis seeks to realign the church's mission on behalf of the poor has been clear from the start of his papacy. He described his choice of papal moniker this way: "That is how the name came into my heart: Francis of Assisi. For me, he is the man of poverty, the man of peace….How I would like a Church which is poor and for the poor!"[1]

In his first major document, *Evangelii Gaudium* (EG),[2] Francis proposed "new paths for the Church's journey in years to come."[3] Selfish consumerism, he wrote, cuts those affected off from the poor: "Whenever our interior life becomes caught up in its own interests and concerns, there is…no place for the poor."[4] He attacked the "economy of exclusion" in stark terms:

> Such an economy kills….Today everything comes under the laws of competition and the survival of the fittest, where the powerful feed upon the powerless. As a consequence, masses of people find themselves excluded and marginalized: without work, without possibilities, without any means of escape.[5]

An adequate response cannot be limited to personal acts of asceticism and charity.[6] Ultimately, Francis wrote, social policies that uphold inequality must be changed:

> We can no longer trust in the unseen forces and the invisible hand of the market. Growth in justice…requires decisions, programs, mechanisms and processes specifically geared to a better distribution of income, the creation of sources of employment and an integral promotion of the poor which goes beyond a simple welfare mentality.[7]

This emphasis on economic structural change to address poverty has alarmed many of the pope's conservative critics,[8] and at the same time, this focus on the poor has contributed considerably to Francis's popularity within and beyond the church.

Pope Francis on Women

If Pope Francis's commitment to the poor has been clear and unwavering, his statements about women present a mixed message. At the level of generalities, he advocates powerfully for women; as to specifics, he argues mostly for the status quo, shored up by gender stereotypes.

Francis strongly affirms the equal dignity of women and men. In EG, he writes:

> Demands that the legitimate rights of women be respected, based on the firm conviction that men and women are equal in dignity, present the Church with profound and challenging questions which cannot be lightly evaded.[9]

He makes clear that this *does not* mean a change in women's official roles in the church: the bulk of this paragraph reiterates the church's exclusion of women from ordination. And while women are needed "where important decisions are made, both in the Church and in social structures,"[10] when he set up an unprecedented advisory board tasked with church reform, no women were deemed necessary.

This giving with one hand and taking away with the other is found throughout his papacy.[11] In an impromptu airplane interview, Francis called for a deeper theology of women, a theme he reiterated to several Jesuit-run publications later the same year.[12] In an address to participants in a conference on complementarity, he seemed to want to nuance the notion: "When we speak of complementarity between man and woman…we must not confuse the term with the simplistic idea that all the roles and relationships of both sexes are confined to a single and static model."[13] He called for equal pay for women and men (on grounds of complementarity), calling the wage gap "an absolute disgrace!"[14]

But when Francis writes about women, he employs the clichés of the Theology of the Body. In EG, he praises women for their "indispensable contribution" to society, but asserts that this is from a special "sensitivity" and "intuition" that women possess, not, for example, for their intelligence, dedication, or skill.[15] Commenting on John Paul II's *Mulieris Dignitatem*, he lauds that document's "solid" anthropology, warning against "promoting a kind of emancipation that, in order to fill areas that have been taken away from the male, deserts the feminine attributes with all its precious characteristics."[16]

Those characteristics center on motherhood, which is far more than biological in scope: women who are not mothers are unfulfilled.

Using women as a metaphor for the church, he said that when the church does not evangelize, "she lacks joy, she lacks peace, and so she becomes a disheartened church, anxious, sad, a church that seems more like a spinster than a mother, and this church doesn't work....The joy of the Church is to give birth."[17] Even celibate women are defined in maternal terms: "The consecrated woman is a mother, she must be a mother, not a 'spinster'!"[18]

Francis frequently uses language of sensitivity, intuition, and a related "feminine genius" in referring to women: "Woman has a particular sensitivity to the 'things of God,' above all in helping us understand the mercy, tenderness and love that God has for us."[19] Even when he named an unprecedented five women to the International Theological Commission (calling them "the icing on the cake"),[20] he reiterated that the core of their "feminine genius" was their sensitivity and intuition—odd praise for academic theologians.

What about those expanded roles in the church? In May 2015, Pope Francis raised the tantalizing possibility of women leading curial dicasteries, saying, "Yes, they can, in certain dicasteries they can; but what you are asking is simple functionalism."[21] He went on to describe women's true role is to act in accord with the "feminine genius." Intuition is key:

> When we face a problem among men we come to a conclusion, but when we face that same problem with women the outcome will be different. It will follow the same path, but it will be richer, stronger, more intuitive. For this reason women in the Church should have this role, they must clarify, help to clarify the feminine genius in so many ways.

That sounds like an argument for women in high church positions, but a month later, Pope Francis slammed that door shut, saying that appointing women to dicastery leadership would be mere "functionalism,"[22] not a real advance for women.

In an interview with Jesuit publications, he warned against "'female machismo,' because a woman has a different make-up than a man."[23] And while it is important that women have greater opportunities in society, their real importance is in the home (a statement never made about men) because of their distinctively feminine traits: "the gifts of refinement, particular sensitivity and tenderness, with which the woman's spirit is richly endowed."[24] How to do both? He is not sure:

> How can one increase an effective presence in so many areas of the public sphere…and at the same time maintain a presence and preferential and wholly special attention to the family? And this is the field for discernment which, in addition to the reflection on the reality of women in society, requires assiduous and persevering prayer.[25]

For Pope Francis, while things must change for women in the church and society, when it comes down to specifics, he has little to suggest beyond equal pay. Women are defined by motherhood, literal and symbolic, and what is distinctive and necessary about women's participation in church and society is connected to a "feminine genius" that echoes John Paul II's sentimental and stereotypical vision of women. Women's first place is in the home. Re-inscribing an unrevised complementarity as the norm for understanding women's roles and character, Francis has made clear that women's "equality" is theoretical, and their station is clearly secondary, defined in biological and emotional terms, and circumscribed by roles determined by men.

The Problem: The Poor Are Women

Women are overrepresented among the poor. In the United States, 3.5 percent more women than men live in poverty, more than 1 in 7 women overall. At age 65 and over, the gap widens: 11.6 percent of women live in poverty, versus 6.8 percent of men.[26] The poverty rate for female-headed (no adult male present) households with children is a stunning 30.6 percent.[27] The more than fourfold higher number of female-headed households over male-headed households means that the poverty gap is especially devastating for children: 19.9 percent of children in the United States—1 in 5—live in poverty.[28] More than half of all related children living in a female-headed household live in poverty.[29]

Several factors conspire to trap women in poverty. Women earn less than men for their work.[30] Perhaps even more significantly, women tend to be shunted into lower-wage "pink collar" jobs;[31] 80 percent of workers in low-wage jobs are women.[32] Discriminatory or otherwise inadequate policies relating to family and child-care, along with the so-called "mommy tax"[33] further burden working women. Moreover, women are disproportionately counted on for low- or unpaid care of children, people with disabilities, and dependent elders.[34]

The factors that drive women's greater poverty in the United States are present in the developing world, often to a greater degree.[35] The employment gap between men and women—13 percent in the developed world—reaches 28.1 percent in developing regions.[36] An education gap affects women: while parity between boys and girls has been achieved in primary education, and overall girls are not far behind boys in secondary education, substantial regional gaps persist.[37] The UN Women's Millennium Development Goals list a number of other factors that need attention internationally, including:

> women's disproportionate share of unpaid care work, women's unequal access to assets, violations of women's and girls' sexual and reproductive health and rights, their unequal participation in private and public decision-making beyond national parliaments and violence against women and girls.[38]

UN Women marked the 20th anniversary of the Beijing Platform for action with these words:

> While both men and women suffer in poverty, gender discrimination means that women have far fewer resources to cope. They are likely to be the last to eat, the ones least likely to access healthcare, and routinely trapped in time-consuming, unpaid domestic tasks. They have more limited options to work or build businesses. Adequate education may lie out of reach. Some end up forced into sexual exploitation as part of a basic struggle to survive.[39]

While poverty assaults the human dignity of men and women, it is women who bear the brunt, both in numbers and in the social and public policy obstacles that differentially afflict women. To ignore the ways poverty specially targets women is to ignore the pervasive influence of the structural sin of sexism.

What's a Pope to Do?

"Among our tasks as witnesses to the love of Christ is that of giving a voice to the cry of the poor."[40] Pope Francis has been eloquent and forceful in emphasizing the need for the ministry of the church to focus on the poor. Francis is not calling only for renewed acts of charity, but for a transformation of the structures that entrap the poor. However, when those structures are exposed, we see that women have been unequally victimized—the voice of the poor tends toward the treble end of the scale. As the Pope knows, confronting unjust social structures is a matter of deliberate empowerment of the marginalized. It is a matter, as he said, of "decisions, programs, mechanisms and processes" that address the structural roots of the evil.

Francis affirms the need for women's greater participation in decision-making in the Church and society. However, he undercuts that message by delimiting women's contributions, both in specific ways—for example, they cannot be ordained, so are ineligible for the most ordinary form of servant leadership in the church[41]—and by repeating unchanged the formulations about women that justify their marginalization. Women are lauded for maternity, not political savvy, for intuition, not intellectual acuity. Their most important role is at home, not in Congress, parliament, or on the papal advisory committee.

He cannot have it both ways. Either he must abandon his hope for a true church for the poor, or he must address with clarity and specificity ways in which women may be empowered in church and society. To continue the status quo will render his dream for the church a mirage, or, worse, a cynical stance that affirms women with one hand while holding them back with the other. To confront the structures of sexism that afflict men and women requires courage: It is the courage to listen with an open heart to the experience of women. It is the courage to name and redress historical and contemporary acts of violence against women, and to name and eliminate the structures that justify that violence. It is to invite women to take their rightful place alongside their brothers in the church and in society, not as "icing on the cake," but as collaborators in the work of the kingdom of God. It is to trust in the spirit of God that She will be with us always, leading us, consoling us, and encouraging us as we work for the justice in the world for which Jesus lived and died and lives anew.

Notes

1. Pope Francis, Address of the Holy Father, March 16, 2013, http://w2.vatican.va/content/francesco/en/speeches/2013/march/documents/papa-francesco_20130316_rappresentanti-media.html, Francis also noted his namesake's care for creation, an emphasis he explored in his encyclical *Laudato Si'*.

2. The first encyclical issued under his signature, *Lumen Fidei*, was drafted in Pope Benedict XVI's pontificate; that encyclical's reflection on faith completed Benedict's writing on the theological virtues started with *Spes Salvi* (2007) and *Caritas in Veritate* (2009). *Evangelii Gaudium* is Pope Francis's first major document.

3. Pope Francis, Apostolic Exhortation on the Proclamation of the Gospel in Today's World, *Evangelii Gaudium* (2013), par. 1. Cited hereafter as EG.

4. EG, par. 2.

5. EG, par. 53.

6. While personal steps *alone* are inadequate, Pope Francis does call for personal as well as political action: "Poverty today is a cry. We must all think about whether we can become a little poorer." His own example underscores that message: this is the pope who travels in a Ford Focus and lives in a Vatican guesthouse. Pope Francis, "Address of Pope Francis to the Students of the Jesuit Schools of Italy and Albania," Q&A (June 7, 2013), http://w2.vatican.va/content/francesco/en/speeches/2013/june/documents/papa-francesco_20130607_scuole-gesuiti.html.

7. EG, par. 204.

8. Two quick examples: right-wing provocateur Rush Limbaugh called him a Marxist, (https://www.reuters.com/article/us-pope-interview/im-no-marxist-pope-francis-tells-conservative-critics-idUSBRE9BE08H20131215) while blogger and former White House speechwriter Mark W. Davis at *US News and World Report* labeled him dangerously naive ("Pope Francis' Poverty Naivete," May 27, 2015, https://www.usnews.com/opinion/blogs/mark

-davis/2015/05/27/pope-francis-naive-views-on-poverty-and-capitalism-are-dangerous).

9. EG, par. 104.

10. EG, par. 103.

11. For a useful and pointed summary, see Miriam Duignan, "In His Thoughts and in His Words: Francis on Women," in *Conscience* 35, no. 4 (2014): 19–23.

12. Antonio Spadaro, "A Big Heart Open to God," *America* magazine, September 30, 2013, http://americamagazine.org/pope-interview. Jesuit Tom Reese said this meant that: "Pope Francis threw John Paul's theology of women under the bus." Thomas Reese, "Where Pope Francis Stands When It Comes to Women," in *National Catholic Reporter*, March 20, 2015, https://www.ncronline.org/blogs/faith-and-justice/where-pope-francis-stands-when-it-comes-women.

13. Pope Francis, "Address of His Holiness Pope Francis to Participants in the International Colloquium on the Complementarity between Man and Woman Sponsored by the Congregation for the Doctrine of the Faith," November 17, 2014, http://w2.vatican.va/content/francesco/en/speeches/2014/november/documents/papa-francesco_20141117_congregazione-dottrina-fede.html.

14. Pope Francis, General Audience, April 29, 2015, http://w2.vatican.va/content/francesco/en/audiences/2015/documents/papa-francesco_20150429_udienza-generale.html.

15. EG, par. 103.

16. Pope Francis, Address to Participants in a Seminar Organized by the Pontifical Council for the Laity on the Occasion of the 25th Anniversary of *Mulieris Dignitatem*, October 12, 2013, https://w2.vatican.va/content/francesco/en/speeches/2013/october/documents/papa-francesco_20131012_seminario-xxv-mulieris-dignitatem.html.

17. Pope Francis, Homily at Morning Mass, December 9, 2014, quoted by David Gibson, "Seven Pope Francis Quotes That Make Women Wince," in *Huffington Post Religion*, June 1, 2015, https://www.huffpost.com/entry/pope-francis-women_n_6307822.

18. Pope Francis, "Address of Pope Francis to the Participants in the Plenary Assembly of the International Union of Superiors General, (I.U.S.G.)," May 8, 2013, https://w2.vatican.va/content/francesco/en/speeches/2013/may/documents/papa-francesco_20130508_uisg.html. He does not use language of lack of human fulfillment of men who, like himself, forego fatherhood, nor does he warn celibate men to avoid the masculine equivalent of spinsterhood.

19. Pope Francis, "Address to Participants in a Seminar Organized by the Pontifical Council for the Laity on the Occasion 62 of the 25th Anniversary of *Mulieris Dignitatem*." That special sensitivity for the things of God, helping

people understand God's mercy and care, is a curious quality to laud in people barred from priesthood.

20. Pope Francis, "Address of His Holiness Pope Francis to Members of the International Theological Commission," December 5, 2014, https://w2.vatican.va/content/francesco/en/speeches/2014/december/documents/papa-francesco_20141205_commissione-teologica-internazionale.html. Women now make up 16 percent of the members of the ITC.

21. Pope Francis, "Address of His Holiness Pope Francis to Consecrated Men and Women of the Diocese of Rome," May 16, 2015, http://www.news.va/en/news/to-religious-people-of-the-diocese-of-rome-16-may.

22. Joshua J. McElwee, "Francis Again Rejects Women as Heads of Vatican Offices," *National Catholic Reporter*, June 21, 2015, https://www.ncronline.org/news/vatican/francis-again-rejects-women-heads-vatican-offices. So what, exactly is "functionalism" for Francis? In an address to the participants in the general assembly of the Pontifical Missionary Societies, he warned participants not to become like NGOs, not to put functionalism at the center of their work, but instead the spirit of Christ (News.va, June 5, 2015, http://www.news.va/en/news/pontificalmissionary-societies-opening-up-to-geog.) In other words, if they do their work absent a vibrant connection to Jesus, they are merely acting out their role, not fully living it. It is not clear how this use applies to women in Vatican leadership, unless exercising ecclesial leadership—something Francis has called for—inherently contradicts the "feminine genius."

23. Spadaro, "A Big Heart Open to God." Francis seems to engage in a kind of thinking critiqued by early feminists, who noted that whenever women wanted to expand their range into areas traditionally restricted to men (by men), they were accused of wanting to be men.

24. Pope Francis, "Address of Pope Francis to the Participants in the National Congress Sponsored by the Italian Women's Centre," January 25, 2014, http://w2.vatican.va/content/francesco/en/speeches/2014/january/documents/papa-francesco_20140125_centro-italiano-femminile.html.

25. Pope Francis, "Address of Pope Francis to the Participants in the National Congress Sponsored by the Italian Women's Centre."

26. Joan Entmacher, Katherine Gallagher Robbins, Julie Vogtman, and Anne Morrison, National Women's Law Center, "Insecure and Unequal: Poverty and Income among Women and Families, 2000–2013" (Washington, DC: NWLC, 2014), 1, https://www.nwlc.org/sites/default/files/pdfs/final_2014_nwlc_poverty_report.pdf. While not my topic here, it must not be forgotten that race matters, too: black, Hispanic, and Native American women have poverty rates about three times higher than that of white, non-Hispanic men.

27. Carmen DeNavas-Walt and Bernadette D. Proctor, U.S. Census Bureau, Current Population Reports, P60-249, *Income and Poverty in the*

United States: 2013, U.S. Government Printing Office, Washington, DC, 2014, pgs. 15–16.

28. DeNavas-Walt and Proctor, U.S. Census Bureau, Current Population Reports, 14.

29. DeNavas-Walt and Proctor, U.S. Census Bureau, Current Population Reports, 14.

30. AAUW, *The Simple Truth about the Gender Pay Gap* (Washington, DC: AAUW, 2015), 3. The statistical benchmark here is women's vs. men's median earnings for full-time work, overall. The wage gap is also exacerbated by race for most groups.

31. Trond Petersen and Laurie A. Morgan, "Separate and Unequal: Occupation-Establishment Sex Segregation and the Gender Wage Gap," *The American Journal of Sociology* 101, no. 2 (Sept. 1995): 329–65. This paper compares people in similar jobs and corrects for several variables not accounted for in the blunter comparison of women's vs. men's median earnings.

32. Bread for the World, "Hunger and Poverty among Women and Children," 2014, http://www.bread.org/media/pdf/women-children-us-2014.pdf.

33. Justine Calcagno, "The 'Mommy Tax' and 'Daddy Bonus': Parenthood and Income in New York City 1990–2010," Center for Latin American, Caribbean & Latino Studies Graduate Center, CUNY, May 2014, https://www.gc.cuny.edu/CUNY_GC/media/CUNY-Graduate-Center/PDF/Centers/CLACLS/Parenthood-and-Income-in-New-York-City-1990-2010.pdf.

34. Nancy Folbre, ed., *For Love and Money: Care Provision in the United States* (New York: Russell Sage Foundation, 2012), xi.

35. The oft-cited "70% of the world's poor are women" lacks substantiation. In part, little data exists to address the question directly. For example, when studies focus on numbers of poor families, it is hard to determine the distribution of goods *within* those families, where women may receive less than a fair share. Even studies that assert (apparently also without data) that men and women are equally represented among the poor point to differential structural disadvantages facing women. See Pedro Olinto, Kathleen Beegle, Carlos Sobrado, and Hiroki Uematsu, "The State of the Poor: Where Are The Poor, Where Is Extreme Poverty Harder to End, and What Is the Current Profile of the World's Poor?," Poverty Reduction and Economic Management Network, the World Bank, October, 2013, http://siteresources.worldbank.org/EXTPREMNET/Resources/EP125.pdf.

36. United Nations Statistics Division, UN Women, "Millennium Development Goals: Gender Chart; Special Edition for the 58th session of the Commission on the Status of Women, New York, Goal 1," March 10–21, 2014, http://www.unwomen.org/~/media/headquarters/attachments/sections/library/publications/2014/gender%20 gap%202014%20for%20web%20pdf.ashx.

37. Sub-Saharan Africa is the worst region for girls' secondary education, with a gender parity index of 0.83. United Nations Statistics Division, UN Women, "Millennium Development Goals: Gender Chart, Goal 2."

38. UN Women, "Millennium Development Goals: Gender Chart, Goal 3."

39. UN Women, "Women and Poverty," Beijing 20, http://beijing20.unwomen.org/en/for-later/poverty.

40. Pope Francis, "Address of Holy Father Francis to His Grace Justin Welby, Archbishop of Canterbury and Primate of the Anglican Communion," June 14, 2013, http://w2.vatican.va/content/francesco/en/speeches/2013/june/documents/papa-francesco_20130614_welby-canterbury.html.

41. Interestingly, by ruling out women's ordination, Francis leaves himself with a far more difficult problem. For women to have real voice in the church without admitting them into the structures of leadership that exist now would require a near-total reordering of the hierarchical structure of church leadership. Lay people, for example, would need to be able to contribute with vote as well as voice in decisions on doctrinal matters, and perhaps on priest-personnel decisions as well. Ordaining women would seem to be the *less* radical change Francis could make to include women meaningfully in the leadership of the church.

8. Floodwaters and the Ticking Clock

The Systematic Oppression and Stigmatization of Poor, Single Mothers in American and Christian Theological Responses

Julie A. Mavity Maddalena

This chapter first appeared in *CrossCurrents* (2013): 158–73.

The predominant current in America moves to hold all people morally and practically responsible for self-sufficiency, regardless of whether the currents actually move against them. Some voices have challenged the validity of the ideal of self-sufficiency, but they remain largely unheard.

Temporary Assistance for Needy Families (TANF), 1996

In the early 1990s, the claim of the moral good of self-sufficiency was directed with increasing intensity toward poor mothers and their children in the months leading up to the welfare reforms promised by Presidential candidate Bill Clinton. When Clinton was elected in 1993, he immediately set a course for reform that would force welfare recipients into the paid workforce. Supporters of this movement attributed the poverty experienced by welfare recipients to single parenthood, welfare dependency, and, most fundamentally, unwillingness to work. Despite parallel statistics of birth and divorce rates with their middle- and upper-middle-class counterparts, detractors leveled cruel, inaccurate accusations and insinuations of laziness, sexual promiscuity, and parental irresponsibility at mothers who accepted the direct aid offered by Aid to Families with Dependent Children (AFDC). Members of Congress blamed women receiving welfare for various social ills; Dan Quayle suggested poor, unmarried women with children were at least partially responsible for the "lawless anarchy" of the Rodney King Riots.[1] Vice President Quayle undoubtedly missed the ironic reversal of the equally hyperbolic, offensive conclusion of a 1931 "study," which linked "truancy, incorrigibility, robbery, teen tantrums, and difficulty managing children" to a "mother's absence from her job" of staying home to raise children.[2]

The same conservatives who would honor and value the privileged mother's choice to remain out of the paid workforce in order to focus solely on family work of nurturing and caring for her children suggested that children would receive greater intellectual stimulation and social development if mothers of poor children work for pay beyond their family work. These advocates related stories of "proud children" proclaiming the "joy" of having a mother who does not "just stay home all day" and the satisfaction of having an answer when "schoolmates ask about what their parent does for a living."[3] In contrast to a woman who does not need direct assistance from the government to stay home to raise her children, poor women who also believe the work of caring for their children is a better choice for their families than work outside the home are labeled "lazy, crazed trying to meet their own selfish needs."[4]

Diane Dujon and Ann Withorn followed media coverage in the months leading up to the passing of welfare reform legislation with disturbing findings. Their overview begins with a February 2, 1995, *Newsweek* article citation, which blames the "sexually irresponsible culture of poverty" on television, which is "the only sustained communication our society has with the underclass."[5] Television, the article continues, idealizes sexual irresponsibility as its most powerful message.[6] Isolating poorer families, envisioned primarily as families of color, into "the underclass" generates troubling "us" and "them" language, which, as Sidel notes, is neither helpful nor accurate in evaluating existing social programs or in devising new ones.[7] Focus on the malicious, stereotyped differences within our communities inhibits empathy or recognition of injustice for the other, which blocks widespread vision or movement for the ultimate common, social good. The same day of the *Newsweek* article, Diane Sawyer interviewed a group of teenage mothers (who comprise less than 10 percent of welfare recipients) on *Prime Time Live*. Assuming the role of the "angry taxpayer," she asked, "Why should taxpayers pay for your mistake?" When one of the mothers pointed out that welfare spending constitutes less than 1 percent of the budget (far, far less than defense spending), Sawyer immediately redirected the interview to the mothers' irresponsibility. Dujon and Withorn wryly hope that Sawyer might direct the same fury and tenacity at CEOs and heads of state, implying that Sawyer, and the American public she represents, has channeled its mounting rage at the failing of our economic structures at the easiest targets, those who lack the power to effect real change in working conditions, income inequalities, tax codes that disproportionately benefit the wealthy, violence, and other social ills.[8]

The outrages of the media coverage continue. The Fairness and Accuracy in Reporting (FAIR) organization studying media coverage of welfare reform December 1, 1994–February 24, 1995, in six major new outlets noted that 71 percent of the writers were male, few of whom were experts and most of whom were moralizing the issue from traditional wisdom over concerns about "values." Most stories recounted words and actions of politicians rather than stories of poor women and their children. In this coverage, 24 percent of the sources were members of Congress (72 percent Republican voices, 28 percent Democratic voices), 24 percent were state and local officials, and 9 percent were persons representing the Clinton administration. E. Clay Shaw, Jr., chair of the house subcommittee that drafted the Personal Responsibility and Work Opportunity Act (PRWOA), enjoyed the widest coverage. Shaw's quoted sentiments included the notion that the current welfare program simply functioned to "pamper the poor."[9] As with Quayle, Shaw missed the irony that recipients of AFDC were trying to survive on incomes at half the federal poverty line even with AFDC direct aid.

Recipients of AFDC assistance comprised 10 percent of media sources though even then the portrayal of recipients was highly selective and distorting. Interviewees were most often of ages 17–19 though that age bracket represented less than 6 percent of recipients. Further, overt racism appeared in such instances as the *World Report* story on January 16, 1995, which showcased seven women in its cover story. Six of these women were black and the lone white woman was described as clinically depressed. Recipients were most often asked insulting, invasive questions and were never invited to share their stories beyond leading questions portraying them in the least sympathetic light possible. Finally, a *Boston Globe* article on April 16, 1995, asked the question, "A family that works does not get a raise for having a child. Why then should a family that doesn't work?"[10] Apparently, the $2,450 tax credit along with tax subsidies for childcare received for each child by families not receiving AFDC funds does not qualify as a raise. Further, were these forms of assistance recognized within the debate, it is doubtful that anyone would suggest that middle-class families base their childbearing decisions on publicly funded perks. Finally, the FAIR report cites 9 percent of sources for the media as research and advocacy groups. While these groups offered studies demonstrating no causal relationship between birth rates and benefit levels, statistics and evidence were largely overlooked in favor of "conventional wisdom and morality sound bites."[11] Couture explains this seemingly irrational phenomenon, claiming that Americans in general and Christians in particular who subscribe to these prejudices are much more comfortable expressing and understanding traditions and beliefs than hard data and concrete policy proposals. They find social scientific data overwhelming and the resultant complexity difficult to evaluate.[12]

Given the cumulative weight of historical bias, the pervasiveness of the cultural ethos and myth of self-sufficiency, and the power of media misrepresentation, it is unsurprising that the 1996 Temporary Assistance for Needy Families (TANF) program linked cash assistance to work requirements and created a lifetime limit for the time poor families could receive assistance to five years.

Almost a decade after its inception, though before the economic crash of 2008, Sharon Hays offered an exploration of the TANF program and the families it professes to serve. She begins by illuminating the conflicting, imbedded values of the program: the work ethic and the traditional family, which, together, "condemn the 'dependence' of poor women and children on the state and celebrate their dependence on miserly employers and men."[13] Most Americans, and most TANF workers, are unaware that the preamble to the PRWOA includes a congressional edict on family. Goals for the restoration of this fabled middle-class, traditional, heterosexual family include a reduction in out-of-wedlock pregnancies and the promotion of marriage, which will allow for the "care of children at home."[14] While the program offers no marriage enrichment training or dating advice to its staff or recipients, the message remains: the U.S. Congress would like poor women to find husbands who earn wages sufficient to allow them to stay at home, and they will enforce these values to the extent that they can by teaching women, through the stringent, inflexible, unrealistic demands of TANF, that they really need a man for their own well-being and that of their children.[15]

Hays spent considerable time in TANF offices observing staff, recipients, dynamics, and literature. She notes two dominant themes, the ticking clock that is the time limit for assistance and the priority of paid work above all else. Pamphlets exhort such pithy aphorisms as "work is better than welfare," "all jobs are good jobs," and "work is the first priority, any earnings are good." A large banner hanging in the TANF offices Hays visited asks the question, "How much time do you have left?" The image of the ticking clock appears in most TANF literature as well.[16]

TANF arrived complete with penalties for non-compliance and few exemption allowances per state (states are allowed to exempt 20 percent of their TANF clients from work requirements; this includes exemptions for disability, mental illness, illness, behavior problems of children, and domestic abuse; exemption slots disappear almost immediately given high rates of all these realities among poorer members of society). States enjoy considerable leeway to develop their programs, which has some advantages but also presents considerable challenges to families moving between states and anyone seeking to measure outcomes of the program. Each of the states, however, shares the rules requiring a job search entailing 30 applications in a month, submission of all paternal information so the state can pursue child support, acceptance of the first job offer one receives, and retention of said job. A woman may choose to pursue job or vocational training part-time for a year in lieu of full-time work (she still must work part-time), but only for a year, and any studying must be supervised in order to count as part of her training hour credits. TANF offers subsidies for childcare as well as cash assistance once the mother has found paid work, both temporary, helpful measures that presumably function to give her the time and leverage to transcend the bounds of poverty.

Strings are attached. Not only can states cap families so that a woman who gets pregnant cannot receive benefits on behalf of that child, she will be penalized for any time she takes off when she gives birth. Therefore, she receives no assistance during her maternal leave from the paid workforce, *and* those unpaid months count toward her five-year maximum TANF assistance. If a woman fails to submit the required paternity information (whether she was raped, uncertain about her child's parentage, or fearful of retribution and abuse), she will not receive assistance. If a woman leaves a job, whether because she cannot find childcare that fits her work schedule, the location of the job (or childcare) makes the situation unmanageable, working conditions are unacceptable (documented sexual harassment rates remain high), or wages are insufficient to meet her family's needs, she will be punished by having her TANF funds withheld. And the clock keeps ticking. If a woman is waiting for a childcare subsidy to become available (only one-third of TANF recipients nationwide receive childcare assistance, and there is an incredible shortage of facilities relevant to need), she must be employed or she will be punished. With the clock still ticking.

In addition to significant deficiencies in the realms of human dignity, compassion, privacy, and sheer economic plausibility, the fiscal realities of TANF ought to trigger a flare for conservatives. Given the high cost of childcare, the price tag for childcare subsidies for low-income women far exceeds the costs of paying the same women for the work of raising their own children. Similarly, the child support enforcement effort costs tax-payers $745 million in 1996. Clearly, paternal support is important, and neglect is crippling, but most mothers receiving TANF assistance do receive some sort of support from the fathers of their children (many of whom are working for extremely low wages themselves), whether it be diapers, occasional cash, or gifts, which function to maintain relations with the children and aid the mother (who, incidentally, only receives $50/month if the government does manage to extract child support, with the rest reimbursing TANF). Often these fragile relationships crumble entirely (often violently) when a mother submits to TANF requirements to identify her child's father. The costs clearly outweigh the benefits from multiple angles.[17]

But let us return to the still more troubling dimensions of TANF. The goals of the program are to reduce welfare assistance, not to reduce poverty. The rhetoric about self-sufficiency is just that. Rhetoric. The exposure of this underlying goal renders this study important for *all* poor, single mothers, whether they receive direct aid or not, because it reveals the attitudes and perceptions shaping the entire cultural, political, and economic system in which they live.

States receive significant incentives for reducing their rolls, so many have incorporated a powerful diversionary system. By disqualifying people or rendering them ineligible for assistance, whether or not they need or qualify for assistance, states can access enormous bonuses.[18] Potential applicants must attend a meeting (typically with no childcare provided) in which they are discouraged from applying for TANF funds. Hays observed many instances of partial, confusing, and misleading information, which led many attendees to decline an application.[19] Yet supporters have hastily proclaimed the "success" of TANF based on drastic reductions in the numbers of recipients. Indeed, the number of families receiving welfare benefits has declined by two-thirds from 1994 to 2008. Studies belie this success with reports from individual states that suggest the percentages of people exiting TANF with work hovers around 50 percent. This 50 percent, moreover, includes anyone who has earned $100 or more in the last three months. Further, the number of poor children receiving TANF benefits has plummeted from over 60 percent prior to the introduction of TANF to 23 percent in 2007.[20] The Children's Defense Fund reports that 70 percent of poor children are living in families in which someone is working full- or part-time. The same report indicates that over half the families with children poor enough to qualify for TANF do not receive assistance due to the various barriers to enrollment.[21] Since the recession of 2009, the numbers are much bleaker. Not only have TANF benefits been cut, in all but two states, the actual value of TANF benefits is less than it was in 1996 after adjusting for inflation. In 2011, TANF benefits fell below 50 percent of the poverty line in all 50 states, and both state and federal governments have made TANF benefit cuts in their budgets. Any paid work or raises directly offset TANF benefits, so families do not see any increase in their incomes as they move off TANF.[22]

This clear failure to "solve the problem of poverty" by propelling poor mothers into the job market was anticipated by those with any ability to calculate the sheer impossibility of supporting one child much less multiple children on minimum wage or near-minimum wage incomes. The minimum wage of $5.15/hour yields an annual income of $10,712, which is below the federal poverty line.[23] This, of course, assumes steady, 40-hour workweeks with no sick or vacation time, which, for anyone who has children, is virtually impossible. Obviously, these jobs offer no healthcare benefits (whose premiums would likely be prohibitive even if available) or unemployment insurance. Further, poverty wages leave no space for unexpected medical, transportation, family emergency, or hundreds of other snowballing costs.[24] Dujon and Withorn offer the metaphor of *Jumanji*:

> …where every role of the dice yields yet another unplanned disaster: a month with consecutive cases of the chicken pox without backup childcare, a returning mate who falls off the wagon and disrupts the family entirely, a sister's car that breaks down so she can't shuttle the kids to camp, rents raised, premiums raised….[25]

What we have sentenced poor women to is a low-wage workforce utterly unwilling to allow a single mother enough control and flexibility in the workplace to accommodate her dual responsibilities for family work and paid work. Most low-wage jobs demand that work be one's primary responsibility, relegating familial responsibilities to secondary, private matters.

> The more worthy goals of work—its promise of independence, citizenship, valued contributions to the collective good—have been debased or discarded. What remains is the individualistic ethic of self-sufficiency and an image of the "good society" as one full of unfettered individuals busily pursuing their daily bread in the marketplace, fending for themselves without a care or concern for others.[26]

Through all of this, the families and their stories have remained largely absent from the views of middle, upper-middle, and upper-class Americans. We have set single mothers up in a double bind, able to neither fully financially support their children despite full-time employment nor fully care for their children with adequate time, energy, and resources.

And little has changed throughout this sordid history. In the recent Presidential campaign, these classist, racist, sexist, and heterosexist attitudes emerged on full display as Presidential candidate Mitt Romney and his wife, Ann, offered public statements about the relative value of family work and paid work contingent on the marital and socioeconomic status of the mother. Defending her decision to engage only in family work (in response to CNN pundit Hilary Rosen's critique), Ann said she "knew what it was like to struggle" and that Mitt would often come home and say, "Your job is more important than mine." She continued to say, "We have to respect women in all the choices that they make."[27] Romney himself responded by including the statement in a speech to the NRA that he firmly believes that "all moms are working moms."[28] Make that middle- and upper-class women. Because Mitt made his feelings about respect and choice regarding poor, single mothers quite clear the previous January. MSNBC's Chris Hayes released a clip of Mitt talking about his positions regarding families (read: women) receiving TANF direct aid and paid work. Mitt touted his advocacy for increasing the work requirements for families receiving TANF so that these women would know the "dignity of work." He also said he would gladly increase child-care subsidies so that women could go back to work "on day one."[29]

Not only did this blatant hypocrisy garner little popular, national attention, the Romney campaign seemed to largely get a pass on its flagrant lies about the Obama administration's proposed changes to TANF regulations. While the Obama administration has not proposed any substantive changes to the TANF work requirements, the political power of such a suggestion/accusation proves the continued presence of the attitudes that created the initial program.

Very few voices have been attentive enough to ask questions about or to the poor, single, mothers who receive these sorts of direct aid or who live close to those economic thresholds: What does it do to the psyche to be constantly labeled, ostracized, and stigmatized? What happens when women do not recognize themselves in the distorted cultural representations and are forced to develop a sort of dual consciousness in order to survive? What does it mean when your family, simply because it lacks a male "head," is seen as deficient, defective, disrupted, and broken?

What are the long-term effects of shame, guilt, and anger? What does it say about a mother's commitment and love for her child, about her courage and tenacity, about her perseverance to face these assaults and indignities again and again in her determination to do whatever it takes to survive? What is it like to be watching rising floodwaters from behind locked gates while the guards holding up a ticking clock ask why you are not helping yourself?

What's Christian Theology Got to Do with It?

Christian theologians and ethicists have challenged the treatment and perception of poor mothers and their children throughout history even as they have also been complicit in perpetuating the status quo of sexist, classist, heterosexist, and racist attitudes and systems. In light of disheartening statistics, cold social policies, and bleak forecasts for the lives of poor women and their children, I turn to the helpful voices in the Christian faith, past and present. While Luther's attempts to discredit the theologically suspect and fundamentally untenable idealization of self-sufficiency have mostly receded into the annals of history, Couture has helpfully retrieved their wisdom and applied it to the deficiencies of welfare reform. Returning to Luther's early awareness of the interdependence of government, local community, the family, and the individual, Couture insists that contemporary language of self-sufficiency is "inadequate to the task" of creating a nurturing, just society. Couture offers the following definition of oppression: "When social expectations are set so high that individuals' personal efforts cannot possibly attain what society considers normative."[30] Clearly the projected, compulsory goal of self-sufficiency is oppressive, effectively "denying poor women the language they need with which to appeal for help."[31] Conservative and liberal clamors for self-sufficiency function as the rhetoric of socially powerful people, creating unrealistic expectations for the capacities of poor people, who are disproportionately women and persons of color, to transcend poverty within existing economic structures.[32]

Couture also criticizes the goals of economic self-sufficiency in TANF for blurring the distinction between psychological needs for self-esteem and fundamentally unequal sociological realities, seeking to ameliorate the unhelpful legacy of the early feminist insistence on self-sufficiency. "The norm the mothers will be employed and raise families can be considered progressive only when mothers' domestic labor is recognized as work which contributes to society, and when family policy provides the support base for single mothers' employment."[33]

As Couture recaps her historical and theological treatment of various reformers and theologians (which includes an important engagement with John Wesley's efforts on behalf of the poor), she identifies the healthier cultural legacy of the idea of shared responsibility for poor women and their children, through personal practice and the shaping of culture and society. The notion of self-sufficiency as it appears in welfare reform, she declares, is "theologically bankrupt," detaching persons from one another in a manner that not only cuts off the route to the divine, but also leaves little room for the care of children and other vulnerable members of society. Finally, "self-sufficiency devalues parenting and creates a perversion in gender relations."[34]

Having debunked the abusive nature of self-sufficiency, Couture suggests a model of interdependence in which domestic and public realms mingle, providing basic care for everyone while encouraging each person's unique social contribution. Couture does offer a highly qualified recognition of the value of self-sufficiency in certain forms, albeit bracketed by her commitment to interdependence as the overarching norm. It is so artfully crafted in its nuanced articulation to warrant a lengthy quotation:

> Within a context of interdependent social practices, self-sufficiency can be conditionally reaffirmed. Self-sufficiency is alluded to when feminists have argued for self-sufficiency for women. That is, a sense of relative personal self-sufficiency is psychologically necessary for all men, women, and children to develop a sense of power over their own lives. Self-sufficiency becomes problematic when our sense of self-sufficiency denies our necessary interpersonal relationships and ignores the basic socioeconomic supports which for most of us are not provided by our self-sufficient efforts....When, out of the denial of our essential interdependence, policy makers turn self-sufficiency into the primary norm of distributive economic justice, this obligation eradicates the

> possible psychic benefits of a personal sense of relative self-sufficiency because it denies the reality of the human condition. An ethic of care through shared responsibility allows room for the psychic empowerment of self-sufficiency by locating it within the larger context of interdependence.[35]

Feminist theological ethicists have also embraced fundamental commitments to interdependence as opposed to self-sufficiency. The editors of *Welfare Policy: Feminist Critiques* share a commitment to the ontological existence and moral responsibilities of the relationality of all things. While drawing from many images, they feel particular affinity for the Pauline metaphor of the body of Christ and to the United States Catholic bishops' statement that the human person is social and has obligations to all of society. They, too, condemn the absence of any acknowledgment of relationality in the welfare debates and deem this antithetical to feminist and Christian thought; they also maintain the importance of autonomy and individual worth within the bounds of interdependent relations, particularly in light of a woman's right to the dignity of self-determination over her physical and emotional self.

Adding another important theological and ethical dimension to the dialogue, Christian feminist ethicists argue that the welfare discussion must engage justice. As feminist theologians, Bounds, Brubaker, and Hobgood see justice as a fundamentally relational word, marked by accountabilities to others. Utilizing this motif, they effectively unmask the more insidious effects of welfare reform.

> In the welfare debates, this notion of justice as a mutual negotiation of needs was silenced in favor of an individualist model where, if one could not be "responsible" for providing for one's own needs, one should turn to charity. Yet charity… is preeminently a relationship among unequals, where the givers enhance their power and moral "goodness" and the receivers are considered dependent and morally inferior.[36]

The editors of *Welfare Policy* offer overarching normative claims and fundamental moral considerations based on feminist ethics of interdependence, justice, and care. These values and concrete proposals represent a good starting place, a moral framework, to ground future studies and discourse regarding economic justice and single mothers. They seek, as their ultimate goal, the "ability of women to achieve some measure of dignity and self-determination to provide for their own well-being and the well-being of those they love and for whom they are responsible."[37] I highlight these goals because they appear in various forms in a fairly wide reading of sociologists, anthropologists, ethicists, advocates, welfare recipients (also themselves advocates), feminists, and theologians, all committed to honoring the courage, worth, and struggle of the unnamed, marginalized, poor mothers who continue to value their family work despite a society that does not. Their realization would also demonstrate the theological expression of repentance on the part of a predominant, complicit Christian society.[38]

These most basic priorities include the following: (1) Full recognition and economic reimbursement for the work of caring for the young, the elderly, and the sick. "The mental, physical, and emotional caring labor that is absolutely necessary to maintain life and enhance its quality should secure for every household a tax-free income up to the actual cost of a decent standard of living."[39] (2) Full employment at living wages in work environments that recognize and support the needs of families and promote basic human dignity and worth. (3) A social context committed to full communal flourishing and fundamental human rights, which recognizes the need for such goods and services as universal health care, quality public education, affordable housing, and public transportation (even when they do not coincide with competitive, free market, profit-driven values). (4) A social security system that fully supports the needs of persons unable to engage in wage-earning activities (which includes care-taking). (5) A policy-making process that recognizes the value and expertise of past and current welfare recipients.[40] These voices have been silenced entirely too long.

The final theo-ethical resource I would like to briefly bring to bear on this issue is the role of the faith community and its commitment to economic justice as envisioned by Dr. Martin Luther King, Jr. King devoted considerable time later in his ministry to exposing the injustices of the economic system and its particular exploitation of marginalized groups and persons. Like feminist theologians and ethicists, King recognized the interdependent nature of reality and the need for human dignity, characterizing his calls for mutuality a matter of survival rather than utopian dreams.[41] King knew that the churches and their leaders must take active roles in advocating prophetically for just social changes because power does not yield its privileges easily; this is one of the most consistent biblical messages overlooked by those benefiting from current social, political, and economic arrangements. While King did not specifically address the needs of economic justice for single mothers, the thrust of his economic critique and the theology of his Beloved Community could easily apply.

Thus, I conclude with what I hope is only a beginning. The model of self-sufficiency imposed on poor, single mothers has generated false, insidious perceptions and expectations that have yielded crippling systems that obscure the real sources and solutions of economic insecurity. Welfare reform that produced the TANF program is the epitome of the sexism, classism, heterosexism, and racism intrinsic to US economic assumptions and arrangements. Given the dominant presence of persons who identify as Christians in positions of power, it seems fitting to appeal to Christian theo-ethical resources as alternative sources for envisioning a more just, relational, compassionate society. Finally, for a tradition that claims to be held accountable for its treatment of "the least of these," it is past time Christians take seriously the experiences, the work, and the economic vulnerabilities of poor, single mothers.

Notes

1. Ruth Sidel, *Unsung Heroines: Single Mothers and the American Dream* (Berkeley: University of California Press, 2006), 2–3.

2. Ruth Sidel, *Women and Children Last* (New York: Penguin Books, 1987), 55.

3. Lawrence Mead, "Welfare Reform and Children," in *Children, Families, and Government: Preparing for the Twenty-first Century*, ed. Edward Zigler, Sharon Lynn Kagan, and Nancy W. Hall (New York: Cambridge University Press, 1996), 70.

4. Sidel, *Unsung Heroines*, 22. It should also be noted that families that do not receive direct assistance in the form of AFDC, then, and TANF now, receive government subsidies for their children in the form of tax breaks and refunds—often in larger amounts than the TANF direct aid.

5. Diane Dujon and Ann Withorn, *For Crying Out Loud: Women's Poverty in the United States* (Boston: South End Press, 1996), 30.

6. Dujon, *For Crying Out Loud*, 30.

7. Sidel, *Keeping Women and Children Last*, 170.

8. Dujon, *For Crying Out Loud*, 30–31.

9. Dujon, *For Crying Out Loud*, 31–32.

10. Dujon, *For Crying Out Loud*, 33.

11. Dujon, *For Crying Out Loud*, 33–35.

12. Pamela Couture, *Blessed Are the Poor? Women's Poverty, Family Policy, and Practical Theology* (Nashville: Abingdon Press, 1991), 18–20.

13. Sharon Hays, *Flat Broke with Children: Women in the Age of Welfare Reform* (New York: Oxford University Press, 2003), 30–31.

14. Hays, *Flat Broke with Children*, 34.

15. Hays, *Flat Broke with Children*, 35–36.

16. Hays, *Flat Broke with Children*, 34–38.

17. Hays, *Flat Broke with Children*, 35–81.

18. Sidel, *Keeping Women and Children Last*, 203.

19. Hays, *Flat Broke with Children*, 84.

20. Gene Falk, "The Potential Role of the Temporary Assistance for Needy Families (TANF) Block Grant in the Recession," Congressional Research Service, prepared for Members and Committees of Congress, February 24, 2009, Summary.

21. "Child Poverty in America," the Children's Defense Fund, August 26, 2008.

22. "TANF Benefits Fell Further in 2011 and Are Worth Much Less than in 1996 in Most States," Center on Budget and Policy Priorities, http://www.cbpp.org/cms/?fa=view&id=3625.

23. $5.15 has been the minimum wage for most of the life of TANF. In 2007, Congress raised minimum wage in a series of three raises over the course of three years. It is now $7.25/hour, which is substantively improved, particularly coupled with the new federal poverty levels, which come much closer to recognizing financial challenges facing poor families. That said, the basic challenges to low-income single mothers remain largely unchanged, particularly in light of the current recession.

24. The gradual implementation of 2010's Affordable Care Act should help to some degree but is certainly no panacea.

25. Dujon, *For Crying Out Loud*, 20.

26. Hays, *Flat Broke with Children*, 85.

27. "Ann Romney Responds to Hillary Rosen," Fox News, April 12, 2012.

28. "Romney: Welfare Parents 'Need to Go to Work,'" http://www.nbcnews.com/video/up/47053681.

29. "Romney: Welfare Parents 'Need to Go to Work.'"

30. Couture, *Blessed Are the Poor?*, 69.

31. Couture, *Blessed Are the Poor?*, 69.

32. Couture, *Blessed Are the Poor?*, 70–71.

33. Couture, *Blessed Are the Poor?*, 70.

34. Couture, *Blessed Are the Poor?*, 164–65.

35. Couture, *Blessed Are the Poor?*, 168–69.

36. Elizabeth M. Bounds, Pamela K. Brubaker, and Mary E. Hobgood, "Welfare 'Reform': A War Against the Poor," in *Welfare Policy: Feminist Critiques*, ed. Elizabeth M. Bounds, Pamela K. Brubaker, and Mary E. Hobgood (Eugene, OR: Wipf and Stock Publishers, 1999), 17.

37. Bounds et al., "Welfare 'Reform,'" 18.

38. This claim is not to perpetuate problematic Christian privilege in denial of a pluralistic culture, but to recognize the role and power of the Christian Right in promoting many of the attitudes and policies exposed here.

39. Bounds et al., "Welfare 'Reform,'" 18.

40. Bounds et al., "Welfare 'Reform,'" 18–19.

41. Martin Luther King, Jr., *Where Do We Go from Here: Chaos or Community?* (Boston: Beacon Press, 1967), 61–63.

9. What Causes Inequality?

Dean Baker

This chapter first appeared as "Rising Inequality: It's Not the Market." *Journal of Catholic Social Thought* 12, no. 1 (2015): 5–17.

There is little dispute that there has been a sharp rise in inequality in the United States in the years since 1980. After a long period from the end of World War II to the mid-seventies in which the country prospered and inequality was lessened, the country has seen three decades in which those at the top have garnered the bulk of the gains from economic growth. Recent research based on tax records has given us a more precise picture of this breakdown. The top 1 percent of the distribution saw a much sharper rise in their income than the top 10 percent and the top 0.1 percent saw sharper gains than the top percentile as a whole. The top 0.01 percent did even better.[1]

There is not much dispute about this trend in inequality, the general contours of which have been documented by a number of different researchers using a variety of data sources. However there is serious dispute about the causes of this increase in inequality. A common view is that the rise in inequality is a natural result of market outcomes, specifically that technology and globalization have led to a reduction in the demand for manufacturing workers and the other middle-skilled jobs that provided a middle-class living standard for tens of millions of workers in prior decades.

This paper challenges this view. It argues that while technology and globalization have both been factors in the rise in inequality, this is more attributable to how these forces were shaped by policy rather than any intrinsic development in the economy. Furthermore, it argues that other conscious policy decisions, such as the decision to tolerate high rates of unemployment, the decision to weaken labor unions and workers' bargaining power, and the strengthening of intellectual property protections have played a substantial role in increasing inequality.

The Wrongly Accused: Technology and Globalization

The rise in inequality over the last three decades is often attributed to developments in technology and globalization. The argument is that technology has destroyed many formerly middle-class jobs in manufacturing and other areas, forcing these workers to take lower paying jobs in sectors like retail. In the same vein it is argued that globalization has eliminated barriers that protected workers in the United States. This has further disadvantaged workers in the middle since it has exposed them to competition with much lower paid labor in the developing world.

From this perspective inequality is unfortunate, but it is the result of the natural workings of the market, not something that was brought about by deliberate policy decisions. While this perspective can be comforting to those who support the status quo, it rests on sloppy thinking rather than a solid basis in evidence.

The fact that new technologies are displacing workers, and disproportionately less-educated workers, is not new. We have long had technological change, and in fact it proceeded at a considerably more rapid pace in the early post-war period than in the years since 1980.[2] In the post-war golden age, the benefits from rapid productivity growth translated into rapidly rising wages and improvements in living standards. The fact that they are now associated with unemployment and rising inequality today cannot be blamed in any simple way on technology.[3]

The claims on globalization are similarly weak. It is true that millions of manufacturing workers have lost their jobs due to competition with low-paid workers in the developing world; however, there was nothing natural about this process. There are hundreds of millions of people in the developing world who are willing to work in manufacturing for a fraction of the pay of U.S. workers, but these countries also have tens of millions of very bright people who would be happy to train to U.S. standards and work as professionals in the United States. The reason factory workers in the United States face competition from low-paid workers in China, but our doctors don't face competition from hundreds of thousands of doctors from India is the result of deliberate policy choices.

Trade agreements like NAFTA were explicitly structured to put our manufacturing workers in direct competition with their counterparts in the developing world. Manufacturing firms were consulted on the obstacles that prevented them from investing in Mexico and setting up operations there. The purpose of these agreements was to remove these obstacles. Trade agreements could have been crafted for the purpose of removing barriers that prevent smart students in the developing world from studying to meet U.S. standards and then having the option to work in the United States just like U.S.-born doctors, lawyers, and dentists.

This would have presumably meant more uniformity in licensing standards across states, a more standardized system of testing (e.g., core rules for being admitted to a national bar in the United States), and the opportunity to take professional licensing exams in the home country (administered by U.S. examiners). The economic argument for trade agreements along these lines is the same as the economic argument for the agreements that were actually implemented. Freeing up trade in professional services would reduce the cost of health care, legal services, and other work performed by highly paid professionals.

This would lead to large gains for consumers and the economy as a whole at the same time it drove down the wages of the most highly educated workers.[4]

The fact that our path to globalization put less-educated workers in competition with the developing world—with the predictable effect of lowering their wages—while leaving our most highly paid workers largely protected from such competition was a policy choice, not a natural development. It is misleading and inaccurate to claim the path of globalization that we have chosen was in any way inevitable; it was a conscious policy choice.

Other Causes of Inequality

Technology can be ruled out as a major cause of inequality, as can globalization as a natural force (but not as policy choice). However, there are many other factors that played an important role in increasing inequality over the last three decades. I will briefly discuss the most important items on my list:

1. Unemployment;
2. The decline of unions;
3. Longer and strong patent protection; and
4. The growth of finance.

Unemployment

Unemployment plays an important role in the distribution of income because it affects the bargaining power of workers at middle and especially the bottom end of the income distribution. The logic of this is straightforward. When the unemployment rate increases, the workers who are most likely to be laid off are the workers at the bottom of the pay ladder. It is likely to be assembly line workers in manufacturing or counter clerks in retail. The management, and especially top management, are the ones least likely to see their employment affected. The result is that in periods of relatively high unemployment, workers at the middle and bottom of the pay distribution have little bargaining power and are therefore poorly situated to secure their share of productivity gains.

It is easy to see casual evidence of this phenomenon from examining the path of wage growth over the last two decades. Workers at the middle and bottom of the wage distribution saw little or no real wage gains through the first half of the 1990s and virtually all of the last decade.[5] The one exception to this pattern was the late 1990s, when the unemployment rate fell below 6.0 percent, the widely accepted measure of the non-accelerating inflation (NAIRU) rate of unemployment at the time. In the last four years of the 1990s, the unemployment rate fell below 5.0 percent in 1997 and eventually reached 4.0 percent as a year-round average in 2000.

This four-year period was the only time since the early 1970s when workers at the middle and bottom of the wage distribution achieved sustained wage gains. This was the result of a tight labor market leading to a real shortage of labor for those at the bottom of the wage ladder. There were accounts in the media of employers chartering busses to take people from the inner cities to work at hotels and restaurants in the suburbs. There were also accounts of employers hiring people they would not ordinarily look to hire, such as people with disabilities or former prisoners. In short, this tightness in the labor market hugely improved the bargaining position of workers at the bottom.

In our book *Getting Back to Full Employment*,[6] we tested this result more formally and found solid evidence that lower unemployment rates were associated with higher wages for those at the middle and especially the bottom. Holding other factors constant, we found that a sustained one percentage point drop in the unemployment rate was associated with a 9.8 percent increase in the wages of workers at the 10th percentile of the wage distribution, a 4.2 percent increase in the wages of workers at the 50th percentile of the wage distribution, and zero change at the 90th percentile.[7]

In addition to having important distributional implications, the rate of unemployment is also to a substantial extent a policy variable. Through fiscal and monetary policy the government has enormous power to raise or lower the unemployment rate. For example, a more expansionary fiscal policy will be associated with a lower rate of unemployment, especially for an economy that is operating below its potential level of output.[8] This has a trade-off in terms of higher budget deficits, at least in the short-run. But even if policymakers opt not to take steps to reduce unemployment because they don't want to incur a larger budget deficit, this is still a policy choice.

The same holds true of monetary policy. The Federal Reserve Board's policy has been sharply focused on reducing inflation rather than sustaining high employment in the years since 1980. This focus was formalized with its explicit adoption of a 2.0 percent inflation target under Ben Bernanke's tenure as chair. Whatever the merits of this anti-inflation policy, it does involve an explicit choice. The Fed is prepared to tolerate a higher level of unemployment rather than risk an increase in the inflation rate above its targeted level.

In fact, the unemployment rate has been notably higher in the years since 1980 than in the years before 1980. From 1949 to 1979, the unemployment rate was a cumulative 15.0 percentage points above the NAIRU as measured by the Congressional Budget Office (CBO).[9] In the years from 1980 to 2012, the unemployment rate was a cumulative 31.0 percentage points above the NAIRU. Even if the years of the Great Recession are excluded, the unemployment rate was 16.0 percentage points above the NAIRU in the years from 1980 to 2007. Whatever the rationale, we have had substantially higher unemployment in the years since 1980 than in the decades before 1980, and there is good reason to believe that this higher unemployment has been a major factor behind the increase in inequality.

There is one other aspect to the macroeconomics of unemployment that is worth noting. In the years prior to 1980 we generally ran trade surpluses or modest deficits, the latter mostly being the outgrowth of the surge in oil prices in 1973 and 1978. In most of the last three decades we have run trade deficits, and in the years since 1997 we have run large trade deficits. These deficits peaked at almost 6.0 percent of GDP in 2005 and remain near 3.0 percent of GDP as of 2014. These trade deficits are associated with a gap in demand, as the deficit corresponds to incomes that are generated in the United States but are creating demand in other countries. There is no easy way to fill this sort of demand gap. In the late 1990s, the gap was filled by the demand generated by the stock bubble. In the last decade, the gap was filled by the demand generated by the housing bubble. However, in the absence of an asset bubble, there is no mechanism in the private sector that is likely to fill this sort of gap in demand. (The government could fill the gap with a larger budget deficit, but as noted before there are serious political obstacles to going this route.)

The trade deficit is also to a substantial extent the result of government policy. It is easy to link the sharp increase in the trade deficit in the late 1990s to the rise in the value of the dollar that followed the East Asian financial crisis. This was to large extent the result of deliberate policy decisions by the International Monetary Fund and the Treasury Department over the conditions of the bailout for the countries of the region. The Clinton administration team, which directed the bailout, insisted that the countries of the region would repay their debts, but they would be allowed to hugely increase their exports to get the foreign exchange to make this possible. This meant a plunge in their currencies against the dollar.

While the exports of the countries of the region to the United States soared following the bailout, other countries in the developing world also followed the same pattern. The conditions of the bailout were seen as so extreme that other developing countries sought to accumulate large amounts of reserves in order to avoid being in the same situation.[10] As a result there was a sharp rise in the amount of reserves held by countries throughout the developing world, which was associated with a large increase in the value of the dollar. This caused the trade deficit of the United States to hugely expand as the run-up in the dollar made our goods and services less competitive internationally.

Even now the trade deficit is still to a large extent a matter of policy. The normal adjustment process in a system of floating exchange rates would be that a country with a large deficit, like the United States, would see a decline in the value of its currency as the supply of dollars in world markets exceeds the demand. This drop in the dollar does not occur because a number of countries (most importantly China) actively buy up dollars to prop up the dollar against their currencies, thereby sustaining their trade surpluses.

The United States could almost certainly negotiate a lower value of the dollar, if this was an important policy goal. The United States routinely pressures its trading partners on a wide variety of issues from greater protection of U.S. patents and copyrights to increased market access for financial and retail firms. If the United States were to instead prioritize reducing the value of the dollar in order to bring its trade deficit closer to balance, it is difficult to believe that it could not achieve substantial progress in this area. However, it is clear from both its actions and public statements that a lower valued dollar is not a top priority in negotiations. As a result, the United States is likely to run a substantial deficit for at least several more years. This means higher unemployment, with the resulting implications for distribution, and also reduced employment in manufacturing since this sector still accounts for the bulk of international trade.

To sum up, we have seen substantially higher unemployment in the last three decades than in the prior three decades. The higher rates of unemployment during recent decades have been the result of conscious policy decisions to focus on other priorities. The result has been a substantial upward redistribution of income.

Unions

The importance of unions in the economy has shrunk rapidly over the last three decades. In the 1970s, close to 20 percent of private sector workers were represented by unions. In recent years, the share has fallen below 7.0 percent. While most countries have seen a decline in unionization rates during this period, no country has seen as sharp a decline as in the United States. For example, Canada still has an overall unionization rate of more than 30 percent. Given the similarities in the language and culture of the United States and Canada, it is not plausible that a wave of anti-union sentiment came over the United States while barely affecting Canada. It is also striking that there has been little decline in the percentage of public sector workers who are in unions, which still stands close to 35 percent.

These facts suggest that a drop in unionization rates was not due to a change in workers' attitude toward unions but rather the fact that it has become much more difficult for workers to organize and sustain unions over the last three decades. This can be explained both by direct changes in government policy and also a failure of the government to respond to changes in practices by private employers that have the purpose of making it more difficult for workers to organize.

The most obvious policy change was the weakening of the protections provided to workers by the National Labor Relations Board (NLRB). At a time when employers were increasingly defying the law, for example by firing workers involved in organizing drives, President Reagan cut funding for the NLRB and allowed staff positions to go unfilled, creating an enormous backlog and long delays.

The delays directly benefited employers. The sanction for wrongly firing a worker for organizing is reinstatement at the job and compensation for lost wages, measured as the difference between the wages a worker would have received at the job from which they were fired, compared to the wages they received at a new job. Since most workers can't survive without a paycheck, after being fired they would generally try to get a new job quickly. This would mean that the lost wages would be a trivial penalty from the standpoint of employers since the difference in wages between the worker's former job and their new job may be very little. The only real sanction to the employer would be if the worker got back their job quickly and could resume the organizing drive.

With a weakening NLRB this was not likely to happen. Instead workers would see that the union was unable to protect a union activist and likely to conclude that unionization was a risky and probably hopeless strategy. It has now become standard practice among employers resisting unions to fire those it identifies as leading the effort.

The other major change in this period in labor management relations was the practice of hiring replacement workers to take the jobs of workers who went on strike. This hugely weakened the value of strikes as a weapon for unions, since it now meant that workers' jobs were put at risk. While it had always been legal to hire workers to replace strikers, in prior decades it was very rarely done. The conventional practice was that companies shut down or operated with a skeletal staff of management personnel until a contract was negotiated with the union.

This changed in the summer of 1981, when the air traffic controllers went out on strike. Since government employers are generally prohibited from striking, the strike was likely illegal. However, past strikes by public sector workers had reached negotiated settlements, even if their legality was questionable. Reagan opted to make an example of the air traffic controllers, ordering them back to work. When they refused to comply, he had the leadership of the union arrested and replaced them with military air traffic controllers.

Major corporations were quick to follow the example. In the next few years a major airline, bus company, meat-packing company, and tire manufacturer all hired replacement workers and fired striking workers. Workers now understood that striking could mean losing a job, which made them far more hesitant to go on strike. This gave management yet more bargaining power in their dealings with unions.

The weakening of unions hits workers directly with fewer workers able to get the benefit of unions in their pay negotiations. The reduction in union membership and the weakening of the union bargaining power also indirectly hurt other workers. Non-unionized workers in an industry tend to have wages that follow the path of union workers. This means that when the pay of union workers is reduced, pay throughout the industry is reduced.

It is worth noting how the law on unions has always had a fundamental asymmetry. Most recourse for management violations of the law require workers to go through the NLRB. Because the power of the

NLRB is limited, potential sanctions are generally minor and often long-delayed. However, when workers violate the law, it is typically possible to get redress through the court system. For example, when the air traffic controllers went out on strike, President Reagan did not go to the NLRB; he went directly to federal court. Union officers were told to order their members back to work. When they refused to do so, they were put in jail for contempt of court and the union's assets were seized.

If management violations were treated with the same seriousness, it is unlikely that there would be so many violations of labor law. Few corporate managers would spend weeks or months in jail rather than hire back union organizers. Similarly, if major fines were imposed on companies that violated labor laws, most corporations would show them greater respect.

Patent Protection and Upward Redistribution

In the last three decades, the government has taken a number of steps to make patent and copyright protection stronger and longer. This has been done both domestically and internationally through trade agreements. While patent policy does not often get mentioned in the context of discussions of inequality, this is a major oversight. It likely has been an important factor in this process.

Taking the case of prescription drugs, which is probably the most important example, the country spent more than $380 billion in 2013 (@ 2.3 percent of GDP) on pharmaceutical products. If drugs were sold in a free market with patent and related protections, it is likely that the cost would have been close to one-tenth of this amount.[11] The high patent-protected price of drugs creates many absurd moral problems. For example, it is debated whether the government or private insurers should have to pay for cancer drugs that can cost over $100,000 a year for people who are already elderly or in poor health.

While that may seem a tough question, when we remember that the research for the drug has already been done, the real question is whether it is worth paying the price of manufacturing an additional person's dosage. That cost will almost never be more than $1,000 and often less than $100. This makes the answer very simple.

In addition to raising the price of drugs, the enormous rents created by patent monopolies provide drug companies with incentive to mislead the public about the safety and effectiveness of their drugs, something they do with great regularity. This method of financing drugs also distorts research since drug companies will have little incentive to pursue evidence suggesting that the best way to treat a condition is by diet, exercise, or a long off-patent drug.

In the absence of patent supported research it would be necessary to use alternative mechanisms for financing the research and development of new drugs (like expanding the sort of public funding that goes through the National Institutes of Health), but these alternatives would almost certainly mean far less money spent on drugs. That would mean less money out of workers' wages and less money going to top executives and shareholders at the drug companies. The net effect of moving away from patent support for prescription drugs would mean a boost to the wages of workers at the expense of those at the top end of the income distribution.

Patent protection likely leads to waste and excessively high prices in other sectors as well. This seems most apparent in the tech sector, where Samsung and Apple compete as much in the courts as in the marketplace. It has become a standard practice to use patent suits to block competitors. This raises the price of products and makes successful patent lawyers wealthy, but it does not benefit the economy. While patents have played a valuable role in the economy in the past and may still do so going forward, patent protection is almost certainly an impediment to economic growth in its current practice. Since patent protection unambiguously redistributes income upward (no low-income people benefit from getting patent rents), its expansion in the last three decades can be viewed as a policy that has slowed growth while furthering the upward redistribution of income.

The Growth of the Financial Sector

The financial sector has expanded rapidly relative to the rest of the economy over the last three decades. The narrowly defined financial sector, investment banking and security and commodity trading, has more than quintupled relative to the size of the economy since the 1970s. The growth in the financial sector has largely been at the expense of the rest of the economy since it would be difficult to argue that the financial sector does its core function of allocating capital and facilitating savings better today than it did in the 1970s. The growth has been fostered by one-sided deregulation. While the restraints in areas like bank size, interstate banking, or the cross-over between investment banking and commercial banking were removed, the government supported the industry by providing implicit "too big to fail" insurance. This means that the largest banks are allowed to borrow at below market interest rates because investors assume that their loans will be backed by the government if the bank were to fail. This implicit guarantee became explicit during the financial crisis when the government openly intervened to support several large banks that surely would have gone bankrupt if the unfettered market was allowed to do its work

The International Monetary Fund recently estimated the size of this implicit subsidy at $50 billion a year.[12] In addition, the financial industry also benefits as a result of being largely exempted from taxes imposed on other industries, most obviously the sales tax. To redress this imbalance, the I.M.F. recently proposed imposing a "financial activities tax," which would be comparable to a value-added tax, on the financial sector that would be intended to raise approximately 0.2 percent of GDP (@ $34 billion a year).

The subsidies and low tax treatment support the profits of firms in the sector and the pay of top executives. The finance sector includes many of the highest-paid individuals in the country, so this has been a major contributor to inequality.

There are two other ways in which the government has promoted inequality through its special treatment of the financial sector. The carried interest tax deduction has allowed hedge fund and private equity fund managers to have most of their earnings taxed as capital gains. These are people who would have been paying tax at the 35 percent top marginal rate (39.6 percent now), who had most of their income taxed at just a 15 percent rate (20 percent now). This is an enormous tax savings to people earning tens or even hundreds of millions of dollars a year.

The other way the tax code has enriched people in the financial sector has been by creating an industry for tax avoidance. This is largely what explains the growth of the private equity (PE) industry. While PE companies do occasionally turn around small and mid-size companies that need an infusion of capital and new management, they more typically profit by bringing sophisticated tax avoidance schemes to companies that had been focused on productive activity. There is a long list of strategies used by PE companies but the simplest and most important is the exploitation of the interest deduction. They routinely leverage the companies they buy to the greatest extent possible. In this way they can usually recover most of the capital they invested and transfer the risk to the creditors and other stakeholders in the firm.[13]

A simpler, cleaner tax code would quickly eliminate most of the opportunities for gaming exploited by the PE industry. Simply limiting the amount of leverage that is tax deductible would go a long way here.

Conclusion

There is no dispute that there has been a substantial upward redistribution of income in the years since 1980. As a result the vast majority of the gains from economic growth over this period have gone to the richest 10 percent of the population, with the richest 1 percent getting an even more disproportionate share of the gains. Contrary to what is often claimed, this upward redistribution was not the result of the natural working of the market but rather a series of conscious policy choices.

This point is crucial because changes in distribution that were brought about by policy decisions can be reversed by policy decisions. This is not a question of having the government interfere with the market; it is a question of having government policies that structure the market in ways that cause it to provide benefits to the bulk of the population rather than just a small minority. An alternative set of policies can lead to both more efficient outcomes and greater equality.

Notes

1. Thomas Piketty and Emmanual Saez, "Income Inequality in the United States, 1913–1998," updated through 2012 (University of California, Berkeley, 2013). https://eml.berkeley.edu/~saez/pikettyqje.pdf.

2. "Usable productivity growth" was 3.1 percent annually from 1947 to 1973. Since 1980 it has averaged just 1.3 percent. Even in the years since the 1995 speedup it has averaged just 1.8 percent. "Usable productivity" is an adjustment that I developed to measure the extent to which productivity growth can translate into wage growth. It accounts for the difference between the GDP deflator and the CPI and gross and net output growth (see Dean Baker, *The Productivity to Paycheck Gap: What the Data Show* [Washington, DC: Center for Economic and Policy Research, 2007] http://cepr.net/documents/publications/growth_failure_2007_04.pdf).

3. The argument that the nature of technology has changed to the benefit of highly educated workers, or led to a hollowing out of the middle, has been shown to be wrong. In fact, since 2000 the most rapid employment growth has been in low-paid occupations with occupations at both the middle and top of the wage distribution seeing declining employment shares. This issue is examined in Larry Mishel, John Schmitt, and Heidi Sheirholz, *Don't Blame the Robots: Assessing the Job Polarization Explanation for Wage Inequality* (Washington, DC: Economic Policy Institute, 2013).

4. It would be a simple matter to impose a modest tax on the earnings of foreign-born professionals working in the United States, which would be repatriated to the home country. This money could be used to train two or three professionals for everyone that emigrated, ensuring that developing countries benefited as well from this trade.

5. See Larry Mishel, Josh Bivens, Elise Gould, and Heidi Sheirholtz, *State of Working America, 2012–2013* (Washington, DC: Economic Policy Institute, 2012) for detailed data on wage growth at various points along the distribution.

6. Dean Baker and Jared Bernstein, *Getting Back to Full Employment: A Better Bargain for Working People* (Washington, DC: Center for Economic and Policy Research, 2013), figure 2-5.

7. These results are based on analysis with the Current Population Survey. We controlled for age, gender, education, and time trends.

8. There have been economists that dispute this claim, but there have been a number of studies in recent years that solidly establish this result. See Olivier Blanchard and Daniel Leigh, "Growth Forecast Errors and Fiscal Multipliers." IMF Working Paper No. 13/1, International Monetary Fund, 2013; Bradford DeLong and Larry Summers, "Fiscal Policy in a Depressed Economy," *Brookings Papers on Economic Activity* (Spring 2012): 233–97; and Jaime Guajardo, Daniel Leigh, and Andrea Pescatori, 2011, "Expansionary Austerity: New International Evidence," IMF Working Paper No. 11/158. International Monetary Fund.

9. This can be found in Baker and Bernstein, *Getting Back to Full Employment*, figure 2-2. The calculation simply adds the differences quarter by

quarter between the actual unemployment and the NAIRU as estimated by the CBO.

10. Dean Baker and Karl Walentin, "Money for Nothing: The Increasing Cost of Foreign Reserve Holdings to Developing Countries" (Washington, DC: Center for Economic and Policy Research, 2001).

11. This figure comes from Bureau of Economic Analysis, National Income and Product Accounts, Table 2.4.5U, Line 119.

12. International Monetary Fund, 2014.

13. See Eileen Appelbaum and Rose Batt, *Private Equity at Work: When Wall Street Manages Main Street* (New York: Russell Sage Foundation, 2014) for a fuller discussion of the extent to which PE firms rely on gaming the tax code for their profits.

Part Six

PRISON

10. Engaging the U.S. Bishops' Pastoral on Crime and Criminal Justice

From Atomism to Community Justice

Robert DeFina and Lance Hannon

This chapter first appeared in *Journal of Catholic Social Thought* 8 (2011): 77–91.

Introduction

The U.S. Catholic Bishops' November 2000 Pastoral titled *Responsibility, Rehabilitation, and Restoration: A Catholic Perspective on Crime and Criminal Justice* offers a perspective on the ways in which Catholics and other people of good will should think about the criminal justice system. The document is remarkable in many ways, not the least of which is its prophetic stance against what has elsewhere been termed "mass incarceration."

Since the early 1970s, the prison population in the United States has grown tremendously. There are currently 753 per 100,000 people in the U.S. in prison or in jail. Indeed, the U.S. now incarcerates a higher percentage of its residents than any other country in the world. The mass incarceration has been especially devastating to people of color. According to noted sociologist Bruce Western, about 60 percent of African American men aged thirty to thirty-four who have not graduated high school have been in prison. The implications for imprisoned individuals, their families, and communities can be devastating.

For the Bishops, the Church's scriptural, theological, and sacramental heritage, both in themselves and as distilled in the principles of Catholic social thought (CST), would understand our current approach as disordered. The clear emphasis on punishment, the harsh and dehumanizing conditions of prisons, and the lack of help to prisoners attempting re-entry into society violate the principles of human dignity, of solidarity, and the common good. In stark opposition, the Bishops call for a new direction, one that privileges restorative justice and re-integration.

While certainly prophetic, the Bishops' letter is just a starting point for thinking about the criminal justice system. This is not a criticism but rather an observation on the purpose of CST documents. They are meant to be general frameworks and guidance, not complete reference materials. Moreover, they are intended as part of a living tradition in which new knowledge is incorporated and applied, bringing faith into contact with reason, in ways that ensure the tradition is constantly relevant to current and ongoing challenges.

With this in mind, this study seeks to directly engage the Bishops' Pastoral on crime and criminal justice. As we will detail below, we intend to focus on policy recommendations in the letter with the purpose of both deepening their arguments and broadening their vision so as to allow new avenues for scrutiny of justice in light of faith. Specifically, we bring into the discussion a variety of studies that emphasize the community-level effects of mass incarceration, as opposed to focusing attention primarily on the individual prisoner. In this way, we want to directly and positively contribute to CST by bringing the most recent theoretical and empirical social science to bear on the issues and to strengthen the foundation on which the Bishops' letter is based.

The Bishops on Incarceration

The Bishops' Pastoral is wide ranging and touches on many important subjects related to crime and criminal justice. These include a major section on *Policy Foundations and Directions*, with several paragraphs concentrating on the impact of prisons on individuals (1, 2, and 7) and placing crime in a community context (3 and 11). It is on these *Policy* discussions that we will focus our attention and efforts, analyzing the Bishops' understanding of the effects of prisons on those imprisoned and collateral effects of communities. We begin by briefly recounting the aspects of the Pastoral that are most relevant for the present study. We then explore ways in which these ideas can be broadened and deepened based on current social science research to allow a more forceful prophetic statement about prisons and punishment.

Prison and the Individual Inmate

The Pastoral is particularly concerned about how the experience of prison affects the individual prisoner and the ultimate ability of a former prisoner to successfully re-integrate into society once his or her time is served. In paragraph 1 of the *Policy* sections, for example, the Bishops emphasize that punishment must have a purpose, and not be carried out for its own sake. Certainly protecting the community is one such legitimate objective. Deterrence, to the degree it actually occurs, would also seem a reasonable goal. The Bishops do note, though, that regardless of the end served, any punishment should be coupled with treatment and restitution whenever possible.

Paragraph 2 notes that the causes of crime are complex, implying that crime-fighting strategies must also be adequately nuanced. Policies such as "three strikes and you're out" and mandatory sentencing are to be avoided. Instead, there should be sufficient discretion to tailor sentences and punishment to better accomplish what ought to be the desired result of punishment—rehabilitation, re-integration, and restoration of justice to the community and individual dignity. The Bishops state with great clarity that children must never be treated as fully formed adults. Simply stated, they are not and so cannot be held to the same standards of knowledge and maturity when assessing culpability, nor are they able to withstand the same degree and type of punishment as adults can.

Finally, in paragraph 7, the Bishops elaborate on the ideas in paragraph 2, noting that prisons must be about more than just punishment. Prisons must be structured so as to help inmates prepare for life after incarceration. Education, rehabilitation, and substance abuse treatment programs should all be part of the prison experience. Similarly, prisons should be easily accessible by family, friends, and religious communities who can each support the authentic development and growth of prisoners. And importantly, prisoners should retain their ability to vote once their sentences have been served.

Prison and the Community

In paragraph 3, the Bishops rightly comment that crime has many structural causes. These include poverty, discrimination, and substandard schools that ill prepare youth for full participation in legitimate activities. Any useful interventions aimed at reducing crime must include actions to mitigate these factors, and cannot rely solely on deterrence and incapacitation strategies, such as policing and incarceration. Along these lines, paragraph 11 argues that communities need to organize themselves better to actively combat crime and its social antecedents. Outreach efforts targeted toward at-risk youth, gang interventions, community policing, and neighborhood watch programs can all aid in preventing crime and creating an environment in which crime is less likely in the first place.

Moving Beyond an "Atomistic View"

Clearly, the Bishops policy suggestions have merit and coincide with a more progressive perspective on crime, punishment, and prevention. It would, we believe, be hard to argue against their prescriptions or the moral basis that underpins them. If anything, as we will explain, the critiques and prescriptions in the Pastoral are too limited. New thinking and evidence in the sociological and criminological literature has raised several additional concerns about the causes and consequences of imprisonment. In sum, incarceration appears to be a much more formidable barrier to authentic human development than previously thought. This section of the paper outlines some of the more important ideas and connects them to the Bishops' concerns as expressed in the Pastoral. We then suggest ways in which the basic principles of CST can be brought to bear on the findings to provide a more effective critique of current practices.

In general, the Bishops analyze the effects of prisons using what Todd Clear[1] (1996) has called an "atomistic view." That is, they focus on the individual prisoner and the impact that both prison and community actions have on the likelihood of the prisoner's successful re-integration and rehabilitation. Recent research indicates that this perspective is limited in at least two important ways. First, as Clear[2] notes, atomistic reasoning fails to account for broader social effects of large-scale imprisonment on the families and neighbors of the people imprisoned. Incarcerating vast numbers of people from a restricted number of communities can create adverse social dynamics within the affected neighborhoods that can actually foster more crime. Second, imprisonment itself can increase the likelihood that ex-convicts will commit crimes once released. Thus, imprisonment can "backfire" and worsen the problem it was meant to contain.

The notion that concentrated mass incarceration can backfire reasonably applies to more than just the prevalence of crime.[3] Indeed, as Roberts[4] notes, mass imprisonment of a community's population "damages social networks, distorts social norms and destroys social citizenship." All of these consequences can interfere with the healthy functioning of communities in myriad ways by diminishing members' economic, social, and political standing. In essence, then, the damage to authentic development of individuals goes far beyond whatever impacts an individual prisoner might experience. The well-being of whole communities is at risk due to our current set of incarceration policies. It is here that CST can expand its inquiry and offer a vision of a better system.

The Community Effects of Mass Incarceration

At the conceptual level, mass incarceration can adversely affect communities in at least six broad ways: engendering losses of family purchasing power; shifting community norms concerning mainstream activities such as work, saving, and participation in legitimate activities; reducing the political power of imprisoned communities; diminishing the health of community residents; decreasing the likelihood of marriage; and community multiplier effects. In part these effects operate directly through the individuals who have been imprisoned, and in part they occur via the collateral effects on the families and communities from which the prisoners are removed and to which they return. Each effect can diminish the common good—the sum total of all resources that individuals need to authentically develop. Concerning the impacts of mass incarceration, this includes income, taxes, the amount and quality of public goods, such as schooling, housing and health care, and political power.

Perhaps most obviously, incarceration removes earnings from the prisoners' families.[5] Research reveals that most of those incarcerated were breadwinners at the time of their arrest, contributing significantly to their families' legitimate income.[6] This reduction in family resources immediately raises the probability that family members will suffer financial hardships and their sequellae. Likewise, incarceration may severely limit the earnings of individuals even after their time is served, via erosion of skills, the evaporation of social networks, the acquisition of destructive attitudes and behaviors, and the stigma associated with incarceration. Thus, mass incarceration can create an intensely disadvantaged segment of low-wage workers. Impacts include lower wages, reduced future wage growth, and worse employment prospects.[7]

The potential loss of family income is not limited to the foregone earnings of the prisoner, however. The loss of one parent also limits the earning potential of the remaining parent. The need to care for the children can significantly decrease the time and flexibility needed to obtain and successfully hold a job. Moreover, time will be spent visiting the prison, both for the sake of the spouse and the children.[8] Research has shown, moreover, that children with a parent in prison suffer physical, emotional, and psychological difficulties, such as anxiety, shame, and depression.[9] Attending to these additional needs of the children further impedes labor force participation.

In a related vein, but at the community level, mass incarceration can disrupt valuable social networks that are needed to obtain employment.[10] The loss of an adult family member, especially one with some employment experience, reduces the number of information-rich "weak ties," and increasingly narrows the network to "strong ties" that have largely redundant information.[11] And as emphasized by Sampson and Raudenbusch,[12] entire communities subject to mass incarceration can become stigmatized, further decreasing the likelihood of their members being employed.

Roberts,[13] Rose and Clear,[14] Lynch and Sabol,[15] and Bursik and Gramsick[16] have suggested that excessive incarceration disrupts a neighborhood's informal mechanisms of social control and social support, and can erode social norms. Reduced collective efficacy and shifting norms, in turn, can significantly reduce income. The removal of substantial numbers of formerly employed adults from neighborhoods can, for example, eliminate important role models that help illuminate and reinforce the expectations of work, school, and participation in legitimate activities. It can also help rationalize and normalize the use of welfare.

Fragmentation of families and friendships undermines the extent of positive pressures that can be put on community members to conform. In addition, a growing perception that the criminal justice system is unfairly concentrating on low-income and minority communities, and imprisoning family members and friends, can contribute to an oppositional culture in which mainstream activities and institutions such as legitimate work are devalued. At a minimum, the significant loss of adults and the resulting increase in social disorganization can obfuscate community norms and decrease the chances of mainstream behaviors. These detrimental effects of mass incarceration on a community's collective efficacy may ultimately lead to a type of "durable inequality" where residents cannot escape what might otherwise be only episodic poverty.[17]

Mass incarceration can also damage the common good by diminishing the political power of the community. Mass incarceration, for example, reduces the sheer numbers of people in communities, and hence the extent of the constituent neighborhoods' representation, because those in prison generally are disenfranchised. Furthermore, some states disallow voting while on probation and parole while others permanently disenfranchise ex-convicts.[18] Uggen and Manza[19] demonstrate the practical importance disenfranchisement can have for communities. And due to the peculiarities of Census counting procedures, prisoners are recorded as residing in the jurisdiction containing the prison.[20] Thus, not only does political power in lower-income and minority communities fall directly, the power is transferred via increases in population to generally rural and whiter communities. This transfer of power, together with the stigma that whiter communities can attach to "incarcerated communities," means less empathy and concern in the realm of budgeting, law making, and enforcement of rules and regulations. The result of the decreased political power can be less support for social safety net programs, job retraining programs, health care and childcare facilities, and ultimately, the common good.

Several researchers[21] have pointed to another important mechanism through which mass incarceration can disrupt communities: its impact on marriage. That is, it can reduce the probability of marriage before and after childbirth by dramatically reducing the number of marriageable males. Additionally, the prison experience itself can make men less suitable for marriage. As mentioned earlier, single parents face a considerable number of obstacles to employment. Thus, decreased marriage rates and increased single parenthood can be important factors undermining community and authentic development.

Mass incarceration has also been associated with growing and serious community health problems. The transmission of AIDS in poor communities has, for example, been linked to mass imprisonment.[22] The problems arise due to sexual violence that occurs in prison and the transmission of the disease once infected prisoners are released. The greater prevalence of the disease in "incarcerated communities" together with the diminished capacity of those communities to handle it implies a particularly severe vulnerability driven by mass incarceration.

Finally, mass incarceration can harm the economic prospects of communities as the effects of lost income are magnified and multiplied. The decreased spending caused by lost income will result in fewer businesses that are able to remain solvent. As businesses weaken or go under, more job and wage losses occur and poverty worsens. Similarly, crucial non-business institutions that support the community such as libraries, counseling centers, and places of worship can be diminished as well. Because these institutions provide goods and services that promote the common good, their loss can inflate and broaden the other problems related to mass incarceration.

There are, in sum, many reasons to expect that mass incarceration has disrupted communities and social solidarity. Alternatively, there are at least two ways that mass incarceration could help, at least theoretically. It should be noted from the onset that empirical support for these possibilities is weak. One is that mass incarceration has led to significantly less crime. Standard neo-classical economic reasoning argued that greater incarceration increases the cost of criminal activity to the criminal and, hence, would produce fewer crimes. Others noted that crime should also fall simply because incarceration prevents criminals from committing crimes they otherwise would have perpetrated had they not been incapacitated. Nonetheless, empirical support for these ideas has been equivocal, and increasingly shows the lack of any effect. For a range of views, see Devine, Sheley, and Smith; Marvell and Moody;

Levitt; Currie; Lynch; Arvanites and DeFina; DeFina and Arvanites; Kovandzic and Vieraitis; and Vieraitis, Kovandzic, and Marvell.[23]

The second possibility has been termed "addition by subtraction."[24] In this scenario, the removal of criminals from the community has a beneficial effect.[25] Bad role models and disruptive influences are eliminated and positive community norms are emphasized. Although this idea has intuitive appeal, its logic is questionable in the context of mass incarceration. That is, the removal of a few "bad apples" might well have positive implications for the community as the social and economic dynamics created by large-scale imprisonment are not initiated. But once the scale of incarceration rises to the extent it has, the negative dynamics are likely to swamp whatever positive effects from imprisonment otherwise might be available.

Indeed, empirical evidence is accumulating that indicates the community-wide impacts are sizable. DeFina and Hannon[26] find, for example, that the mass incarceration of the last few decades has meant millions more people living in poverty than otherwise would have experienced. These impacts were found both for the official poverty measure and alternative measures that define poverty using both the depth of poverty and the distribution of income among the poor, as well as the number of people officially defined as poor. In a related follow-up study, DeFina and Hannon[27] likewise found that the mass incarceration of adults significantly increased child poverty in North Carolina counties.

Other studies have presented evidence on the criminogenic effects of prison. These potentially arise both because of the adverse effects on communities to which prisoners return, as well as the environment that prisoners are exposed to while incarcerated. This includes violence, lack of opportunity to maintain or enhance skills, exposure to an emergent criminal network, and isolation from networks of legitimate opportunity. L. M. Vieraitis, T. Kovandzic, and T. Marvell[28] studied the effects of imprisonment on crime at the state level and found that imprisonment actually increases the incidence of various types of crime. DeFina and Hannon[29] extend their results to show that any crime-reducing incapacitation effect of imprisonment is limited to the present; it lasts only as long as offenders are behind bars. The crime-promoting consequences of mass imprisonment, on the other hand, rapidly accumulate over time, and can extend many years into the future. For example, those released from prison five years ago can still be affected by the criminogenic label of an incarceration record today.

Catholic Social Thought and the Community Effects of Mass Incarceration

Overall, the community level effects of mass incarceration are both pernicious and widespread. How might CST address the situation? The most basic concern centers on the damage to the common good. As mentioned, mass incarceration diminishes the amounts of resources—material (schools, jobs, health), symbolic (social prestige and status), and emotional (love, family life)—available both to prisoners and to the entire communities from which they are drawn. Such profound losses constitute perhaps insuperable barriers to authentic development. Thus, CST can offer a powerful rebuke and critique of the current system.

Mass incarceration also opposes the social nature of the person. The fracturing of families and of the broader community directly contravenes a basic foundation of the person's social development. This is in addition to the lengthy removal of the prisoner from the community for crimes that are better dealt with in alternative ways, such as drug rehabilitation and youth counseling.

Mass incarceration further inhibits the full participation of individuals in society and limits their contribution to the common good. As mentioned, the community disruption, loss of jobs and public goods means that important avenues by which individuals and communities can contribute are closed off. This limitation is exacerbated by the stigma suffered by prisoners, their families, and the entire communities in which they live.

There is a deeper, perhaps more subtle way by which mass incarceration impedes participation. It concerns its underlying basis. On the surface, mass incarceration appears to be a normal response to the problem of crime. That is, the amount of imprisonment is simply a passive response to the amount of criminal activity in society. As pointed out by many researchers,[30] however, the main drivers of mass incarceration have been changes in the laws and in probation and parole policy. A particularly important driver was the War on Drugs. Variations in the crime rate, by contrast, played a considerably more minor role. Indeed, while incarceration has risen steadily throughout the last thirty years, the amount of crime has both risen and fallen; the overall crime rate is currently about where it was thirty years ago, while the incarceration rate has more than tripled.

In the minds of some leading experts, the change in policies that have caused the rise in imprisonment were undertaken in the wake of the civil rights movement. They thus represent a means of social control that replaced now-outlawed forms of control—blatant job discrimination, Jim Crow laws, housing segregation, and so on. Imprisonment, in other words, is a strategy to isolate members of a devalued social group, so as to limit their access to valued resources.

To the extent that this explanation of mass incarceration is accurate, then it directly violates several principles of CST, including the dignity of the person, the social nature of the person, participation, solidarity, and the universal destination of goods. Through the lens of CST, mass incarceration should be considered more than something that is ineffective and to be improved through things like skill development programs. It should be denounced as a thoroughly sinful, repugnant, and disordered structure worthy of wholesale replacement. In fact, section 3 of the Policy section in the Pastoral could be expanded to include prisons themselves as one of the disordered structures that leads to crime and devaluation of the person, along with discrimination, poverty, and poor schooling.

Promoting Community Justice

The current emphasis of CST on the re-integration of prisoners and their restitution to the community is a legitimate goal, one consistent with the basic principles. But as we have seen, it leaves much of the problem with mass incarceration untouched. In the future, we believe that CST should broaden its focus to include community justice.

By community justice we mean the consideration of the community as an organic whole whose treatment should be subject to the demands of justice. A response to this statement might be that CST already does this, insofar as it applies to all members that comprise a community. The point here, however, is somewhat different. We are arguing that communities are *sui generis* entities to which the principles of CST are to be applied. Understanding communities this way is common for sociological analysis, but not perhaps for economic analysis and the kind of atomistic framework used in the CST social documents.

This perspective, consistent with the CST principles of the social nature of the person, solidarity, and the common good, opens an array of new questions, issues, and "signs of the times" that CST can scrutinize. Certainly, in the case of mass incarceration, one can reasonably argue that it is entire communities that integrally have been damaged—their collective organization and efficacy, their collective identities, their collective social, cultural, and physical capital. It has not simply been the case that the total damage equals the sum of individual harms.

We believe that using a concept of community justice leads to a devastating critique of the current system of justice in the U.S. That critique is much more profound than the one offered by the Bishops' Pastoral. While the atomistic vision engendered by the Pastoral suggests reformist policies to improve a generally sound system, the community justice perspective reveals a system in need of fundamental change. That is, the rehabilitation, re-integration, and restoration called for by the Bishops require as a pre-condition a healthy well-functioning community to offer support to the ex-prisoner and the families and neighbors of the imprisoned. The good news is that once a perspective of community justice is used, the principles of CST offer clear guidance on how to reconstruct the system so that it functions in a moral and ethical way.

Specifically, and consistent with the principle of the common good, policies should be enacted that strengthen the collective efficacy of communities so that their ability to exercise social control and offer social support are enhanced. Foremost among these is the access to decent and legitimate employment opportunities and those things that directly support work such as quality child care and available and reasonably priced transportation alternatives. This perspective underscores another way in which the Pastoral is atomistic; it addresses crime as a problem separate and distinct from the larger social system in which it is embedded. Thus, ideas aimed at improving the justice system must include improvements in the larger social environment that give rise to crime in the first place.

Concentrating on the community as a whole opens new possibilities for greater community justice than more limited concerns with the justice system per se. For example, efforts can include government support of community gardens, recreation centers, parks, and public murals in low-income neighborhoods. Community self-efficacy can also be underpinned by changes in states' laws concerning the ability of ex-felons and those on probation and parole to fully participate in civic life, including the right to vote. We note that the Bishops identified an individual's right to vote as an important aspect of welcoming ex-felons back to the community. However, we are emphasizing here the importance of the vote for political power and community building. In the context of mass incarceration, the aggregate effects of disenfranchisement go far beyond the effects on the individual ex-felon.

According to a study done by the Sentencing Project and Human Rights Watch, 3.9 million Americans (about 1 in 50 adults), had either currently or permanently lost their right to vote in 1998. There was, in addition, a clear racial imbalance in this loss—in several states, close to one in four black men of voting age were permanently disenfranchised due to incarceration.[31] Overall about one in seven black men had either currently or permanently lost the right to vote. Such a loss of political power makes communities much less able to effectively organize themselves and promote the authentic development of their members.

In a similar vein, ex-felons are barred from a large selection of occupations, which runs against the CST principle of participation and limits their ability to contribute to the common good. In New York, for example, ex-felons are excluded from being emergency medical technicians, and in Florida they are barred from being speech-language pathologists and cosmetologists (Samuels and Mukamal 2004).[32] In thirty-seven states, employers can consider arrests without conviction when making hiring decisions. Fifteen states have laws that impose an outright ban on anyone with a criminal record from becoming an adoptive or foster parent. All these restrictions should be scrutinized and those not demonstrably necessary to ensure community safety should be lessened from their current lifetime status to a shorter horizon, if not removed outright.

Along the same lines, ex-felons' access to the social safety net is curtailed. Several states, such as Texas and Missouri, disallow ex-felons the use of food stamps, public housing, and TANF. As with other components of the common good, these and other social programs should be made available to all, including those who have served their time.

The principles of CST have proven to be a useful framework for reflection and guidance for numerous social problems. The arena of criminal justice is no exception. The Bishops' Pastoral has served as a powerful reminder that justice involves more than just punishment, but also the hard work of supporting the common good. In part, as the Bishops point out, this entails help for and focus on the individual ex-felon and his or her re-integration into the community. Yet, as we have stressed, there must simultaneously be a strong and vibrant community available to reintegrate with. As CST highlights in its principle concerning the social nature of the person, ex-felons as others can only develop authentically with the help of others.

We have tried here to broaden the view presented in the Bishops' Pastoral to recognize that incarceration not only can harm the individual but also the community at large, especially when undertaken on the scale seen during the past few decades in the U.S. Thus, reconstructing the criminal justice system in ways consistent with the principles of CST means undoing the harm it has done to communities as well as to individuals. In this manner, both the common good and the authentic development of the individual will be respected.

Notes

1. T. Clear, "Backfire: When Incarceration Increases Crime," *Journal of the Oklahoma Criminal Justice Research Consortium* 3 (1996): 1–10.

2. Clear, "Backfire"; T. Clear, *Imprisoning Communities: How Mass Incarceration Makes Disadvantaged Neighborhoods Worse* (New York: Oxford University Press, 2007).

3. T. Clear, "The Social Consequences of Mass Incarceration," *Social Research* 74 (2007): 2–18.

4. D. Roberts, "The Social and Moral Cost of Mass Incarceration in African American Communities," *Stanford Law Review* 56 (2004): 1281.

5. P. E. Oliver, G. Sandefur, J. Jakubowski, and J. E. Yocom, "The Effect of Black Male Imprisonment on Black Child Poverty." Working Paper, 2004; B. Western and K. Beckett, "How Unregulated Is the U.S. Labor Market? The

Penal System as a Labor Market Institution," *American Journal of Sociology* 104 (1999): 1030–60.

6. C. J. Mumola, "Bureau of Justice Statistics Special Report: Incarcerated Parents and their Children," U.S. Department of Justice, Washington, DC, 2000.

7. Western and Beckett, "How Unregulated Is the U.S. Labor Market?"; B. Western, J. R. Kling, and D. F. Weiman, "The Labor Market Consequences of Incarceration," *Crime and Delinquency* 47 (2001): 410–27; D. Pager, "The Mark of a Criminal Record," *American Journal of Sociology* 108 (2003): 937–75; and B. Western, *Punishment and Inequality in America* (New York: Russell Sage Foundation, 2006).

8. D. Braman, "Families and Incarceration," in *Invisible Punishment: The Collateral Consequences of Mass Imprisonment*, ed. Marc Mauer and Meda Chelsey-Lind (New York: The New Press, 2002), 117ff.

9. D. Johnson, "Effects of Parental Incarceration," in *Children of Incarcerated Parents*, ed. Katherine Gabel and Denise Johnson (New York: Lexington Books, 1995), 59–88.

10. Braman, "Families and Incarceration"; T. Clear, D. Rose, and J. Ryder, "Incarceration and the Community: The Problem of Removing and Returning Offenders," *Crime and Delinquency* 47 (2001): 335–51; D. R. Rose and T. Clear, "Incarceration, Social Capital and Crime: Implications for Social Disorganization Theory," *Criminology* 36 (1998): 441–78.

11. M. S. Granovetter, "The Strength of Weak Ties," *American Journal of Sociology* 78 (1973): 1360–80; R. S. Burt, "The Contingent Value of Social Capital," *Administrative Science Quarterly* 42 (1997): 339–65; N. Lin, "Social Networks and Status Attainment," *Annual Review of Sociology* 25 (1999): 467–87.

12. R. J. Sampson and S. W. Raudenbusch, "Seeing Disorder: Neighborhood Stigma and the Social Construction of 'Broken Windows,'" *Social Psychology Quarterly* 67 (2004): 319–42.

13. Roberts, "Social and Moral Cost of Mass Incarceration."

14. D. Rose and T. Clear, "Incarceration, Reentry and Social Capital: Social Networks in the Balance," in *Prisoners Once Removed: The Impact of Incarceration and Reentry on Children, Families and Communities*, ed. Jeremy Travis and Michelle Waul (Washington, DC: Urban Institute Press, 2004), 314–42; D. Rose and T. Clear, "Who Doesn't Know Someone in Prison or Jail: The Impact of Exposure to Prison on Attitudes toward Formal and Informal Social Control," *The Prison Journal* 82 (2004): 208–27.

15. J. P. Lynch and W. J. Sabol, "Assessing the Effects of Mass Incarceration on Informal Social Control in Communities," *Criminology and Public Policy* 3 (2004): 267–94.

16. R. Bursik and H. G. Grasmick, *Neighborhoods and Crime: The*

Dimensions of Effective Community Control (New York: Lexington Books, 1993).

17. R. J. Sampson and J. Morenoff, "Durable Inequality: Spatial Dynamics, Social Processes, and the Persistence of Poverty in Chicago Neighborhoods," in *Poverty Traps*, ed. by S. Bowles, S. Durlauf, and K. Hoff (Princeton, NJ: Princeton University Press, 2006), 176–203.

18. Roberts, "Social and Moral Cost of Mass Incarceration."

19. C. Uggen and J. Manza, "Democratic Contraction? Political Consequences of Felon Disenfranchisement in the United States," *American Sociological Review* 67 (2002): 777–803.

20. P. Karlan, "Convictions and Doubts: Retribution, Representation and the Debate Over Felon Disenfranchisement," *Stanford Law Review* 56 (2004): 1147–70.

21. T. Clear and D. Rose, "Individual Sentencing Practices and Aggregate Social Problems," in *Crime Control and Social Justice: The Delicate Balance*, ed. D. F. Hawkins, S. L. Myers, and R. N. Stone (Westport, CT: Greenwood, 2003), 27–53; W. Sabol and J. Lynch, "Assessing the Longer-Run Consequences of Incarceration: Effects on Families and Employment," in Hawkins et al., *Crime Control and Social Justice*, 3–26; Braman, "Families and Incarceration."

22. Rucker Johnson and Steven Raphael, "The Effects of Male Incarceration Dynamics on AIDS Infection Rates among African-American Women and Men," 2005. Online at http://citeseerx.ist.psu.edu/viewdoc/download?doi=10.1.1.531.4420&rep=rep1&type=pdf.

23. Joel Devine, Joseph Sheley, and M. Dwayne Smith, "Macro Economic and Social Control Policy Influences on Crime Rate Changes," *American Sociological Review* 53 (1988): 407–20; Thomas Marvell and Carlisle Moody, "Prison Population Growth and Crime Reduction," *Journal of Quantitative Criminology* 10 (1994): 109–40; Steven D. Levitt, "The Effect of Prison Population Size on Crime Rates: Evidence from Prison Overcrowding Litigation," *Quarterly Journal of Economics* 111, no. 2 (1996): 319–51; E. Currie, *Crime and Punishment in America* (New York: Owl Books, 1998); Michael Lynch, "Beating a Dead Horse: Is There Any Basic Evidence for the Deterrent Effect of Imprisonment?" *Crime, Law and Social Change* 31 (1999): 347–62; T. Arvanites and R. DeFina, "Business Cycles and Street Crime," *Criminology* 44 (2006): 139–64; R. DeFina and T. Arvanites, "The Weak Effect of Imprisonment on Crime: 1971–1998," *Social Science Quarterly* 53 (2002): 407–20; T. Kovandzic and L. Vieraitis, "The Effect of County-Level Prison Population Growth on Crime Rates," *Criminology and Public Policy* 5 (2006): 213–44; and L. M. Vieraitis, T. Kovandzic, and T. Marvell, "The Criminogenic Effects of Imprisonment: Evidence from State Panel Data, 1974–2002," *Criminology and Public Policy* 6 (2007): 589–622.

24. T. Clear, "The Problem with 'Addition by Subtraction': The Prison

Crime Relationship in Low-Income Communities," in *Invisible Punishment: The Collateral Consequences of Mass Imprisonment*, ed. Marc Mauer and Meda Chelsey-Lind (New York: The New Press, 2002), 18–194.

25. J. Hagan and R. Dinovitzer, "Collateral Consequences of Imprisonment for Children, Communities, and Prisoners," in *Crime and Justice: A Review of Research* 26, ed. M. Tonry and J. Petersilia (Chicago: University of Chicago Press, 1999), 121–62.

26. R. DeFina and L. Hannon, "The Impact of Mass Incarceration on Poverty," *Crime and Delinquency* 59 (2013): 562–86.

27. R. DeFina and L. Hannon, "The Impact of Adult Incarceration on Child Poverty: A County-Level Analysis, 1995–2007," *The Prison Journal* 90 (2010): 377–96.

28. Vieraitis, Kovandzic, and Marvell, "The Criminogenic Effects of Imprisonment."

29. R. DeFina and L. Hannon, "For Incapacitation, There Is No Time Like the Present: The Lagged Effects of Prisoner Reentry on Property and Violent Crime Rates," *Social Science Research* 39 (2010): 1004–14.

30. M. Mauer, "The Causes and Consequences of Prison Growth in the United States," in *Mass Imprisonment: Social Causes and Consequences*, ed. David Garland (New York: Sage Publishers, 2001), 4–14; Western, *Punishment and Inequality in America*; and Western and Beckett, "How Unregulated Is the U.S. Labor Market?"

31. Also, see C. Uggen, J. Manza, and M. Thompson, "Citizenship, Democracy and the Civic Reintegration of Criminal Offenders," *The Annals of the American Academy of Political and Social Science* 605 (2006): 281–310.

32. P. Samuels and D. Mukamal, *After Prison: Roadblocks to Reentry; A Report on State Legal Barriers Facing People with Criminal Records* (New York: Legal Action Center, 2004).

11. Reconstructing the Moral Claim of Racially Unjust Mass Incarceration

Alison Benders

This chapter first appeared in *Today I Gave Myself Permission to Dream: Race and Incarceration in America*. Edited by Erin Brigham and Kimberly Rae Connor. San Francisco: University of San Francisco Press, 2018.

The participants of this Roundtable...have explored the criminalization of black and brown bodies from a diverse array of positions: formerly incarcerated people; employees of social service-reintegration organizations; prison ministers; social ethicists; lawyers and legal justice advocates; and sociologists. My contribution from theological anthropology can seem sterile and distant because theoretical foundations seem to lack pragmatic impact. Theological anthropology explores who we are as human beings in light of our faith commitments, who we are before God and who we are to each other. However, in and through prophetic exploration, theology can objectify our underlying conceptual framework for critique and reformulation. More adequate concepts can yield more effective exchanges in our day-to-day lives. So this essay attempts to demonstrate that a better theological anthropology can disclose the social sin of mass incarceration and elevate its moral claim upon all of us in American society.

My experimental contribution begins by situating the theological discussion within the evidence that mass incarceration criminalizes people of color. This criminalization rests on an "arm-chair" theology that valorizes human autonomy and equates disobedience with sinfulness. The second section presents an alternate theology of human identity based upon our social context of shared community and intersubjectivity. The next section shows what can happen when our understanding of the human person shifts from autonomous individualism epitomized in freedom to human community in which we are loved and we love others into full human flourishing. It focuses particularly on our obligation to address social sins because we are socially constituted. The concluding point is that, by understanding our humanity socially, our moral integrity compels us to claim social injustices as our own responsibility and address them.[1]

The Criminalization of People Because of Skin Color

Since the 1980s our nation has seen the skyrocketing rate of incarceration nearly quadrupling in 35 years to 7 million people under supervision by corrections departments, and more than 2.2 million in jails.[2] The Sentencing Project's 2013 report to the United Nations Human Rights Commission documents the racial disparity in the U.S. criminal justice system. A few statistics, quoted directly from the report, provide ample evidence:

- "Roughly 12% of the United States population is black. Yet in 2011, black Americans constituted 30% of persons arrested for a property offense and 38% of persons arrested for a violent offense." (3)
- "Between 1980 and 2000, the U.S. black drug arrest rate rose from 6.5 to 29.1 per 1,000 persons; during the same period, the white drug arrest rate increased from 3.5 to 4.6 per 1,000 persons." (4)
- "The Bureau of Justice Statistics found…black drivers were twice as likely to experience the use or threat of violent force at the hands of police officers than both white and Hispanic drivers." (5)

The report concludes, based upon deeper statistical analysis, that implicit racial bias at every level of the criminal justice system is the predominant cause for the hyper-enforcement of criminal laws against men and women of color.

More problematically, utilizing the criminal justice system to control men and women of color represents the contemporary manifestation and state-sanctioned reinvention of slavery, Jim Crow segregation, northern ghettoization, and unrelenting race-based violence. It expresses America's white supremacist culture built *ab initio* upon the dehumanization, exclusion, and criminalization of non-white people.[3] The trajectory from slavery to today's prison system leads Loïc Wacquant to judge:

> The astronomical overrepresentation of blacks in houses of penal confinement and the increasingly tight meshing of the hyperghetto with the carceral system suggests that, owing to America's adoption of mass incarceration as a queer social policy designed to discipline the poor and contain the dishonored, lower-class African-Americans now dwell, not in a society with prisons as their white compatriots do, but in the first genuine prison society in history.[4]

There are many approaches to address the racial discrimination in the criminal justice system. Some seek to reform the system directly by challenging facially neutral laws with disparate impact.[5] Bryan Stevenson's personal account in *Just Mercy: A Story of Justice and Redemption* and Michelle Alexander's magisterial study *The New Jim Crow*[6] are two instances of the vast scholarly and personal literature about the implicit bias and other injustices in the system itself. Moving from direct witness against racial injustice, a second approach seeks to reform the impact of the penal system more comprehensively by replacing its crippling adherence to retributive justice with a restorative justice model. Restorative justice augments a rights-punishment analysis with a focus on the dignity of the victims and offenders and on their community context in order to promote long-term social stability and even reconciliation.[7] All remedial efforts rest upon irrefutable evidence that our so-called justice system incarcerates people of color, especially black men, because of their skin color: it is a crime in our nation to have black or brown skin.

Reframing Our Understanding of the Human Person

Our common-sense concepts of sin and crime derive almost as an intellectual reflex from an ill-informed theological position. An untutored reading of Genesis can glean from the story of "the Fall" that human beings are first and foremost free and autonomous individuals[8] who have disobeyed the only command God gives them. Sin is personal, intentional disobedience or transgression that offends God and/or other people.[9] An atonement theology, following upon the premise of freedom, reduces to the idea that God creates human beings to be free and obedient to God's will; human beings sin by disobeying God; human beings should bear the consequences of their sin; and, if not for Christ's sacrificial death, human beings would suffer death as a consequence of sin. In this reductionist model, conformity with God's law constitutes the measure of human worthiness, love, and ultimately, salvation. Its logic affirms for both sinners and criminals: those who break the law should be punished; those who are punished must have broken the law. Without a more adequate investigation into human identity, this legalistic theological anthropology leads us to accept, rather than abhor, the hyper-incarceration of people of color. Incarceration statistics then reinforce our cultural bias, particularly that dark skin equates with criminality.

Human Beings as Intersubjectively and Socially Constituted

The problem with reducing human identity to freedom, and the resulting emphasis on punishment is that it rests on a foundational notion of human identity that prescinds from our lived experience. An alternate starting point is to recognize that our humanity is in fact forged intersubjectively—in relationship.[10] We are rooted by our very existence in social relationships and mutual care. As co-creators with God, humanity's highest calling is to love other people into full human flourishing, just as God's love creates and sustains us. We ourselves are loved into our humanity by our parents, teachers, friends, and most intimate partners. When we begin our theological anthropology here, interpersonal justice is the virtue that "perfects our relationships with other people," according to moral theologian James Keenan, SJ.[11] Thus, freedom is subsumed and contextualized within interpersonal and community relationships.

Catholic social teaching glosses the embodiment of justice by highlighting a moral obligation to solidarity. As Pope John Paul II explains:

> [Solidarity] is not a feeling of vague compassion or shallow distress at the misfortunes of so many people, both near and far. On the contrary, it is a firm and persevering determination to commit oneself to the common good; that is to say, to the good of all and of each individual, because we are all really responsible for all.[12]

M. Shawn Copeland writes:

> Solidarity is a task, a praxis through which responsible relationships between and among persons (between and among groups) may be created and expressed, mended and renewed....The fundamental obligations that arise in the context of these relationships stem not from identity politics or from the erasure of difference, but rather from basic human creatureliness and love.[13]

With this reframing, the primary indicator of authentic humanity is the quality of our love as lived in relationship with others.[14] Human freedom is no longer untethered and privatized but is located within a social nexus and the overarching obligations of solidarity and common good. This reframing still allows for a culturally contextualized investigation of freedom and responsibility, but it must be anchored in a particular community's history, traditions, and values. When personal freedom and responsibility are abused, we investigate not just individual choices, but more importantly, how our communities practice interpersonal justice and embody mutual care, solidarity, and justice for all members.

An Intersubjective Anthropology Reveals Social Sin

An intersubjective theological anthropology also clarifies what social sin is and our responsibility for it. Preoccupied with individual freedom and culpability, the criminal justice system only rarely asks about compulsion or "bondage of the will," mostly in particular situations of mental illness or abuse. With a similar focus, sin "properly so called" is individual sin. Social sin has been understood as sin only analogously, because people cannot be blamed for harm for unintentional acts.[15] Individual sin looks backward in time toward a past injury to assign culpability and impose penance for disobedience to God's law. An individual focus precludes inquiry into the facticity of our social environment and the way the conditions of the world (i.e., original sin) truly constrain our freedom to act justly and lovingly. This approach to sin has tended to over punish individuals for transgressions and over exculpate individuals for sinful systems and structures, precisely as displayed in the racial injustice of mass incarceration.

Human intersubjectivity and solidarity in community disclose our responsibility for the sin embedded in our institutions; they reveal to us our responsibility to create and sustain the common good and goodness in community. Exploring the implications of social sin, moral theologian Kenneth Himes parses responsibility for social sin according to three categories: causal, culpable, and remedial.[16] *Causal responsibility* identifies the agents whose actions produce the physical or psychological harm. Causal responsibility may or may not be blameworthy, as in accidents where inattention causes harm. *Culpability* designates the agents who are to blame for the harm. The theological tradition distinguishes a personally and morally culpable act (a sin) based on intent to cause harm; moral condemnation for a "personally wrongful act" attaches only to intended injuries.[17] *Liability*, or remedial responsibility, specifies which agents are obliged to ameliorate harm; liability might be direct for one's own actions or vicarious for another's acts due to legal or cultural conventions. These distinctions of responsibility allow a more effective analysis of the complex dialectic between individual and social responsibility, particularly with respect to liability for social sins.

In moving from blame to liability, Himes asks: "Why should a person not be expected to do something to oppose a perceived [or proven] injustice?"[18] He suggests that the liability to remediate a cultural injustice attaches to everyone in the culture, and particularly to those who benefit most or who "unconsciously encourage [social sins] through a variety of folkways and social institutions."[19] He concludes: "Those who have benefitted from the past structures should strive to assist those who have been disadvantaged by the culture. No judgment of blameworthiness is needed, only an assessment that the present cultural institutions…are institutions which [we] have more or less supported."[20] Regardless of whether we caused an injustice in the first place, we are liable for ameliorating social or institutionalized harms and reconstituting the interpersonal justice and common good that are the theological foundations of human community.

A More Compelling Moral Claim

The theological and experiential understanding of the human person as intersubjectively constituted in and through our relationships to others has tremendous power. So, what can happen when our theological understanding of the human person shifts from autonomous individualism epitomized in freedom to human community in which we are loved and we love others into full human flourishing? Most significantly, a foundational commitment to intersubjectivity and solidarity highlights, through incongruity, the immorality of our society. It shows the hypocrisy of our professed commitment to interpersonal and social justice when one group of people is disproportionately oppressed and imprisoned. Rather than interrogate an offender, "What did you do wrong?" we must ask, "What are we doing wrong that this group of people is perpetually criminalized?" Rather than demand of those incarcerated, "How will you atone for this?" society must consider, "How will we assure the restoration of these people to full inclusion in our shared future?" These questions compel us to reexamine the underlying social inequities that drive so-called criminal behavior, and to search for something other than retribution and punishment as preferred methods of social control.

Particularly in the present discussion, beginning with intersubjectivity strengthens the moral claim that mass incarceration makes upon us because we are complicit in the injustice.[21] Regardless of the culpability of individual offenders, statistical evidence and human suffering testify that hyper-incarceration is a tool to criminalize people of color in their very existence. In the context of mass incarceration, social sin reveals itself precisely in documented patterns of injustice and discrimination. Thus, simply by being members of American society, we must act. If not, we are guilty of a sin of omission, either because we avoid recognizing what is common knowledge in the public sphere (vincible ignorance); or, we absolve ourselves with the usual justifications of indifference: "my efforts are too small to make a difference"; "others are taking care of this"; "I can't think of what to do"; or "it's not my area."[22] A just response requires, at the very least, support for efforts to reform the system, to reintegrate those who have served their time, and to eliminate the underlying inequities that created the problem.

Granted, this is a tall order. Still, only by acknowledging that our criminal justice system is unjust—by acknowledging that our nation excludes and criminalizes people for the color of their skin—can we take seriously the moral obligation rooted in our identity as cocreators of human community with God. Taking responsibility to mitigate the racial injustice in the prison system means intentionally cultivating new skills to become more personally active in restoring justice according to our means and opportunities. These demands must be particularized according to our individual situations, skills, and capacities, but they cannot be ignored.

Theology is not an abstract drill. Rather it is a lever for personal and social change when we integrate our faith commitment into concrete action. A first step, offered here for all people whatever our situation, is a renewed theology, a better understanding of how we define ourselves as human beings. If we are to root out racial injustice, especially our own indifference, we must view human community intersubjectively—this means, in common parlance, that we must practice love. To love and to create the common good for our community means looking at the world through a lens of solidarity. Christ tells us to love one another as he has loved us. As people created in the image of God and imitating Christ's own abounding love, we must respond to the moral claim that sinful social structures make upon us as individuals, as a Church and as a nation. In short, a theological anthropology grounded in intersubjectivity and solidarity in community reveals the sinfulness of hyper-incarceration of people of color—and we must respond.

Notes

1. The reflection here is particularly relevant to expanding efforts to repent for and redeem American culture from its "original sin" of racism. I recognize that this topic far exceeds the limits of the Lane Center Roundtable

Discussion; it is a tiny contribution that might respond to Black Catholic theologians' call for Christian theology to make anti-black racism a compelling theological issue.

2. "Report of the Sentencing Project to the United Nations Human Rights Committee Regarding Racial Disparities in the United States Criminal Justice System," 2013, published in full at the Sentencing Project, www.sentencingproject.org, 1.

3. Loïc Wacquant, "From Slavery to Mass Incarceration: Rethinking the 'Race Question' in the US," *New Left Review* 13 (2002): 55–56. See also Michelle Alexander, *The New Jim Crow: Mass Incarceration in the Age of Color Blindness* (New York: New Press, 2011).

4. Wacquant, "From Slavery to Mass Incarceration," 60.

5. On the discriminatory impact of facially neutral policies and practices, see Eduardo Bonilla-Silva, *Racism without Racists: Color-Blind Racism and the Persistence of Racial Inequality in the United States* (Lanham, MD: Rowman & Littlefield Publishing, 2010).

6. Bryan Stevenson, *Just Mercy: A Story of Justice and Redemption* (New York: Spiegel and Grau, 2015); and Alexander, *The New Jim Crow*.

7. Two examples are William O'Neill, "Imagining Otherwise: The Ethics of Social Reconciliation," *Journal of the Society of Christian Ethics* 22 (2002): 183–99; and Howard Zehr, *The Little Book of Restorative Justice*, rev. and updated ed. (New York: Good Books, 2014).

8. There is a much larger discussion here about whether freedom is a theoretical presumption for human identity or a primal experience. Regardless, the call by many contemporary theologians of color to root human identity in concrete and particularized experience represents a vital imperative. See, e.g., M. Shawn Copeland, *Enfleshing Freedom: Body, Race, and Being* (Minneapolis: Fortress Press, 2010); Ada María Isasi-Díaz, *En la Lucha (In the Struggle): A Hispanic Women's Liberation Theology* (Minneapolis: Augsburg Fortress, 1993); and James H. Cone, *A Black Theology of Liberation* (Maryknoll, NY: Orbis Books, 1970). To revision the starting point of theological anthropology does not deny the experience of freedom to be an inextricable aspect of humanity; it merely recognizes that the meaning and expression of freedom cannot be abstracted from its cultural context.

9. See Kenneth R. Himes, "Social Sin and the Role of the Individual," *The Annual of the Society of Christian Ethics* 6 (1986): 183, quoting Langdon Gilkey, "The language about Adam and Eve in the garden has represented the language of freedom, choice, act and responsibility; the language about our common inheritance [original sin] has represented that of necessity, fate, and so of

universality and inevitability," from *Message and Existence: An Introduction to Christian Theology* (Eugene, OR: Wipf and Stock Publishers, 2001), 112. Thus, "sin" can refer to individual transgression or the given (and distorted) conditions in our human world. See also Bryan N. Massingale, *Racial Justice and the Catholic Church* (Maryknoll, NY: Orbis Books, 2014), 91–96; and Neil Ormerod, *Grace and Disgrace: A Theology of Self Esteem, Society and History* (Sydney, Australia: E. J. Dwyer, 1992), generally part B.

10. For a recent collection of diverse approaches to theological anthropology, see Lieven Boeve, Yves De Maeseneer, and Ellen Van Stiebel, eds., *Questioning the Human: Toward a Theological Anthropology for the Twenty-First Century* (Oxford: Oxford University Press, 2014).

11. Lisa Fullam and Gina Hens-Piazza, unpublished paper, citing James Keenan, SJ, "Proposing Cardinal Virtues," *Theological Studies* 56, no. 4 (2004): 724.

12. John Paul II, *Sollicitudo Rei Socialis*, December 30, 1987, 38.

13. M. Shawn Copeland, "The New Anthropological Subject at the Heart of the Mystical Body of Christ," *Proceedings of the Catholic Theological Society of America* 53 (2013): 37.

14. Rooting human identity in intersubjectivity evokes notions of Trinity and the loving relationship among Father, Son, and Spirit. Such a theological analysis is far beyond the scope of this discussion.

15. See, e.g., Mark O 'Keefe, *What Are They Saying about Social Sin?* (New York: Paulist Press, 1990); and Kristin E. Heyer, "Social Sin and Immigration: Good Fences Make Bad Neighbors," *Theological Studies* 71, no. 2 (2010): 415–20. See also Himes, "Social Sin and the Role of the Individual," at 196–97, who does not rule out the possibility of assigning individual blame for collective action to group members but cautions that this requires a careful analysis of causal contribution, voluntariness, one's role within the group, and the accrual practices and policies of the group.

16. Himes, "Social Sin and the Role of the Individual," 189–91.

17. Himes, "Social Sin and the Role of the Individual," 187.

18. Himes, "Social Sin and the Role of the Individual," 205. We need not turn the page on the past policies and actions that led to the mass incarceration or abandon reintegration and reconciliation measures. As noted in the introduction to this essay, these are vital and complementary aspects of a comprehensive battle against mass incarceration on individual, systemic, political, and cultural and religious levels.

19. Himes, "Social Sin and the Role of the Individual," 211.

20. Himes, "Social Sin and the Role of the Individual," 212.

21. Alexander Mikulich, Laurie Cassidy, and Margaret Pfeil, *The Scandal of White Complicity in US Hyper-incarceration: A Nonviolent Spirituality of White Resistance* (New York: Springer Books, 2013).

22. David Ford analyzes three levels of indifference relating to the sin of omission: awareness, acknowledgment, and action. *Sins of Omission: A Primer on Moral Indifference* (Minneapolis: Fortress Press, 1990). I have grouped awareness and acknowledgment together as vincible ignorance.

Part Seven

RACISM

12. The Systemic Erasure of the Black/ Dark-Skinned Body in Catholic Ethics

Bryan Massingale

This chapter first appeared in *Catholic Theological Ethics, Past, Present, and Future: The Trento Conference*. Edited by James F. Keenan. Maryknoll, NY: Orbis Books, 2011.

One of the questions I address in my scholarly work is this: *What would Catholic theological ethics look like if it took the "Black Experience" seriously as a dialogue partner?* To raise the question, however, is to signal the reality of absence, erasure, and "missing" voices. The question is necessary only because the "Black Experience"—the collective story of African American survival and achievement in a hostile, exploitative, and racist environment—and the bodies who are the subjects of this experience have been all too often rendered invisible and therefore "missing" in U.S. Catholic ethical reflection.[1]

The Historical Omission of Racism and Racial Justice

An example illustrates this invisibility, which, I contend, amounts to a systemic erasure. In 1948, the eminent U.S. moral theologian Gerald Kelly considered the question of whether the Sunday Mass obligation ceased for a Negro who was excluded from the local "white church."[2] Kelly judged that such racial discrimination was "unjust, impious, and scandalous." He also expressed regret at the harm given to "the Negro's spirit" and sense of church membership. Nonetheless, Kelly concluded that such discrimination within the church "does not of itself excuse him from hearing Mass. That question must be solved on the basis of the difficulty of getting to another church."

He did reiterate that white Catholics were duty bound to extend ordinary courtesy and respect to black people, noting that the refusal to do so was "a sin against charity."[3] Note, however, that Catholics were not duty bound to protest against the social evil of racial segregation itself, whether in society or in the church. Nor was there any expressed obligation for Catholics to engage proactively in the struggle to change this sinful situation. Nor was there but the most fleeting attention given to the perspective of the dark-skinned victim of such ecclesial exclusion.

A review of the two major professional journals of U.S. Catholic theological ethicists—namely, the authoritative "Notes on Moral Theology" published by *Theological Studies* (1940–96) and *The Proceedings of the Catholic Theological Society of America* (1946–96)—confirms the stark and glaring omission of the issue of white racism. U.S. Catholic moral theology's past reveals embarrassing omissions whereby theological ethicists were seemingly oblivious to the major social movements occurring around them (such as the Civil Rights and Black Power Movements of the 1960s). One searches these journals in vain for in-depth analyses or reflections on the reality of racism or race relations. The Civil Rights Movement, the catalyst for some of the most epochal social transformations in U.S. history and a paradigm for many other justice struggles globally, passed unnoticed by U.S. Catholic ethicists who were consumed by other matters—specifically, the controversies surrounding the morality of artificial contraception. Indeed, if one depended solely on these sources for one's knowledge of the period, one would never know of Martin Luther King, Jr.'s life, contributions, or even his death because Catholic moralists of that time scarcely adverted to him.[4]

Thus, one noted scholar, in reflecting on the omission of racial justice in U.S. Catholic ethical reflection, concluded:

> Historically it is impossible to deny that from the end of the Civil War until modern times, an almost universal silence regarding the moral issues involved in segregation blanketed the ecclesiastical scene. The American hierarchy and theologians have remained mute, and this at a time when…

> enforced segregation was growing and extending more and more into all areas of life.[5]

Not Only a "Historical" Omission

The observation that the muting of the Black Experience and the overlooking of ethical attention to the reality of racism is not, unfortunately, a matter of past history has been more recently confirmed. In October of 2008, a conference was held at the Catholic Theological Union and DePaul University in Chicago to explore the task of "Building a Catholic Social Theology for the Americas." As part of the closing panel charged with noting the conference's achievements and remaining tasks, I observed the omission of any consideration of race. For example, although the conference participants examined and lamented the poverty revealed in the United States through the Hurricane Katrina event, they never adverted to race as a decisive factor in how this tragedy unfolded.[6]

The assembled scholars also lamented the difficulty of elaborating a common social theology for the Americas—both North and South—given our differing histories and origins. But such an observation ignored our shared history of racism and slavery—undergone by both African and indigenous peoples—which not only marks both of our continents but also has been decisive in the formation of Latino/a identity. *La raza*—the *mestizo/mestizaje* reality of Latin America—would not exist without the racial mixing that stemmed from the deep wounding and often unacknowledged pain of slavery and economic exploitation. Race-based enslavement, colonialism, and conquest are common histories that are foundational not only for the Americas but for Western culture as well. These cannot be adequately understood without a forthright and in-depth engagement with racial injustice and a naming of white supremacy.

The Erasure of the Black Embodied Voice

Moreover, when the dark bodies of African Americans did appear in Catholic ethical discourse, they were as the objects of white sympathy, charity, and assistance. (I use the word *object* deliberately.) Though the leading moralists of the 1950s agreed that racial segregation was unjust, the solution advocated was to encourage whites to yield or concede rights to blacks, rather than encourage African Americans to press for what was their due.[7] Catholic moral discourse treated black people as *objects* of white study, analysis, and charity—and rarely deemed them as *subjects* capable of independent action or creative initiative. There was no acknowledgment of black *agency*; black people are usually acted upon and seldom the actors in U.S. Catholic moral discourse.[8] Their voice and agency are muted, absent, erased—and at the same time opposed, feared, and resisted.[9] Such practices and attitudes could not but render Catholic ethical reflection in matters of race inadequate and impoverished, if not absolutely erroneous.

This "underside" of history revealed in the erasure and distortion of the Black Experience in Catholic ethical reflection is well expressed by David Tracy:

> There is an underside to all the talk about history in modern religion and theology. That underside is revealed in the shocking silence in most theologies of historical consciousness and historicity alike on the evil rampant in history, the sufferings of whole peoples, the destruction of nature itself.... [It is] a history without any sense of the radical interruptions of actual history, without a memory of historical suffering, especially the suffering caused by the pervasive systemic unconscious distortions in our history—sexism, racism, classism, antisemitism, homophobia, Eurocentrism.[10]

Why the Evasion of the Black Body?

Yet we must deepen our inquiry into this "shocking silence...on the suffering of whole peoples," and particularly of black- and darker-skinned peoples, on the part of Catholic theological ethics by raising the question of *why*. Why, despite the "turn to the subject" and the embrace of historical consciousness, did U.S. Catholic theological ethicists *not* attend to the blatant and endemic racism of American society? Why was the most pressing moral issue of the 1960s artificial contraception and not the Civil Rights Movement or the racial violence of 1967 and 1968 that tore apart that nation's cities and has enduring consequences today? Why was, and why still is, the "radical interruption" of the black body continually overlooked, ignored, and thus erased?

There are multiple reasons for this state of affairs. M. Shawn Copeland suggests that one reason may be that the black body is what she calls a "structural embarrassment,"[11] that is, an uncomfortable reminder of the invisible ghosts of enslavement, colonization, and racial supremacy—that is, the "unjust enrichment" through exploited labor[12]—that haunt and hover over our histories. Another reason for the avoidance of the black body in Catholic theological and ethical discourse is that a forthright engagement with it would bring to the surface the deep complicity and collusion of Western Christianity in the suffering, abuse, and horror that attended European and American colonial expansion.[13] Yet perhaps the most profound reason for avoiding the black body is that challenging its invisibility would entail making white bodies visible as "white," that is, as sites of conferred racial dominance and privilege.

Marking white theologians as "white" means naming and facing the deforming effects of culture on the consciousness of North American and European theological ethicists. It means facing not only the possibility but indeed the probability that Catholic ethicists of the past (and too often in the present), being (de)formed by the systemic distortion of Western racism, did not and could not have regarded persons of African descent as numbered among the "subjects" to whom they should "turn."[14]

This probability is neither idle nor speculative. Social scientists have uncovered the reality of what they call "racially selective sympathy and indifference," that is, "the *unconscious* failure to extend to a minority the same recognition of humanity, and hence the same sympathy and care, given as a matter of course to one's own group."[15] It is important to underscore, however, that this "selective indifference" is not necessarily a matter of conscious decision or intentional willing. It results, rather, from the unnoted effects of socialization in a culture of racism and the corrosive impact of a racialized ethos on one's identity and consciousness.

As the historian Taylor Branch notes, "Almost as color defines vision itself, race shapes the culture eye—what we do and do not notice, the reach of empathy and the alignment of response."[16] And because of such social conditioning, certain lives become easier to ignore or, put another way, certain bodies have a higher claim upon a community's energy and concern, even among Catholic theological ethicists.[17]

Thus, a forthright engagement with the black body in Catholic theological ethics would demand making white ethicists visible as "white" and confront the challenges this poses for personal integrity in a compromised social system. These challenges are neither uncomplicated nor easily faced.

Systemic Erasure and Compromised Ethical Reflection

However, the "missing" voices of our darker sisters and brothers are significant not only for the personal integrity of Catholic moral theologians but also for the integrity and adequacy of Catholic ethical reflection. Because of this silencing and invisibility, there are not only voices that have not been heard, there are moral questions that have not been asked by Catholic theological ethicists of previous generations, such as the following: "What does it mean to be a disciple of Jesus in a racist society?"; "In a world where 'black' is an illegitimate or inferior mode of being human, what are the social implications of believing that Black Americans are made in the image of God?"; "How are persons of African descent to live ethically in a society that denies, questions, or attacks our humanity?"; "How do we tell those whom society ignores, fears, and disdains that they are sons and daughters of God?" Not adverting to such questions in a society of endemic racism makes one's ethical project not only inadequate and incomplete, it also strains credibility.[18]

Moreover, the invisibility of black bodies and darker voices masks methodological deficiencies in Catholic ethical reflection. I highlight, for example, Catholic moral theology's understanding of sin and moral culpability. Its primary focus on obvious acts of conscious and voluntary racial malice blinds us to the deeper and more sinister social evil that afflicts us. The issue is that we are tacitly ensnared in and malformed by a web of evil that we cannot yet even satisfactorily name.

In a recent work, I expressed this concern thus: "Because of the covert nature of racism's transmission, its meanings are internalized without awareness of the source and judged to be…normative."[19] That is, one's sense of right and wrong, one's grasp of morality, one's very conscience become blunted and twisted by one's socialization in a culture of racism. One cannot become aware of the absence or omission of certain voices or perspectives if one believes that such omissions are "normal" and the way things ought to be.

This is not a matter of mere culpable ignorance. Nor do I believe that the issue can be satisfactorily resolved through an appeal to what the tradition calls "invincible ignorance." Such appeals can somewhat deal with individual culpability, but do not attend to the deeper web of injustice that is truly "evil" but for which Catholic theological ethicists have not developed a precise way of naming, nor the church a proper forum for repentance and reconciliation.[20]

Nor does an appeal to "social" or "structural" sin suffice. For I am trying to call our attention to "the underlying set of cultural meanings... that are (re)inscribed in social customs, institutional policies and political processes."[21] Social or structural sin addresses the latter—that is, how social institutions and structures are the causes of unjust suffering—but not the former, namely, the underlying set of cultural meanings and symbols that social institutions reflect. Culture animates the social order, and our moral theology has not yet developed the tools for examining, much less naming, this layer of human-caused evil. Merely calling the "culture of racism" an accumulation of many acts of personal sin (*pace* the *Catechism of the Catholic Church*) fails to do justice to the enormity of entrenched cultural evil and its deleterious impacts. There is a "radical evil" at work in human history that the predominant understanding of sin as a voluntary and conscious act can neither address nor redress—and indeed compounds.

Thus, the systemic erasure of the black- and darker-skinned body in Catholic theological ethics not only implicates the personal integrity of Catholic ethicists, but also compromises our ability to adequately reflect on the challenges of moral living in a multicultural and multiracial world. Taking the Black Experience and darker bodies as serious dialogue partners is a daunting challenge that promises to have profound, necessary, and yet perhaps unknown effects on the discipline of Catholic theological ethics and its practitioners.

Lament as a Way Forward

What, then, are we to do in the face of the weight of history and the complicity of Catholic theological ethics in the silencing of the suffering of peoples? It is tempting to offer a series of concrete proposals that, if followed, would lead Catholic ethicists into an intellectual "promised land." But I have become more convinced that racism engages us viscerally at a "gut" level that cannot be addressed solely through rational discussion. I have become more aware of the limits of discursive or intellectual practices alone. Thus, I believe that we Catholic ethicists need to *lament* the ambiguity and distortions of our history and their tragically deforming effects on ourselves. We need to lament, mourn, and grieve our history.[22]

The scriptures remind us that lamentation is an expression of complaint, grief, and hope rooted in a "trust against trust" that God hears the cry of the afflicted and will respond compassionately to their need. Lamenting holds together both sorrow and hope in ways that defy easy rational understanding. Laments honestly name and forthrightly acknowledge painfully wrenching circumstances, and yet proclaim that in the midst of the pain there is another word to be heard from God—a message of compassion and deliverance. Lament thus facilitates the emergence of something new, whether a changed consciousness or a renewed engagement with external events. It is indeed a paradox of protest and praise that leads to new life.

For example, consider the African American spiritual "Nobody Knows the Trouble I've Seen."[23] Composed by an unknown black enslaved man whose family was rent asunder by being sold to different slave masters, the song piercingly relates that no one could possibly comprehend or "know my sorrow." Yet, the singer ends his lament on an unexpected, even incomprehensible note: "Nobody knows the trouble I've seen. Glory Hallelujah!" Through the practice of honest and forthright protest, the singer finds the strength to bear and endure unspeakable loss and harsh circumstances. History afflicts but does not crush him.

I offer such lament as a possibility for Catholic theological ethicists. Lament has the power to challenge the entrenched cultural beliefs that legitimate racial privilege. It engages a level of human consciousness deeper than logical reason. Lamenting can propel us to new levels of truth seeking and risk taking as we grieve our past history and strive to create an ethical discourse that is more reflective of the universality of our Catholic faith.

Nearing the limits of time and space for this reflection, I conclude on this note: The systemic erasure of dark-skinned bodies and the silencing of black voices in our history are not of concern only for an adequate account of the past. For, as the U.S. novelist William Faulkner noted, "The past is not dead, it is not even past."[24] Race-based enslavement, conquest, and colonialism are common foundational experiences—the "original sins" that link the Americas, Africa, Europe, and Asia. We cannot, then, give an adequate account of present controversies and moral responsibilities—much less develop a Catholic theological ethics for a world church—if we fail to attend to the voices of the dark bodies that hover over and haunt our histories despite our embarrassed silence and studied neglect.

Notes

1. James Cone, the pioneer of black American liberation theology, defines the "Black Experience" thus: "The black experience [in the United States] is the atmosphere in which blacks live. It is the totality of black existence in a white world…in a system of white racism….The black experience, however, is more than simply encountering white insanity. It also means blacks making decisions about themselves….It is the experience of carving out an existence in a society that says that you do not belong." See James Cone, *A Black Theology of Liberation*, 2nd ed. (Maryknoll, NY: Orbis Books, 1986), 24–25.

2. Readers from outside the U.S. context need to recall that ironclad racial segregation was the official legal and social policy of the United States from 1896 to 1965. Justified under the fiction of providing white and non-white peoples "separate but equal" educational, social, and economic opportunities, this racial segregation was a means of advancing white supremacy in political, social, and economic matters. Such racial exclusion was, unfortunately, a reality in the U.S. Catholic Church as well. Black men and women were all but excluded from participation in the priesthood and religious life. Catholic parishes were often designated as "white only" or "black only"—especially but not solely in the Southern United States. For a seminal study detailing the Catholic Church's collusion and complicity in U.S. racialized evil, see Cyprian Davis, *The History of Black Catholics in the United States* (New York: Crossroad, 1992).

3. Gerald Kelly, "Notes on Moral Theology," *Theological Studies* 8 (1947): 112–14. I present this article because it illustrates the standard treatment

that racism received when it was considered by U.S. Catholic theological ethicists. One should also appreciate that, while it is easy to be critical and even dismissive of the limitations of this approach, at least the ethicists of the 1940s adverted to the topic. After 1963, the topic of racial justice all but disappears from *Theological Studies'* annual moral survey until the late 1990s.

4. I detail this sad legacy in Bryan Massingale, "The African American Experience and U.S. Roman Catholic Ethics: 'Strangers and Aliens No Longer'?" in *Black and Catholic: The Challenge and Gift of Black Folk; Contributions of African American Experience and Thought to Catholic Theology*, ed. Jamie T. Phelps (Milwaukee: Marquette University Press, 1997), 79–101.

5. Joseph T. Leonard, "Current Theological Questions in Race Relations," *Catholic Theological Society of America Proceedings* [hereafter, *CTSA Proceedings*] 19 (1964): 82.

6. For the signal impact of U.S. racism in the response to the plight of Hurricane Katrina's victims, see Bryan Massingale, "The Scandal of Poverty: 'Cultured Indifference' and the Option for the Poor Post-Katrina," *Journal of Religion and Society*, Supplement Series 4 (2008): 55–72; and Bryan Massingale, "About Katrina: Catastrophe Exposes U.S. Race Reality," *National Catholic Reporter* 43, no. 18 (2007): 10–13.

7. Citing the eminent U.S. moralist John Ford, "The doctrine of Christ inculcates more insistently that we must *give* rights to commutative justice; nowhere does Christ encourage us to *fight* for what is our due. It would be better for theologians and priests generally to preach to whites that they should give rights due to the Negroes, rather than urge the Negroes to press for the rights that are their due. Otherwise we might be encouraging fights and violence." See C. Luke Salm, "Moral Aspects of Segregation in Education—Digest of the Discussion," *CTSA Proceedings* 13 (1958): 61; emphasis in the original.

8. As noted above, there was very little examination or treatment of the black-led Civil Rights Movement in U.S. Catholic theological ethics. Indeed, in previous work, I detail the suspicion of black initiative and the pervasive white paternalism that typifies the U.S. Catholic engagement with racism. See my *Racial Justice and the Catholic Church* (Maryknoll, NY: Orbis Books, 2010), chap. 2.

9. John LaFarge, S.J., a preeminent advocate for racial justice in the mid-twentieth century, nonetheless was suspicious of and opposed to African American agency and leadership in the quest for racial justice. See David W. Southern, *John LaFarge and the Limits of Catholic Interracialism 1911–1963* (Baton Rouge: Louisiana State University Press, 1996).

10. David Tracy, "Evil, Suffering, and Hope: The Search for New Forms of Contemporary Theodicy," *CTSA Proceedings* 50 (1995): 29.

11. M. Shawn Copeland, *Enfleshing Freedom: Body, Race, and Being* (Minneapolis: Fortress Press, 2009), 3.

12. Joe R. Feagin, *Systemic Racism: A Theory of Oppression* (New York: Routledge, 2006), 18.

13. In the U.S. context, Malcolm X is perhaps the sharpest critic of the collusion of Western Christianity in the racial oppression of dark bodies. I treat his thought in "*Vox Victimarum Vox Dei*: Malcolm X as Neglected 'Classic' for Catholic Theological Reflection," *CTSA Proceedings* 65 (2010): 63–88.

14. Bryan Massingale, "The African American Experience and U.S. Roman Catholic Ethics," 79–101.

15. Charles R. Lawrence III, "The Id, the Ego, and Equal Protection: Reckoning with Unconscious Racism," *Stanford Law Review* 39 (1987): 317–88, at n135.

16. Taylor Branch, *Parting the Waters: America in the King Years, 1954–63* (New York: Simon & Schuster, 1989), cited in Haki R. Madhubuti, *Black Men: Obsolete, Single, Dangerous?* (Chicago: Third World Press, 1990), 264. Madhubuti further declares, "The white response to the majority of the world's people, who are not white, is indeed grounded in race. More than any other factor in the Eurocentric context, *race* defines, categorizes, tracks, destroys, and redefines cultures."

17. I explore the realities of "unconscious racism" and "racially selective sympathy and indifference" in my *Racial Justice and the Catholic Church*, 26–33. I note, however, yet another reason for the invisibility of the black body as "black" in Catholic moral discourse, namely, the myth of—or even aspiration to—so called "color blindness." As the celebrated novelist Toni Morrison explains in another context, "One likely reason for the paucity of critical materials on this large and compelling subject is that, in matters of race, silence and evasion have historically ruled literary discourse.... It is further complicated by the fact that the habit of ignoring race is understood to be a graceful, even generous, liberal gesture. To notice it is to recognize an already discredited difference. To enforce invisibility through silence is to allow the black body a shadowless participation in the dominant cultural body." See Toni Morrison, *Playing in the Dark: Whiteness and the Literary Imagination* (New York: Vintage Books, 1993). This official "color blindness" marks the public policies of many countries, including France and Uruguay, where race-based social and economic disparities among social groups are officially "erased" through a refusal to collect the data that would reveal them. The problem with "color blindness," no matter how well intentioned, is that in a sociocultural context where skin-color difference plays a significant and even decisive role, not to attend to this difference in practice preserves and defends entrenched social privilege.

18. Massingale, *Racial Justice and the Catholic Church*, 160–61.

19. Bryan Massingale, "Author's Response: Review Symposium on *Racial Justice and the Catholic Church*," *Horizons* 37 (2010): 138–42.

20. David Tracy, e.g., states that naming social evils such as racism as "sin" may not be doing justice to the depth and pervasiveness of the evil we confront through an encounter with the systemically silenced and erased. Rather, we need a more radical doctrine of sin—and grace—to do justice to the enormity of entrenched evil present in our history and in the present. See his discussion in *Plurality and Ambiguity: Hermeneutics, Religion, and Hope* (Chicago: University of Chicago Press, 1994), 74–75.

21. Laurie Cassidy, "Review Symposium: *Racial Justice and the Catholic Church*," *Horizons* 37 (2010): 127–28.

22. I treat the practice of lament and its significance for racial-justice praxis in more detail in *Racial Justice and the Catholic Church*, 104–14. The reader is directed there for a more in-depth discussion.

23. Bruno Chenu, *The Trouble I've Seen: The Big Book of Negro Spirituals*, trans. Eugene V. Leplante (Valley Forge, PA: Judson, 2003), 265; and John Lovell Jr., *Black Song: The Forge and the Flame* (New York: Paragon, 1972), 122.

24. Cited in Tracy, *Plurality and Ambiguity*, 36.

13. Anti-Blackness and White Supremacy in the Making of American Catholicism

M. Shawn Copeland

This chapter first appeared in *American Catholic Studies* 127, no. 3 (Fall 2016): 6–8.

And if anyone asks, "What are these wounds?" the answer will be: "The wounds I received in [my own] house [from] my friends."

—after Zechariah 13:6

Critical and sustained interrogation of the social construction of race and white supremacy with their deforming impact on individual, institutional, as well as spiritual and sacramental domains remains a most underdeveloped topic in American Catholic studies. As an African American Catholic and a theologian, this neglect and indifference wounds my heart and insults my intellect. Thus, the epigraph of this essay expresses my emotional, spiritual, and intellectual experience of black Catholic life. In what follows, I put forward theses for comprehending, analyzing, and evaluating the relation of American Catholicism to anti-blackness and white supremacy.

1. Catholic sanctioning of the colonization of and trade in flesh reverberates with acute and painful irony. At the center of Catholic thinking (*read*: theology) and practice (*read*: worship) lies broken and bruised flesh. The doctrine of incarnation "mobilizes" the notions of nature,

essence (*ousia*), *homoousios*, *hypostasis* to mediate the most profound, daring, and dangerous mystery of Christian faith: the Word of God became flesh.[1] At a particular time in the course of human history in a particular geographic place in the person of the Jew Jesus of Nazareth, God became flesh, lived *with* us and *for* us.

2. Despite its reverence for Being and beings; despite its intense sacramental and therefore symbolic character; despite its intimate knowledge of and irrevocable and essential relation to flesh—racialization of flesh has shaped Christianity, and thus Roman Catholicism, almost from its origins: women, Jews, people of color (especially, indigenous and black peoples) have undergone metaphysical violence.[2] In the Americas, this effort to master beings by force nearly exterminated indigenous peoples and dehumanized Africans. In the highly profitable commodification of flesh, this specious union of colonial and ecclesiastical power decidedly abused religion and the religious.
3. This racialization and commodification of flesh were so attached to the black body that the very meaning of being human "was defined continually against black people and blackness."[3] This definition, in turn, spawned subtle and perverse "anti-black logics"[4] that took root in cognition, language, meanings, and values, thereby reshaping nearly all practices of human encounter and engagement. Fatally, these anti-black logics have proved resistant to intelligibility and to critique. Thus, the normative denotation of who was (and is) human referred exclusively to white human beings, although this was expressed concretely as white males.
4. These anti-black logics were so pervasive and so restrictive, so precise and so pleasurable[5] that they overrode the exercise of potentially legitimate authority and seized and displaced Divine Authority, thereby, totalizing and fetishizing whiteness and white human beings. In this process, anti-black logics repressed the demands of conscience,

obscured morality, and eclipsed ethics to induce authority and authorities to kneel before the racialized idol of whiteness. In an even more perilous, totalizing move, these authorities attempted to bleach and domesticate the Divine, to make over the Divine in their image and likeness. Thus, in adhering to the culture and customs of anti-blackness, ecclesial authorities, both episcopal and parochial, bound themselves to the idolatry of whiteness. These men abrogated to themselves interpretive and judicial power to justify geographic and spatial sequestering or segregation of black flesh and bodies. Their accommodation to anti-black logics included the establishment of segregated parishes, schools, and, in some cases, cemeteries; the denial, exclusion, and prohibition of black bodies from religious vows and from priesthood; and the proscription of black religious expression, culture, and spirituality.[6] Their accommodation to anti-black logics not only contested Catholic teaching regarding the *imago dei*, that all human beings participate in the divine likeness, not only defied the effect of Baptism, but interrupted the power of Eucharist to collapse barriers of space and relation.[7]

5. The indifference of Catholic authorities to the care of black bodies and (black) souls neither prevented black human beings from communicating with the Divine, nor drove them from that church which constitutes for them the singular way the Divine Three give their own self and life for the liberation of all. Since the Stono Rebellion[8] and, even, perhaps prior to it, God's black human creatures have improvised authenticity of life and worship in struggle, in ways that were and are spiritually defiant, intellectually imaginative, culturally creative, socially interdependent—in uncommon faithfulness.[9]

In subtle and in crude ways, American Catholicism has and continues to demonstrate contempt for black human creatures who share in the glory, beauty, and image of the Divine. Such contempt veers toward contempt of the Divine, toward blasphemy through enacting, even passively, a metaphysical violence. And such contempt toward being could set American Catholicism on the path of idolatry.

Notes

1. Cf. Jean-Luc Nancy, *Dis-enclosure: The Deconstruction of Christianity*, trans. Bettina Bergo, Gabriel Maleufaut, and Michael B. Smith (New York: Fordham University Press, 2008), 37.

2. Gianni Vattimo's phrase "a violence of metaphysics" refers to the "attempt to master the real by force," in "Towards an Ontology of Decline," in *Reading Metaphysics: The New Italian Philosophy*, ed. Giovanni Borradori (Evanston, IL: Northwestern University Press, 1988), 64.

3. Rinaldo Walcott, "The Problem of the Human: Black Ontologies and 'the Coloniality of Our Being,'" in *Postcoloniality—Decoloniality—Black Critique: Joints and Fissures*, ed. Sabine Broeck and Carsten Junker (New York: Campus Verlag, 2014), 93.

4. Rinaldo Walcott, "The Problem of the Human," 93.

5. Anthony Paul Farley, "The Black Body as Fetish Object," *Oregon Law Review* 97 (1997): 461–535.

6. See Cyprian Davis, *The History of Black Catholics in the United States* (New York: Crossroad Publishing, 1990); Bryan N. Massingale, *Racial Justice and the Catholic Church* (Maryknoll, NY: Orbis Books, 2010).

7. William T. Cavanaugh, "The World in a Wafer: A Geography of the Eucharist as Resistance to Globalization," *Modern Theology* (April 1999): 194.

8. John Thornton, "African Dimensions of the Stono Rebellion," *The American Historical Review* (October 1991): 1101–13. Thornton argues for the participation of black Catholic slaves in this rebellion.

9. See Jamie T. Phelps, *Black and Catholic: The Challenge and Gift of Black Folk; Contributions of African American Experience and Thought to Catholic Theology* (Milwaukee: Marquette University Press, 1997); Diana Hayes and Cyprian Davis, eds., *Taking Down Our Harps: Black Catholics in the United States* (Maryknoll, NY: Orbis Books, 1998); M. Shawn Copeland, LaReine-Marie Mosely, and Albert Raboteau, eds., *Uncommon Faithfulness: The Black Catholic Experience* (Maryknoll, NY: Orbis Books, 2009).

14. White Privilege

Charles E. Curran

This chapter first appeared as "Facing Up to Privilege Requires Conversion." *National Catholic Reporter*, June 18, 2016, 18–19.

This essay, an autobiographical narrative reflecting on my awareness of racism and white privilege in my theological journey, has not been easy to write. In the last few years, I have become somewhat educated about racism and white privilege. I have to face the reality that I barely recognized the problem of racism in my own somewhat extensive writings and was blithely unaware of my own white privilege.

Acknowledging my failure as a Catholic theologian to recognize and deal with the problem of racism in society and the church is only the first step toward a recognition of white privilege. Boston College theologian M. Shawn Copeland has rightly challenged us white theologians to recognize the omnipresent reality of white privilege and how it has affected our understanding of and approach to theology.

White privilege functions invisibly and systemically to confer power and privilege. Only very recently have I been educated to realize the extent and power of white privilege and my participation in it.

Here, too, I now realize the inadequacies and errors in some of my earlier approaches. I have tried to be supportive of minority colleagues in theology. At The Catholic University of America, I purposely went out of my way to encourage the African-American women who were working on their doctorates. I often went to sessions of professional societies when African-Americans and other minorities were presenting so that I could show my support for them.

On one occasion at a Call to Action conference, I went to a session given by an African-American woman theologian who was a former student. I was somewhat embarrassed because I embarrassed her. She saw me come in and sit in the last row and almost immediately told her audience that she was nervous because I had come to her session. She graciously thanked me publicly for the support I had already given her from the time that she was in graduate school.

Yes, I supported African-Americans and other minority Catholic theologians, and I was quite satisfied that I was doing what I could for the cause. But only recently have I become aware of the problem with such an approach. "I" was the subject; "they" were the object. "I" was graciously doing what I could to help and support "them."

In reality, the problem was "I" and not "them." I was blithely unaware of how white privilege had shaped my understanding of what was going on. The invisible and systemic nature of white privilege came through in my absolutizing my own limited, privileged position and making all others the object of my goodwill.

My perspective was the normative perspective from which all others were to be seen. My white theology was the theological standpoint from which all others were to be judged. I finally realized to some extent that I was the problem.

White privilege is invisible, structural, and systemic. Borrowing from Jesuit Fr. Bernard Lonergan, Copeland describes white privilege as biased common sense. Lonergan used the term *scotosis* to describe this reality. There is a need then to shed light on this evil and to overcome its invisibility to the person. White privilege is a structural sin that has to be made visible and removed.

Borrowing from Lonergan and Copeland, there is need for conversion and especially continuing conversion in overcoming white privilege. I have just begun to recognize white privilege as the problem, and I have to continually strive to uncover it in my own life and work.

On the basis of what I have read and experienced, there are three types of conversion involved—personal, intellectual, and spiritual.

With regard to the first conversion, activist Peggy McIntosh's seminal article, "White Privilege: Unpacking the Invisible Knapsack," is an eye-opener on the road to personal conversion. I have to see myself as the oppressor and as the problem. She lists about 50 different ways in which I, as a white person, am privileged because of being white. This privilege exists in practically every aspect of my life. Making matters worse, this privilege comes at the expense of others. I have to become much more aware of the role of white privilege in my daily life brought about by the systemic injustice of racism.

I became somewhat aware of white privilege two years ago when I was teaching a course in moral theology for the Perkins School of Theology at Southern Methodist University in their Houston program. Most of the students were older and second-career folks studying for ministry. There were twenty-one students in the class, including five African-Americans. In the exams and papers, the African-Americans received the lowest grades.

But I also broke the class down into four groups to role-play different cases of quandary ethics. In this role-playing, four of the African-Americans truly excelled. They understood exactly what was involved, went to the heart of the case, and presented the whole issue with intelligence and humor.

The African-American students in this role-playing showed themselves to be just as intelligent, and perhaps even more so, than the others in the class. But they did not have the same skills with regard to reading texts and writing papers. Obviously, they were products of a poor educational system that had never prepared them to read and write that well. In light of that experience, I reflected on my own privilege with regard to education. I was born to a family that took reading and education very seriously. My parents encouraged us to read and to get a good education. I went to good schools and had some excellent teachers. To this day, I still know the names of the sisters who taught me in grammar school.

As a seminary student and priest, the church paid for all my college, theology, and doctoral studies. I did not have to work, take out loans, or worry in any way about how my expensive education was paid for. This was not all due to white privilege, but it obviously was a privilege that very few others have had.

The second conversion is intellectual. Early on, I learned from Lonergan the importance of historical consciousness. The person as subject is embedded in one's own cultural and historical environment. No one can claim to be the neutral, objective, value-free knower. Liberationist and feminist theologies made me all the more aware of social location with its limits and biases.

I learned about the hermeneutic of suspicion and the need to recognize that the strong and powerful create the structures and institutions of our world. But I did not see racism and its connection to my white privilege until I was prodded by recent writings. I was trying to help and encourage African-American theologians to do their work. But I never realized how they could and should help me and my theology.

My failures here indicate the need for both a stronger moral imagination and for the other conversions to affect the intellectual conversion.

The third is spiritual conversion. In reading the literature, I was taken by how many theologians dealing with white privilege emphasize spiritual conversion.

At first, I was fearful that this was an escape to reduce the invisible, structural, and systemic reality of white privilege to the realm of the spiritual. The flight to the spiritual might be a dodge for avoiding the structural and institutional realities of life.

Yes, the flight to the spiritual can be an escape, but not for one who sees the spiritual as the primary area that affects all other aspects of human existence. In moral theology, I have emphasized the role of a fundamental option that gives direction to all aspects of life. But I have purposely not embraced a transcendental understanding of the fundamental option precisely because in my judgment it does not give enough importance to the historical and the concrete.

The spiritual thus influences the other two conversions—the intellectual and the personal.

Here, I remembered what I had forgotten for so long. In 1982, I had praised the radical social ethics approach of Paul Hanly Furfey for clearly recognizing the deep problems existing in American society—poverty, race, and nationalistic violence. The spiritual conversion of the radical Furfey made him see what others did not see. But unfortunately, in the ensuing years, I forgot what I had said then.

What effect will these beginning conversions have on my doing moral theology? At this stage of my life as a "senior" theologian, I am not going to become an expert on racism and white privilege. The best analogy for the future is what I have done with regard to feminist theology. I am not an expert in feminist theology, but I recognize the problem of pervasive patriarchy, I dialogue with feminism, and I have appropriated many of its insights into my own work. I hope to do the same with regard to racism and white privilege.

A spirituality that prays to a God who is also black and female can and should help open my eyes to white male privilege.

15. The Black Lives Matter Movement
Justice and Health Equity

Michael P. Jaycox

This chapter first appeared in *Health Progress* 97, no. 6 (November–December 2016): 42–47.

Sooner or later, the members of any organization with an interest in ethics will ask themselves a critical question: Whose voices, experiences, and concerns usually occupy the center, and whose have been relegated to the periphery?

Examining the relative distribution of power in the group typically helps in answering this question. For example, my work as a white participant in the Black Lives Matter movement has instructed me regarding the importance of placing in the center the voices, experiences, and concerns of black persons, women, and black women in particular, even when members of these groups represent a majority of the people in the room.

The sheer amount of power our racist and patriarchal society confers upon white, educated men like me underlines the fact that I must cultivate a deliberate habit of "de-centering" my own voice, experiences, and concerns in order to make myself less likely to dismiss and more able to hear those of black persons and women.

Practically speaking, the de-centering habit does not require silence so much as a willingness to cede the floor. This is not a contrived self-effacement, but, rather, an appropriate humility about whether or not I am able to know what is true and good solely by consulting my own standpoint. Although this may seem like one more exercise in postmodern moral equivocation or political correctness, the reality is that patterns of systemic oppression and privilege at the societal level make such habits ethically necessary at the interpersonal level, especially, but not exclusively, in the context of grassroots political organizing.

Catholic health care in the United States obviously is a large system with a distinctive institutional culture. Perhaps less obviously, its context is similar to that of grassroots organizations because it has a center and a periphery. Even with its noble mission and its purpose to heal suffering, Catholic health care's status as an inescapably human institution means it, too, is morally implicated in the patterns of privilege and oppression that characterize the society it serves.

Health care professionals, whether in Catholic or in secular facilities, frequently have been guilty of relegating to the periphery the voices, experiences, and concerns of patients who have endured terrible suffering—even while aiming to help them.

Systemic and Structural Causes

Such instances of well-intentioned but ultimately harmful paternalism are not attributable to a few bad apples in the profession; rather, the causes are systemic and structural. For example, we have institutional protections requiring the informed consent of human subjects participating in medical research because we know that researchers, left to their own devices, tend to prioritize interests other than those of the frequently vulnerable populations participating in the research.

Governed by the *Ethical and Religious Directives for Catholic Health Care Services*, the Catholic health care ministry "is rooted in a commitment to promote and defend human dignity."[1]

Basic human dignity is imperiled when members of vulnerable social groups are exploited by those with more power and excluded from participating in their fair share of society's benefits. Catholic health care prioritizes

> by service to and advocacy for those people whose social condition puts them at the margins of our society and makes them particularly vulnerable to discrimination: the poor; the uninsured and the underinsured; children and the unborn; single parents; the elderly; those with incurable diseases and

> chemical dependencies; racial minorities; immigrants and refugees.[2]

From the standpoint of Catholic theological ethics, this prioritization of the needs of the oppressed, even if it means sacrificing the preferences of the privileged, is necessary for promoting and protecting the common good of human society as a whole.

That being said, an ethical and political question remains: How should health care professionals working in Catholic facilities respond to the challenge of the Black Lives Matter movement? How can the vast institutional structure of Catholic health care serve the cause of racial justice?

Health Care Equity

Being a "bottom-up" grassroots coalition of many smaller groups rather than a "top-down" hierarchical organization, the Black Lives Matter movement has no official leadership structure. Political positions and policies are established at the local level and at national conferences by consensus. In addition to proposed reforms of the criminal justice system and policing methods, the movement has expressed concern about health care equity, or, to be more precise, outrage about the persistent threats to the health of black individuals and communities struggling to survive and thrive in U.S. society.

One branch of the movement, The Movement for Black Lives, calls attention in its extensive policy platform to the following health-related challenges: lack of access to quality health care in a prison system that disproportionately jails black inmates; lack of access due to discrimination against black persons who are transgender, queer, or gender nonconforming; lack of proximity to comprehensive health care facilities for black communities in racially and economically segregated neighborhoods; lack of culturally competent health care professionals; lack of access to mental health resources for black communities living with social instability, constant police surveillance, literal and structural forms of violence, and the resulting trauma; persistent racial disparities in insurance coverage, even in the midst of the expansion of Medicaid under the Affordable Care Act; and the political elusiveness of a public, single-payer system as the most realistic path to guaranteeing universal access to health care.[3]

Members of another branch of the movement, the student-led coalition WeTheProtesters, also express outrage that colleges and universities generally are not prepared to address the distinctive mental health struggles of black students, particularly on predominantly white campuses.[4]

Even this brief perusal of the health-related concerns of the Black Lives Matter movement is enough to warrant some caution on the part of health care professionals eager to respond. The temptation to propose premature answers, without first placing the voices, experiences, and concerns of black persons at the center, should be avoided. It is tempting, for example, to propose, fund, and implement new programs or initiatives that focus on increasing awareness of the adverse health effects of trauma or on improving the accessibility of health care resources in black communities. Such programs will indeed continue to be necessary and good, but they ultimately are insufficient for addressing the underlying structural causes of inequity, which are the focus of the movement's outrage.

Structural Racism as a Cause

The 2004 book *Aquinas, Feminism, and the Common Good* (Georgetown University Press) by Susanne DeCrane, PhD, addresses the structural causes of health inequity specifically from the standpoint of black women's health and the Catholic principle of the common good. In it, she called attention to the gaping racial disparity in breast cancer morbidity between white women and black women and diagnosed the structural causes of this disparity as lack of equitable access to preventive care and insurance coverage.

Her common-good approach to addressing the problem prescribed substantial reforms of the U.S. health care system as a whole, some of which have been partially attained by the Affordable Care Act since the time of her writing.[5] A most surprising omission in her analysis, however, is the absence of any speculation about whether racism itself might be a cause of higher breast cancer morbidity in black women and a threat to the common good, whereas she does discuss at length the intersection of patriarchy and capitalism as causes for the disparity.[6]

A similar pattern of omission can be found in an article by Fred Rottnek, MD, published in the July–August 2016 issue of *Health Progress*. Writing in response to the systemic health disparities in the St. Louis region, he references the medical fact that "persistent, toxic stress creates poor health outcomes," particularly when the pattern of allostatic overload begins in childhood and affects early neurological development.[7]

Moreover, he highlights the reality that the presence of violence is a prime cause of chronically elevated stress responses and, thus, is a social determinant of negative health outcomes. His essentially colorblind approach to violence, however, fails to identify clearly structural racism as a root cause of the violence affecting the St. Louis region, inasmuch as this racism is embedded in an economic system, housing system, education system, criminal justice system, and policing system that systematically target, exploit, and marginalize black communities, leaving them with not only very few legal opportunities for employment, but also worse health.[8]

From a structural standpoint, violence is primarily something white communities have done to black communities, not something black communities have done to themselves (a frequent misperception). In other words, the deepest threat to public health is not merely violence but, more profoundly, white dominance. To his credit, Rottnek is aware of the generations of racial and economic segregation in the St. Louis region, but his moral prescription to prevent violence and reduce the impact of trauma through the "Alive and Well STL" program does not reflect his having identified segregation as a root structural cause of the violence and trauma. Surely if the goal is to prevent the violence that traumatizes black communities, then the strategy should be to correct the root causes of violence in the unjust economic and political structures that benefit white communities and constitute the more fundamental threat to the common good.

Chronic Stress, Disparities

By focusing on racism as a social determinant of a variety of negative health outcomes for persons of color, we can see that the available evidence confirms the health-related concerns of the Black Lives Matter movement and reveals the magnitude of the problem to be truly staggering. For example, a 2007 study based on data from the on-going Black Women's Health Study at Boston University's Slone Epidemiology Center found that black women who perceive themselves to be impacted by racial discrimination have a higher risk for breast cancer than black women who do not, and by comparison with white women before age 40 (DeCrane did not have this information at the time of her writing).[9]

We have known since 1997 that the biological fact of lower (on average) birth weight for the children of black mothers is caused by the system of social subordination that is racism, and not putative genetic differences associated with race.[10] Both in the case of higher breast cancer risk and in the case of lower birth weight for their infants, black women are experiencing the biological effects of a chronically elevated stress response to racism (combined with patriarchy) over the entire course of their lives, and not merely during pregnancy or at the time of cellular mutation.[11]

Moreover, because of epigenetic mechanisms we are just beginning to understand, the trauma associated with a chronic stress response to racism can be inherited intergenerationally at the level of phenotypical expression of genes.[12] Black children literally are being born with the effects of racism already in their bodies.

The skeptic might respond by noting that there is some ambiguity in the public health community as to whether being black in the U.S. is, in itself, a significant social determinant of negative health outcomes, regardless of income level. Paul Farmer, the medical anthropologist and co-founder of Partners in Health, who articulated one of the first comprehensive, social-justice-oriented, international health agendas, has written that "where the major causes of death…are concerned, class standing is a clearer indicator than racial classification." Yet when faced with the available data, he says that "race differentials persist even among the [economically] privileged."[13]

In order to speak meaningfully about oppression on the basis of race in the context of U.S. society, one also must speak about oppression on the basis of economic class and vice versa, given that the white domination of black communities has been accomplished historically through the systematic extraction of economic resources and deliberate disinvestment by private and public institutions. Sociologist and Harvard

University public health professor David R. Williams, PhD, in examining the effects of this historical (and contemporary) pattern, observes that "although the majority of poor persons in the United States are white, poor white families are not concentrated in contexts of social and economic disadvantage and with the absence of an infrastructure that promotes opportunity in the ways that poor blacks, Latinos, and Native Americans are."[14]

If the goal is to eliminate health disparities determined by the interlocking oppressions of racism and economic class stratification, then reliance on a public health approach that aims only to increase incomes for all households living in poverty will not reduce racial disparities and may even make them worse.[15] Instead, more research and more input from communities struggling on the ground are both necessary for crafting adequate public health strategies that take into account the distinctive barriers to health that different black communities face, whether lower, middle, or higher income.[16]

Political Intervention

Despite the depth and complexity of the problems, they are not so overwhelming that positive steps are impossible; indeed, the Black Lives Matter movement requires political solidarity from those who have the power to influence the functioning of large social systems. If the vast institutional structure of Catholic health care, in particular, is going to make an impact for the cause of racial justice, what is demanded is not primarily a medical intervention, but rather a political intervention.

Health care professionals working in Catholic facilities have in their box of resources not only the fact that the system in which they participate has a stated commitment to making services more accessible to those who are oppressed, but they also have the considerable amount of educational and professional privilege they exercise as individuals. From a grassroots organizing standpoint, that privilege is an invaluable asset because it gives one political access to powerful people and the capacity to be an advocate for those who do not have such access. Just as white people are needed to challenge other white people to resist racism and take the claims of black organizations seriously, so doctors and nurses are needed to pressure elected officials to support progressive laws and policies capable of changing the economic and criminal-justice status quo that is so harmful to the health of black citizens.

A fine example of such advocacy work can be found in the White-Coats4BlackLives movement, which in 2014 was started by medical students at Icahn School of Medicine at Mount Sinai in New York City, Perelman School of Medicine at the University of Pennsylvania, and the University of California San Francisco School of Medicine. These students called upon health professionals everywhere to confront institutionalized violence against people of color in the policing system as a public health crisis.[17]

Moreover, they have offered a four-point agenda for pursuing racial justice in health care that includes increasing the number of physicians of color, eliminating implicit racial bias toward patients, advocating for a single-payer health care system in the U.S., and working to address structural racism embedded in social, political, and economic institutions.[18]

What if even more clinicians working in the Catholic health care system were to join this movement, and what if they couched their reasoning in terms of participating in a Catholic institutional commitment to racial justice and advocating on behalf of those who are oppressed? The organization already has chapters at the medical schools of Loyola University Chicago and Saint Louis University. Consider the difference that could be made if every Catholic medical school and hospital in the U.S. had a chapter.

Solidarity between Catholic health care institutions and the Black Lives Matter movement really isn't as simple as asking, "What are the actionable items?" Black health cannot make significant improvement in the context of the current economic and political structure of the U.S., at least not in the absence of a radically new distribution of power and resources.

And so, I invite those reading this article to share their own power and resources for the cause of social justice and health equity, which are among the deepest ethical aspirations grounding the ministry of health care.

Notes

1. See United States Conference of Catholic Bishops, *Ethical and Religious Directives for Catholic Health Care Services*, 5th ed. (issued November 17, 2009), part 1, "The Social Responsibility of Catholic Health Care Services," www.usccb.org/issues-and-action/human-life-and-dignity/health-care/upload/Ethical-Religious-Directives-Catholic-Health-Care-Services-fifth-edition-2009.pdf.

2. USCCB, *Ethical and Religious Directives*, Directive 3.

3. See the Movement for Black Lives, "Platform," https://policy.m4bl.org/platform/; and "Universal Health Care: One Pager," https://docs.google.com/document/d/1Ug0uwTZz5KuhoCWdlbLWh7GYin1ReGG-KNgrVG1Lr68/edit.

4. See WeTheProtesters, "The Demands," available at www.thedemands.org/.

5. See Susanne DeCrane, *Aquinas, Feminism, and the Common Good* (Washington, DC: Georgetown University Press, 2004), 149–50.

6. See DeCrane, *Aquinas, Feminism, and the Common Good*, 144–46.

7. Fred Rottnek, "How Can Our Communities Move Ahead after Ferguson?" *Health Progress* 97, no. 4 (July–August 2016): 50.

8. See David R. Williams and Selina A. Mohammed, "Racism and Health I: Pathways and Scientific Evidence," *American Behavioral Scientist* 57, no. 8 (August 2013): 1152–73.

9. See Teletia R. Taylor et al., "Racial Discrimination and Breast Cancer Incidence in U.S. Black Women: The Black Women's Health Study," *American Journal of Epidemiology* 166, no. 1 (2007): 46–54.

10. See Richard J. David and James W. Collins, "Differing Birth Weight among Infants of U.S.-Born Blacks, African-Born Blacks, and U.S.-Born Whites," *New England Journal of Medicine* 337, no. 17 (Oct. 23, 1997): 1209–14; also Richard J. David and James W. Collins, "Disparities in Infant Mortality: What's Genetics Got to Do with It?" *American Journal of Public Health* 97, no. 7 (July 2007): 1191–97.

11. See Michael C. Lu and Neal Halfon, "Racial and Ethnic Disparities in Birth Outcomes: A Life-Course Perspective," *Maternal and Child Health Journal* 7, no. 1 (March 2003): 13–30; and Fleda Mask Jackson et al., "Examining the Burdens of Gendered Racism: Implications for Pregnancy Outcomes among College-Educated African American Women," *Maternal and Child Health Journal* 5, no. 2 (June 2001): 95–107.

12. See Christopher W. Kuzawa and Elizabeth Sweet, "Epigenetics and the Embodiment of Race: Developmental Origins of U.S. Racial Disparities in Cardiovascular Health," *American Journal of Human Biology* 21, no. 1 (January 2009): 2–15.

13. Paul Farmer, *Pathologies of Power: Health, Human Rights, and the New War on the Poor* (Berkeley: University of California Press, 2005), 45–46.

14. David R. Williams, "Miles to Go before We Sleep: Racial Inequities in Health," *Journal of Health and Social Behavior* 53, no. 3 (2012): 284.

15. See David Mechanic, "Disadvantage, Inequality, and Social Policy," *Health Affairs* 21, no. 2 (2002): 48–59.

16. See David R. Williams, Naomi Priest, and Norman B. Anderson, "Understanding Associations among Race, Socioeconomic Status, and Health: Patterns and Prospects," *Health Psychology* 35, no. 4 (2016): 407–11.

17. See White Coats for Black Lives, www.whitecoats4blacklives.org.

18. See White Coats for Black Lives National Working Group, "#Black Lives Matter: Physicians Must Stand for Racial Justice," *AMA Journal of Ethics* 17, no. 10 (2015): 978–82.

Part Eight

WOMEN FROM THE MARGINS

16. *Mujerista* Theology
A Challenge to Traditional Theology

Ada María Isasi-Díaz

This chapter first appeared in Ada María Isasi-Díaz. *Mujerista Theology: A Theology for the Twenty-First Century*. Maryknoll, NY: Orbis Books, 1996.

One of the reviewers of my book *En la Lucha* pointed out that I have spent the last ten years of my life working at elaborating a *mujerista* theology. When I read this, I realized the reviewer was right: the elaboration of *mujerista* theology has been and will continue to be one of my life-projects. Since I know myself to be first and foremost an activist, an activist-theologian, the reason why *mujerista* theology is so important to me is because to do *mujerista* theology is a significant and important way for me to participate in the struggle for liberation, to contribute to the struggle of Latinas in the USA.

What is *mujerista* theology? In the first part of this chapter, after a general description of *mujerista* theology, I will explain some of the key characteristics and elements. In the second part I will deal with the challenges that *mujerista* theology presents to traditional theology. So, what is *mujerista* theology?

Mujerista Theology

General Description

To name oneself is one of the most powerful acts a person can do. A name is not just a word by which one is identified. A name also provides the conceptual framework, the point of reference, the mental constructs that are used in thinking, understanding, and relating to a person, an idea, a movement. It is with this in mind that a group of us Latinas[1] who live in the United States and who are keenly aware of how sexism,[2] ethnic prejudice, and economic oppression subjugate Latinas, started to use the term *mujerista* to refer to ourselves and to use *mujerista* theology to refer to the explanations of our faith and its role in our struggle for liberation.[3]

The need for having a name of our own, for inventing the term *mujerista* and investing it with a particular meaning became more and more obvious over the years as Hispanic women attempted to participate in the feminist Anglo-European movement in the United States. Latinas have become suspicious of this movement because of its inability to deal with differences; to share power equally among all those committed to it; to make it possible for Latinas to contribute to the core meanings and understandings of the movement; to pay attention to the intersection of racism/ethnic prejudice, classism, and sexism; and because of the seeming rejection of liberation as its goal, having replaced it with limited benefits for some women within present structures, benefits that necessitate some groups of women and men to be oppressed in order for some others to flourish. These serious flaws in the Euro-American feminist movement have led grassroots Latinas to understand "feminism" as having to do with the rights of Euro-American middle-class women, rights many times attained at the expense of Hispanic and other minority women. As the early 1992 national survey conducted by the Ms. Foundation in New York City and the Center for Policy Alternatives in Washington, D.C., called the "Women's Voices Project" showed:

> the term feminism proved unattractive, women of color saying it applied only to white women. The survey shows that, while 32 percent of all women reported they would be likely to join a woman's group devoted to job and educational opportunities, or supporting equal pay, and equal rights for women, substantially fewer reported they would join a "feminist" group devoted to these tasks. Thus we must demonstrate to women that "feminism" *means* devotion to the concerns women report, or we must find another term for women's activism.[4]

Mujerista is the word we have chosen to name devotion to Latinas' liberation.

A *mujerista* is someone who makes a preferential option for Latina women, for our struggle for liberation.[5] Because the term *mujerista* was developed by a group of us who are theologians and pastoral agents, the initial understandings of the term came from a religious perspective. At present the term is beginning to be used in other fields such as literature and history. It is also beginning to be used by community organizers working with grassroots Hispanic women. Its meaning, therefore, is being amplified without losing as its core the struggle for the liberation of Latina women.

Mujeristas struggle to liberate ourselves not as individuals but as members of a Hispanic community. We work to build bridges among Latinas/os while denouncing sectarianism and divisive tactics. *Mujeristas* understand that our task is to gather our people's hopes and expectations about justice and peace. Because Christianity, in particular the Latin American inculturation of Roman Catholicism, is an intrinsic part of Hispanic culture, *mujeristas* believe that in Latinas, though not exclusively so, God chooses once again to lay claim to the divine image and likeness made visible from the very beginning in women. *Mujeristas* are called to bring to birth new women and new men—Hispanics willing to work for the good of our people (the "common good") knowing that such work requires the denunciation of all destructive sense of self-abnegation.[6]

Turning to theology specifically, *mujerista* theology, which includes both ethics and systematic theology, is a liberative praxis: reflective action that has as its goal liberation. As a liberative praxis, *mujerista* theology is a process of enablement for Latina women that insists on the development of a strong sense of moral agency and clarifies the importance and value of who we are, what we think, and what we do. Second, as a liberative praxis, *mujerista* theology seeks to impact mainline theologies, those theologies that support what is normative in church and, to a large degree, in society—what is normative having been set by non-Hispanics and to the exclusion of Latinas and Latinos, particularly Latinas.

Mujerista theology engages in this two-pronged liberative praxis, first by working to enable Latinas to understand the many oppressive structures that almost completely determine our daily lives. It enables Hispanic women to understand that the goal of our struggle should be not to participate in and to benefit from these structures but to change them radically. In theological and religious language, this means that *mujerista* theology helps Latinas discover and affirm the presence of God in the midst of our communities and the revelation of God in our daily lives. Hispanic women must come to understand the reality of structural sin and find ways of combating it because it effectively hides God's ongoing revelation from us and from society at large.

Second, *mujerista* theology insists on and aids Latinas in defining our preferred future: What will a radically different society look like? What will be its values and norms? In theological and religious language this means that *mujerista* theology enables Hispanic women to understand the centrality of eschatology in the life of every Christian. Latinas' preferred future breaks into our present oppression in many different ways. Hispanic women must recognize those eschatological glimpses, rejoice in them, and struggle to make those glimpses become our whole horizon.

Third, *mujerista* theology enables Latinas to understand how much we have already bought into the prevailing systems in society—including the religious systems—and have thus internalized our own oppression. *Mujerista* theology helps Hispanic women to see that radical structural change cannot happen unless radical change takes place in each and every one of us. In theological and religious language this means that *mujerista* theology assists Latinas in the process of conversion, helping us see the reality of sin in our lives. Further, it enables us to understand that to resign ourselves to what others tell us is our lot and to accept suffering and self-effacement is not a virtue.

Main Characteristics

Following are descriptions of three main elements or key characteristics of *mujerista* theology that are closely interconnected. I develop the role of *lo cotidiano* at greater length since I have not done so before.

Locus Theologicus. The *locus theologicus*, the place from which we do *mujerista* theology, is our *mestizaje* and *mulatez*, our condition as racially and culturally mixed people; our condition of people from other cultures living within the USA; our condition of people living between different worlds, a reality applicable to the Mexican Americans living in the Southwest, but also to the Cubans living in Miami and the Puerto Ricans living in the Northeast of the USA.

Mestizaje refers to the mixture of white people and native people living in what is now Latin America and the Caribbean. *Mulatez* refers to the mixture of black people and white people. We proudly use both words to refer both to the mixture of cultures as well as the mixture of races that we Latinas and Latinos in the USA embody. Using these words is important for several reasons.[7] First of all, it proclaims a reality. Even before the new *mestizaje* and *mulatez* that is happening here in the USA, we all have come from *mestiza* and *mulata* cultures, from cultures where the white, red, and black races have been intermingled, from cultures where Spanish, Amerindian, and African cultural elements have come together and new cultures have emerged.[8] *Mestizaje* and *mulatez* are important to us because they vindicate "precisely that which the dominant culture, with its pervading racism, [and ethnic prejudice] condemns and deprecates: our racial and cultural mixture."[9] *Mestizaje* and *mulatez* also point to the fact that "if any would understand us, they must come to us, and not only to our historical and cultural ancestors."[10] *Mestizaje* and *mulatez* are what make "it possible for our cultures to survive. 'Culture' is a total way of responding to the total world and its ever changing challenges."[11] Culture has to do with a living reality, and as such it must grow, change, adapt. And our "new" *mestizaje* and *mulatez* here in the USA are just that, our actual ongoing growing, based on our past but firmly grounded in the present and living into our future.

Finally, *mestizaje* and *mulatez* are our contribution to a new understanding of pluralism, a new way of valuing and embracing diversity and difference. Later, we will discuss the issue of differences in greater detail. Suffice it to say here that the kind of pluralism that does embrace differences is about distributing opportunities, resources, and benefits in an inclusive way. To embrace differences at the structural level goes well beyond recognizing the multiplicity of interests and identities that exist in this society and their multiple claims on the institutions of the USA. Embracing differences, real pluralism, is first and foremost about making sure that

> institutional and economic elites are subjected to effective controls by the constituencies whose welfare they affect, that neither the enjoyment of dominance nor the suffering of deprivation is the constant condition of any group, and that political and administrative officers operate as guardians of popular needs rather than as servants of wealthy interests.[12]

Theologically, how do *mestizaje* and *mulatez* function? *Mestizaje* and *mulatez* are what "socially situates" us Hispanics in the USA. This means that *mestizaje* and *mulatez* as the *theological locus* of Hispanics delineates the finite alternatives we have for thinking, conceiving, expressing our theology.[13] For example, because *mestizaje* and *mulatez* socially situate our theology, our theology cannot but understand all racism and ethnic prejudice as sin and the embracing of diversity as virtue. This means that the coming of the kin-dom[14] of God has to do with a coming together of peoples, with no one being excluded and at the expense of no one. Furthermore, *mestizaje* and *mulatez* mean that the unfolding of the kin-dom of God happens when instead of working to become part of structures of exclusion, we struggle to do away with such structures. Because of the way mainline society thinks about *mestizas* and *mulatas*, we cannot but think about the divine in non-elitist, nonhierarchical ways.

Mestizaje and *mulatez* for us Latinas and Latinos are not givens. In many ways it is something we have to choose repeatedly, it is something we have to embrace in order to preserve our cultures, in order to be faithful to our people, and from a theological-religious perspective, in order to remain faithful to the struggle for peace and justice, the cornerstone of the gospel message. Because we choose *mestizaje* and *mulatez* as our theological locus, we are saying that this is the structure in which we operate, from which we reach out to explain who we are and to contribute to how theology and religion are understood in this society in which we live. *Mestizaje* and *mulatez* and the contributions they make to society's understanding of pluralism, therefore, is one of the building blocks of a *mujerista* account of justice.

Latinas' *Cotidiano* as Theological Source. From the very beginning of *mujerista* theology, we have insisted that the source of our theological enterprise is the lived experience of Hispanic women. We have insisted on the capacity of Latinas to reflect on their everyday life and the struggle to survive against very difficult obstacles. When in *mujerista* theology we talk about liberative daily experience, about Hispanic women's experience of struggling every day, we are referring to *lo cotidiano*. *Lo cotidiano* has to do with

> particular forms of speech, the experience of class and gender distinctions, the impact of work and poverty on routines and expectations, relations within families and among friends and neighbors in a community, the experience of authority, and central expressions of faith such as prayer, religious celebrations, and conceptions of key religious figures.[15]

These key religious figures are not only those of Christianity, Jesus and Mary his mother, but also those more exclusively Catholic like the saints, and those of popular religion, such as the orishas of different African religions and the deities of different Amerindian religions.

However, in *mujerista* theology, *lo cotidiano* is more than a descriptive category. *Lo cotidiano* also includes the way we Latinas consider actions, discourse, norms, established social roles, and our own selves.[16] Recognizing that it is inscribed with subjectivity, that we look at and understand what happens to us from a given perspective, *lo cotidiano* has hermeneutical importance. This means that *lo cotidiano* has to do with the daily lived experiences that provide the "stuff" of our reality. *Lo cotidiano* points to "shared experiences," which I differentiate from "common experience." "Shared experiences" is a phrase that indicates the importance differences play in *lo cotidiano*. On the other hand, "common experience" seems to mask differences, to pretend that there is but one experience, one way of knowing for all Hispanic women.[17] And *lo cotidiano* points precisely to the opposite of that: it points to transitoriness and incompleteness.

Lo cotidiano is not a metaphysical category, it is not an attempt to see Latinas' daily lived experience as fixed and universal. Rather it is a way of referring to the "stuff" and the processes of Hispanic women's lives.[18] *Lo cotidiano* is not something that exists a priori, into which we fit the daily lived experience of Hispanic women. *Lo cotidiano* of Latinas is a matter of life and death, it is a matter of who we are, of who we become, and, therefore, it is far from being something objective, something we observe, relate to, and talk about in a disinterested way. Finding ways to earn money to feed and clothe their children and to keep a roof over their heads is part of *lo cotidiano* for Latinas. Finding ways to survive corporal abuse is part of *lo cotidiano*. Finding ways to effectively struggle against oppression is part of *lo cotidiano*.[19]

Besides its descriptive and hermeneutical task, *mujerista* theology appropriates *lo cotidiano* as the epistemological framework of our theological enterprise. Therefore, *lo cotidiano*, the daily experience of Hispanic women, not only points to their capacity to know but also highlights the features of their knowing. *Lo cotidiano* is a way of referring to Latinas' efforts to understand and express how and why their lives are the way they are, how and why they function as they do.[20] Of course there are other ways of coming to know what is real; there are many forms and types of knowledge. Our emphasis on *lo cotidiano* as an epistemological category, as a way of knowing, has to do, in part, with the need to rescue Hispanic women's daily experience from the category of the unimportant. *Lo cotidiano* has been belittled and scorned precisely because it is often related to the private sphere, to that sphere of life assigned to women precisely because it is considered unimportant. Or is it the other way around?

In *mujerista* theology, then, *lo cotidiano* has descriptive, hermeneutical, and epistemological importance. The valuing of *lo cotidiano* means that we appreciate the fact that Latinas see reality in a different way from the way it is seen by non-Latinas. And it means that we privilege Hispanic women's way of seeing reality insofar as the goal of their daily struggle is liberation. This is very important for *mujerista* theology, for, though for us *lo cotidiano* carries so much weight, it is not the criterion used for judging right and wrong, good and bad. It is only insofar as *lo cotidiano* is a liberative praxis, a daily living that contributes to liberation, that *lo cotidiano* is considered good, valuable, right, salvific.[21] Were we to claim *lo cotidiano* as an ethical/theological criterion, norm, or principle we would be romanticizing *lo cotidiano*. Yes, there is much that is good and life-giving in *lo cotidiano* but there also is much that "obstructs understanding and tenderness, allowing to appear an abundance of postures of self-defense that are full of falsehoods, of lies, that turn *lo cotidiano* into a behavior that is not open to life."[22]

The importance we give to *lo cotidiano* steers *mujerista* theology away from any essentialism that would obscure precisely what is at the core of *lo cotidiano*: difference. At the same time *lo cotidiano* moves us from the "add and stir" version of feminist theology. As an epistemological category, *lo cotidiano* goes well beyond adding another perspective and points to the need to change the social order by taking into consideration the way Latinas see and understand reality. *Lo cotidiano* points to the fact that how we Hispanic women, women who struggle from the underside of history, constitute ourselves and our world is an ongoing process. It takes into consideration many different elements that we use to define ourselves as Latinas within the USA in the last years of the twentieth century.[23]

This does not mean, however, that *lo cotidiano* leads us to total relativism.[24] The fact that *lo cotidiano* is not the criterion, norm, or principle we use in *mujerista* theology does not mean that we use no criterion to judge right and wrong. As we have already said, we do recognize and hold liberation to be the criterion or principle by which we judge what is right or wrong, what is good or bad, what is salvific or condemnatory. By insisting as we have done on the "shared experiences" that constitute *lo cotidiano* we are trying to counter the isolationism inherent in individualism, the superiority inherent in claims of uniqueness, the hegemonic effect of false universalisms, all of which are intrinsic elements of absolute relativism. By saying that liberation is the criterion we use in *mujerista* theology, we are insisting on making it the core element, yes, the essential element of Hispanic women's morality and of all morality. In making liberation our central criterion, *mujerista* theology attempts to contribute to an elaboration of morality that revolves around solidarity with the oppressed and the search for ways of an ever more inclusive social justice.[25]

In no way is the specificity of *lo cotidiano* to be taken as an "anything goes" moral attitude. That attitude is possible only in those who have power, in those whose social-political reality is entrenched and, therefore, do not feel threatened by the rest of humanity. That attitude is possible only in those who feel their world is completely stable, that nothing needs to change and that nothing will change. That is why *lo cotidiano* of Latinas is totally unimaginable for the dominant group; that is why they are totally disengaged from *lo cotidiano* of two-thirds of the world; that is why they are incapable of conceiving new ideas, of creating new ways of organizing society, even ways that would help them to perpetuate the status quo.[26]

Our insistence on *lo cotidiano* indeed should be seen as a denunciation of inadequate and false universalisms that ignore Latinas' daily lived experience. It also is a denunciation of the oppression Hispanic women suffer. Our insistence on *lo cotidiano* is an attempt to make our Latinas' experience count, to question the "truth" spoken by those who have the power to impose their views as normative. But our insistence on *lo cotidiano* must not be read as denying the viability and need for shared agendas and strategies. On the contrary, *mujerista* theology is anxious to participate in developing those strategies for liberation, which we know can grow only out of real solidarity, and this, in turn, depends on a real engagement of differences rather than a superficial acknowledgment of them.

In *mujerista* theology, *lo cotidiano* has made it possible to appeal to the daily lived experience of Hispanic women as an authentic source without ignoring social location. On the contrary, *lo cotidiano* makes social location explicit for it is the context of the person in relation to physical space, ethnic space, social space. Furthermore, *lo cotidiano* for Latinas points both to the struggle (*la lucha*) against the present social order and to the liberating alternative that constitutes the core of our historical project: community (*la comunidad*). This means that *lo cotidiano* constitutes the arena where Hispanic women are confronted by the groups of which they are members. This makes it possible for them to judge their own personal understandings, aspirations, ambitions, projects, and goals in their lives. So *lo cotidiano* is where morality begins to play a role for Latinas.[27] *Lo cotidiano* becomes the lived-text in which and through which Hispanic women understand and decide what is right and good, what is wrong and evil.[28] As such *lo cotidiano* is not a private, individual category, but rather a social category. *Lo cotidiano* refers to the way Latinas know and what we know to be the "stuff" (*la tela*, literally, the cloth) out of which our lives as a struggling community within the USA is fabricated.[29]

Lo cotidiano for us is also a way of understanding theology, our attempt to explain how we understand the divine, what we know about the divine. I contrast this to the academic and churchly attempts to see theology as being about God instead of about what we humans know about God. *Lo cotidiano* makes it possible for us to see our theological knowledge as well as all our knowledge as fragmentary, partisan, conjectural, and provisional.[30] It is fragmentary because we know that what we will know tomorrow is not the same as what we know today but will stand in relation to what we know today. What we know is what we have found through our experiences, through the experiences of our communities of struggle. What we know is always partisan, it is always influenced by our own values, prejudices, loyalties, emotions, traditions, dreams, and future projects.[31] Our knowing is conjectural because to know is not to copy or reflect reality but rather to interpret in a creative way those relations, structures, and processes that are elements of what is called reality. And, finally, *lo cotidiano* makes it clear that, for *mujerista* theology, knowledge is provisional for it indicates in and of itself how transitory our world and we ourselves are.[32]

The insistence on *lo cotidiano* brings up the issue of how *mujerista* theology deals with the past. Does *mujerista* theology pay any attention to what Scriptures tell us about God, what the doctrines and dogmas of our churches tell us about the divine, what theologians throughout the centuries have said about God? We certainly reject any and all regurgitation of the past. Reflexive use of the past is *no* good. But reflective use of the past is an important method in *mujerista* theology. Our communities have their own living religious traditions. The religious beliefs and practices of grassroots Latinas are not *ex nihilo*, but rather are rooted in traditions passed on from our ancestors and certainly rooted in Catholic and, more recently, in Protestant religious teachings.

Using *lo cotidiano* of Hispanic women as the source of *mujerista* theology is an act of subversion. Our theology challenges the absolutizing of mainline theology as normative, as exhaustively explaining the gospels or Christian beliefs. Using *lo cotidiano* as the source of our theology means that Latinas are not the object of *mujerista* theology. Hispanic women are the subjects, the agents of *mujerista* theology.

A Specific Kind of Liberation Theology. The third characteristic of *mujerista* theology is that it is a liberation theology, a specific kind with its own characteristics. As in other liberation theologies, for us the unfolding of the kin-dom of God does not happen apart from history. We talk about "salvation-liberation," believing that both are interconnected and that to work for liberation for us Christians, which has to do with establishing justice in concrete ways in our world, is not necessarily different from being good Christians. For Latinas, our religious practices and beliefs contribute significantly to the struggle for liberation, the struggle for survival.

Part of this understanding is the fact that for us theology is a praxis. By praxis I mean reflective, liberative action. To understand theology as praxis means that we accept the fact that we cannot separate thinking from acting. *Mujerista* theology is not reflection upon action but a liberative action in and of itself. The daily actions of our communities as they struggle to survive need intentional thinking, and religion plays a role in the thinking and the motivation for action, as well as in the kind of action done and the reason for doing it. Furthermore, the insistence that grassroots Latinas do *mujerista* theology and that so doing is a liberative praxis indicates that they too are intellectuals. The regular understanding of "intellectual" connotes a social function, a professional category. Unfortunately, however, this meaning is usually extended to mean that intellectuals, in contrast to nonintellectuals, are the ones who are capable of intellectual activity. In reality, however,

> although one can speak of intellectuals, one cannot speak of non-intellectuals, because non-intellectuals do not exist.... Each [one] participates in a particular conception of the world, has a conscious line of moral conduct, and therefore contributes to sustain a conception of the world or to modify it, that is, to bring into being new modes of thought.[33]

Women in general (but, in particular, poor women with little formal education, and even more so women whose first language is not English—as is the case with many Hispanic women) are commonly not considered quite capable of articulating what they think. Yes, many consider that Latinas' ability to think is at best limited. It is clear to see, then, why *mujerista* theology's claim that grassroots Hispanic women are "organic intellectuals," that their articulation of their religious understandings is an element of this theology is in itself a liberative praxis.

Another important element of *mujerista* theology as a liberation theology is the part popular religion plays in it.[34] It is precisely this aspect of the religion of Latinas that provides the greatest impetus for our struggle for liberation. There is no way you can deal with Hispanics, study our culture, or read our literature without encountering popular religion. After the Spanish language, popular religion is the most important identifying characteristic of Latinas, the main carrier of our culture. Hispanic women's Christianity is of a very specific variety. Its main vehicle, the signs and symbols that it uses, and a significant part of its theology are based on medieval Christianity, the pre-Reformation, sixteenth-century Christianity of southern Spain. But this sixteenth-century Spanish Christianity is mingled with the religious beliefs and rituals of African and Amerindian cultures as well.[35]

Now "dominant North Atlantic theology has generally regarded popular religion as a primitive force of religious expression needing to be evangelized."[36] *Mujerista* theology, as most of Hispanic/Latino theology, on the other hand, "recognizes popular religion as a credible experience of the...[divine]; and as a positive reservoir of values for self-determination."[37] In other words, in *mujerista* theology we insist on "the normative, graced, and even universal dimensions of the 'salvific' manifestations of non-Christian religions."[38]

Popular religion plays a significant role in our struggles for survival and liberation. Many of us know from experience that it is mainly due to popular religion that Christianity is alive and flourishing among Latinas in spite of the lack of care and attention we have experienced from the churches. In popular religion we find a sense of embracing diversity that makes it possible for very different elements to influence each other to the point where each element is reformulated, maintaining its own specificity but not without taking into consideration the specificity of the other elements.

Challenges to Traditional Theologies

In pointing out the ways in which *mujerista* theology challenges traditional theologies I do not want to suggest that there is nothing good about traditional theology. But I do want to make it very clear that its relevance to what is going on in our world today is waning mainly because of the way in which it insists on dealing with tradition, because it does not take seriously the religion of the people but seems to prefer the doctrines and dogmas of the church, and because traditional theologies seem to be content with seeing themselves as accountable only, or at least mainly, to the institutional churches.

"Epistemological Vigilance"

The first challenge is born of a need we *mujerista* theologians recognize as primary: we must have "epistemological vigilance."[39] We need to be epistemologically vigilant as indeed traditional theology should also be. But while we recognize this need and embrace it, traditional theology rejects it or simply ignores it. Now, what understandings are encompassed within this term "epistemological vigilance"?

First, we *mujerista* theologians make a very serious and ongoing effort to be aware of our subjectivity. We need to have a "critical consciousness of the limits of our capacity to know reality, and of the 'concealing and distorting' tendencies of this same capacity."[40] We work hard at being aware of our ideological biases and, though it is not easy, we work hard at revealing such biases. This means that we have to be aware of how our own social situation colors our analysis of the religion of our communities and colors the way we say what we say in our theological writings.

Second, epistemological vigilance here refers to the constant need to evaluate how our theological enterprise contributes to the liberation of our people. And here I am referring not only to the results of our theology, our writings, but also to the way in which we conduct our research. The question "Who benefits from this?" should never be far away from our minds. We need to apply a hermeneutic of suspicion to our constructive proposals, to our narratives, to our whole theological enterprise.

Third, epistemological vigilance refers to the need to avoid avoidance. *Mujerista* theologians need to be able to grapple with differences, with contradictions. We need to engage each other, to press each other for greater clarity, to question each other. In order to do this we need to work very hard at maintaining our sense of community, at not giving in to destructive competition or, what is worse, ignoring each other.

Now, all of this is a challenge to traditional theology because one of the key elements of traditional theology is its so-called objectivity, its so-called immutability, its sense of being "official" and, precisely because it is official, of being the only perspective that is correct.

Mujerista theology denounces any and all so-called objectivity. What passes as objectivity in reality merely names the subjectivity of those who have the authority and/or power to impose their point of view. So instead of objectivity what we should be claiming is responsibility for our subjectivity. All theology has to start with self-disclosure. Self-disclosure as part of theology should give all those who in one way or another come into contact with our theological work our "actional route."[41] As a theologian I am obliged to reveal my concrete story within the framework of the social forces I have lived in. I am called to reveal the pivotal forces and issues that have formed me and that serve as my main points of reference. The idea in this kind of self-disclosure is to situate the subject, in this case myself, so that my discourse is understandable to others not only out of their own experience but insofar as they have the ability to go beyond the limits of their experience and see how my experience, because it is part of the processes of living, relates to and intersects with their experience, no matter how different both experiences are. In other words, the particulars of my life might not be something others can relate to easily, but by knowing a little about them, others will be able to find some point of contact, at least because of similarities in the processes of our lives. Thanks to those points of contact, others will be able to understand me and assess what I say without necessarily agreeing with me or limiting me to the scope of their experience.

Because subjectivity embraces the question "Who benefits from this?" *mujerista* theology challenges the so-called objectivity of traditional theology that refuses to recognize that it often tends to benefit the status quo at the expense of those who are marginal in church and society. The status quo is not a natural arrangement but rather a social construct originating with and maintained mainly by white, Euro-American males. Traditional theology offers intellectual backing for religious understandings and practices at the core of our churches, and it is easy to see who are those in charge of our churches.

Finally, *mujerista* theology's insistence on recognizing and disclosing subjectivity challenges the official status of traditional theology that results in avoidance of engagement. Traditional theology has clothed itself with the immutability that it claims is God's. Or does perhaps not that traditional theology make God immutable because it makes God in its own image and likeness?

Theology as a Communal Task

Our second challenge to traditional theology has to do with the centrality that community has in our Latino culture and in our theology. This means that we will continue to use the lived experience of our grassroots communities as the source of our theology. So the themes of our theology are those that are suggested to us by the religious understandings and practices of our communities and not by the doctrines and dogmas of our churches. The goal of *mujerista* theology is not to come up with a *Summa*, or with three volumes entitled *Systematic Theology #1*, *#2*, and *#3*. The themes *mujerista* theology deals with are those that are required by Latinas' struggle for liberation. Thus, in our first book we dealt with what grounds the struggle for many of us, our understanding of God.[42] The second book dealt with issues of self-identity—of ethnicity—and of moral agency.[43] And now we are working on issues of embodiment, for what is most commonly used against us, to oppress us, is our bodies.[44]

Yes, we need to continue to approach theology from the perspective of the religious understandings and practices of our communities. This means that we must resist the temptation to do theology as usual, not only by using different methods but also by resisting the temptation to follow the "regular" themes and divisions of traditional theology. In no way does this mean that our theology is not, should not be rigorous. We owe to ourselves and our communities the very best theology that we can do. But good theology for us *mujerista* theologians is a theology that helps our people in their struggle for survival, not a theology that receives the blessing of the status quo because it follows traditional patterns.

In a way traditional theology, even the best of traditional theology, by insisting on following the patterns established long ago in my opinion, closes itself to the ongoing revelation of the divine in our midst. Those who do traditional theology call their way of proceeding "faithfulness to the past." I call it "blindness to the present" and "ignoring the God-in-our-midst today."

The Importance of Differences

A third challenge *mujerista* theology presents to traditional theology has to do with *mestizaje* and *mulatez*, with how we understand and deal with diversity, with differences. For us differences are not something to be done away with but rather something to be embraced. In our theology we do not aim at assimilation, at making all that is different fit into some preconceived norm or center. That is not how we deal with diversity. Both our understanding of *mestizaje* and *mulatez* as well as our understanding of popular religion and how it functions in *mujerista* theology make explicit what we mean when we talk about embracing diversity.

Let me explain this further here. Usually in mainline discourse, in traditional theological discourse, difference is defined as absolute otherness, mutual exclusion, categorical opposition.[45] This is an essentialist meaning of difference in which one group serves as the norm against which all others are to be measured. Those of us who do not measure up are considered to be deviant, and our ideas are heretical. Difference of opinion, difference of perspective, arising most of the time from different life experiences, any and all differences are defined as exclusion and opposition.

This way of defining difference expresses a fear of specificity and a fear of making permeable the boundaries between oneself and the others, between one's ideas and those of others. Specificity tends to be understood as unique—lending it a certain air of "the unknown" of which one is afraid or which is romanticized as exotic.

In *mujerista* theology we posit embracing differences as a moral option. We work at seeing those who are different from us as mirrors of ourselves and what we think. Ideas that are different from ours are mirrors—not the only ones—we have for our ideas (ideas similar to ours, of course, also are mirrors of our ideas) for they do make us see our ideas in a new light, maybe even make it possible for us to better understand our own ideas, to clarify them for ourselves and for others, a result that might not be achieved if we were to ignore ideas different from ours.

To embrace differences, we have to stop being lazy and have to know what others really think. But that requires self-conscious interaction, and we are afraid of interacting with those with whom we disagree. Also, to be able to interact with others we have to affirm difference as something positive, we have to affirm plurality, to make permeable the boundaries of our categories. All of this requires embracing ambiguity, something those of us who live at the margins know much about. But traditional theology is not willing to do that because instead of risking ambiguity it rests secure in its impermeable and immutable center.

In *mujerista* theology difference, then, means not otherness or exclusive opposition but specificity and heterogeneity. Difference is understood as relational rather than as a matter of substantive categories and attributes. Difference is not then a description of categories, descriptions set one against the other across a barbed wire fence. Rather, difference points to the specificity of each description and seeks ways to relate those different descriptions, different because they come from people with dissimilar life experiences.

Embracing difference, welcoming ambiguity, is not in any way to be conceived as wishy-washiness! We are not advocating total relativity. As a matter of fact, because *mujerista* theology is a strategy for liberation, there is a certain discipline of action that we demand of each other. Also, in Latino culture, tradition is something very important. So tradition is taken into consideration. But the role of tradition is not to impose itself perennially without any changes. The role of tradition is to make present the wisdom of generations past that we are then called to evaluate and apply to the present in view of our need for survival, our need for liberation. And, unfortunately, that is an understanding of tradition that traditional theology is not willing to consider.

Conclusion

In many ways what has guided *mujerista* theology from the beginning are those wonderful words of Miriam in the book of Numbers, "Has Yahweh indeed spoken only through Moses?" (Num 12:2). Well aware of the fact that she suffered severe penalties for daring to scold Moses, for daring to claim that Yahweh also spoke to her and through her, our sister Miriam invites *mujerista* theologians to throw our lot with the people of God and to hope that, just as in her case, the authorities will catch up with us, that they will eventually also see that we have no leprosy, that we are clean. But their declaration of cleanliness is *not* what makes us clean; their saying is *not* what makes *mujerista* theology a worthwhile and important task for us. It is rather the fact that *mujerista* theology is part of the struggle for survival, the struggle for liberation—that is what makes it right and just for us to pursue it. Doing *mujerista* theology is an intrinsic element of our struggle, of our lives, because indeed, for Latinas in the USA to struggle is to live, *la vida es la lucha.*

Notes

1. There is no agreement among Latinas whether to refer to ourselves as "Hispanic women" or as "Latina women." My choosing to use *Latina* is done indiscriminately.

2. In *mujerista* theology heterosexism is understood to be a distinct element of sexism.

3. It is important to notice that we do *not* use the term *mujerismo* since it can be understood to indicate that Latinas' natural entity is based on being women when in fact our natural entity as women is based on being human. See Raquel Rodríguez, "La marcha de las mujeres...," *Passos* 344 (March–April 1991): 11n6.

4. Linda Williams, "Ending the Silences: The Voices of Women of Color," *Equal Means* 1, no. 4 (Winter 1993): 13.

5. Though the rest of this chapter refers more directly to *mujerista* Latinas, we intend here to make explicit that Latino men as well as men and women from other racial/ethnic groups can also opt to be *mujeristas*.

6. Rosa Marta Zárate Macías, "Canto de mujer," in *Concierto a mi pueblo*, tape produced by Rosa Marta Zárate Macías, P.O. Box 7366, San Bernardino, CA 92411. Much of this description is based on this song composed and interpreted by Rosa Marta in response to several Latinas' insistence on the need for a song that would inspire them in the struggle. For the full text of her song in English and Spanish, see Ada María Isasi-Díaz, "*Mujeristas*: A Name of Our Own," *Christian Century* 106, no. 18 (May 1989): 560–62.

7. Our usage of these words goes beyond their original meaning to include the mixing of Hispanics/Latinos in the USA with those of other races-cultures who

live in this country, and the mixing among ourselves Hispanics/Latinos coming from different countries of Latin America and the Caribbean.

8. I use *mulato* and *mulata* in Spanish to indicate that the social connotation that we give to this word is not as derogatory as the one given to it in the USA. By using the Spanish spelling, I also seek not to offend African Americans in this country who find the use of the word *mulatto* offensive.

9. Justo L. González, "Hispanics in the United States," *Listening—Journal of Religion and Culture* 27, no. 1 (Winter 1992): 14.

10. González, "Hispanics in the United States," 15.

11. González, "Hispanics in the United States," 15.

12. Michael Parenti, *Power and the Powerless* (New York: St. Martin's Press, 1978), 28.

13. Otto Maduro, *Religion and Social Conflict* (Maryknoll, NY: Orbis Books, 1982), 42–43.

14. I use "kin-dom" to avoid using the sexist and elitist word *kingdom*. Also, the sense of the family of God that "kin-dom" represents is much more in line with the centrality of family in our Latina culture. I am grateful to Georgene Wilson, OSF, from whom I learned this word.

15. Daniel H. Levine, *Popular Voices in Latin American Catholicism* (Princeton, NJ: Princeton University Press, 1992), 317.

16. Levine, *Popular Voices*, 317.

17. This has very serious methodological implications for *mujerista* theology. See Ada María Isasi-Díaz, *En La Lucha—Elaborating a Mujerista Theology* (Minneapolis: Fortress Press, 1993), chap. 3.

18. Sharon Welch, "Sporting Power—American Feminists, French Feminists and an Ethic of Conflict," in *Transfigurations: Theology and the French Feminists*, ed. C. W. Maggie Kim, Susan M. St. Ville, and Susan M. Simonaitis (Minneapolis: Fortress Press, 1993), 174.

19. I want to make absolutely clear that *lo cotidiano* is not to be understood as housekeeping chores in the sense that women's daily work is usually conceptualized: cleaning, doing laundry, driving the children to extracurricular activities. However, neither do I wish to diminish the importance of those kinds of tasks.

20. Otto Maduro, *Mapas para la fiesta* (Buenos Aires: Centro Nueva Tierra para la Promoción Social y Pastoral, 1992), 17.

21. In *mujerista* theology, salvation and liberation are intrinsically united. There can be no salvation without liberation. The realization of the kin-dom of God, which is what salvation refers to, begins to be a reality in history, and that is what liberation is. Liberation has to do with fullness of life, a prerequisite of the full realization of the kin-dom of God. For a fuller explanation, see *En la Lucha*, 34–45.

22. Ivone Gebara, *Conhece-te a ti misma* (São Paulo: Ediciones Paulinas, 1991), 24.

23. For an explanation of the elements that are key to the self-understanding of Latinas, see *En la Lucha*.

24. My main dialogue partners for these following paragraphs have been Margaret Farley and Leonardo Boff, whom I cite below. See Margaret Farley, "Feminism and Universal Morality," in *Prospect for a Common Morality*, ed. Gene Outka and John P. Reeder (Princeton, NJ: Princeton University Press, 1993), 170–90.

25. Leonardo Boff, "La Postmodernidad y la miséria de la razón liberadora," *Pasos* 54 (July–August 1994): 13.

26. Boff, "La Postmodernidad," 13. I am reminded here of one of the reasons Miguez Bonino gives for the preferential option for the poor and oppressed. According to him, since they have nothing to gain from the present structures, the poor and oppressed are capable of imagining a different future, something those who are set in protecting the present are not capable of doing. See José Miguez Bonino, "Nuevas tendencias in teologia," *Pasos* 9 (January 1987): 22.

27. Cecilia Mino G., "Algunas Reflectiones sobre pedagogia de género y cotinianidad," *Tejiendo Neustra Red* 1, no. 1 (October 1988): 11–12.

28. To claim *lo cotidiano* as lived-text is in no way to say that it is a moral criterion.

29. Though I do not agree with all of Mary McClintock Fulkerson's ideas, her book gives much to think about in our own *mujerista* theological enterprise. See her book *Changing the Subject: Women's Discourses and Feminist Theology* (Minneapolis, MN: Fortress Press, 1994).

30. Maduro, *Mapas para la fiesta*, 137.

31. And in *mujerista* theology we are very clear about our partisan perspective. We make a clear option for the perspective of Latinas based on the fact that we believe the Christian message of justice and peace is based on an option for the oppressed.

32. I have here adapted Maduro's synthesis about knowledge. See *Mapas para la fiesta*, 136–38.

33. Antonio Gramsci, *Prison Notebook*, ed. and trans. Quintin Hoare and Geoffrey Norwell Smith (New York: International Publishers, 1975), 9.

34. Generally, popular religion is understood along the lines of less sophisticated nonsystematic, almost dealing with magic. Here it means nothing of that but simply refers to "the religion of the people."

35. At present certain Pentecostal elements are beginning to be integrated into Latino popular religion.

36. Arturo Bañuelas, "U.S. Hispanic Theology," *Missiology* 20, no. 2 (April 1992): 290–91.

37. Bañuelas, "U.S. Hispanic Theology," 290–91.

38. This quotation is taken from unpublished notes of Orlando Espín and Sixto García for a presentation they made at the Catholic Theological Society of America. An edited version of their presentation/workshop can be found in the *Catholic Theological Society of America Proceedings* 42 (1987): 114–19.

39. This term is used by Maduro. In his work it refers mainly to the meaning I notice in the next paragraph. See Maduro, *Religion and Social Conflict*, 27–29.

40. Maduro, *Religion and Social Conflict*, 27.

41. Mark Kline Taylor, *Remembering Esperanza* (Maryknoll, NY: Orbis Books, 1990), 1–18.

42. Ada María Isasi-Díaz and Yolanda Tarango, *Hispanic Women: Prophetic Voice in the Church* (San Francisco: Harper & Row, 1988; reprint, Minneapolis: Fortress Press, 1992).

43. *En la Lucha*.

44. We are in the process of doing reflection weekends with Latinas all around the country to collect material on how Latinas understand and relate to our bodies.

45. I am indebted to the work of Iris Marion Young on the issue of diversity. See Iris Marion Young, *Justice and the Politics of Difference* (Princeton, NJ: Princeton University Press, 1990), particularly chap. 6.

17. Faith of Our Mothers
Catholic Womanist God-Talk

Diana L. Hayes

This chapter first appeared in *Uncommon Faithfulness: The Black Catholic Experience*. Edited by M. Shawn Copeland, 129–46. Maryknoll, NY: Orbis, 2009.

She is clothed with strength and dignity,
  and she laughs at the days to come.
She opens her mouth in wisdom,
  and on her tongue is kindly counsel.

(Prov 31:25–26)

It can be argued that I am using these verses somewhat out of context, for they are taken from a section of Proverbs that describes the ideal wife! But my purpose is not to consider the qualities of the "ideal wife" but to consider how for centuries, especially in the United States, women of color, and especially African American women, whether Protestant or Catholic, were seen as "ideal" only as models for slavery, sexual abuse, racial discrimination, and any and all other forms of degradation and dehumanization. Yet somehow they remained women "clothed with strength and dignity" who, through their shared wisdom and that of their ancestors, were instrumental not only in preserving themselves but in building up and preserving the black community as a whole—women, men, and children.

The daughters of Africa who now make their home in the United States have had almost five hundred years in which to be perfected as women of God. They came nameless and unknown, identified only as "Negro woman, age about six or twelve or twenty-two." They may have come with family and/or friends, caught up in the sudden invasion of their village life and daily round of farming or grazing, cooking and weaving, or they came alone, sharing little but fear of the unknown with those captured and traded with them.

New relationships were forged as they were thrown, often unclothed, always defenseless, into the holds of countless ships with names like *Jesus* or *Blessed Redeemer*, but which they saw and experienced as floating hells, places of licentiousness and terror, as they were raped, fed slops, and often, at the first sign of "bloody flux," thrown overboard alive, food for the always accompanying sharks.

When they landed, off-loaded from the "big canoe" that had taken them over the "river without banks," they found their situations had not improved but worsened. They were separated from family and friends, from those who understood their language or shared their culture, and sold to men with lust in their eyes, to serve as breeders, field hands, wet nurses, and maids of all work. Cuffed and shackled, they were taken to distant farms and plantations and quickly realized that this was to be their fate in life: to work from "can't see to can't see"; to be treated as farm animals, mere beasts of labor; to be bred to strangers, to give birth only to see their offspring sold from them over and over again. In other words, they lived and died as property. Not for them was the protected pedestal of "true womanhood." They were not seen as "ideal" women or wives, even for their fellow slaves. This myth, used to protect but also confine white women, "stressed piety, purity, submissiveness,[1] and domesticity for women as well as innocence and modesty." African American women, however, were not included in this understanding, as they were required to work in the same fields as their men. At the same time, purity and innocence were unattainable because of the uses to which they were put by greedy men and unscrupulous women.

The social and legal institution of slavery that assigned ownership of slave women's bodies to their owners officially denied slave women of the right to reject any sexual overtures and, by extension, also denied the presumption of virtue to black women (free or slave), who often had to deal with the sexual advances of white men.[2]

Yet they did not despair, nor did they turn away from all hope. They had not come empty-handed to this new world but had brought with them a deep and abiding faith in a God of creation, a God of justice and honor—however God was named in their particular communities. They were survivors, not in the silly sense of today's so-called reality shows, but in the deepest sense of those who survived experiences conducive to death. It is Hagar, the slave woman and concubine of Abraham, who exemplifies black women's experience of survival. For Hagar experiences what Delores Williams calls the "wilderness experience," an experience that all African Americans have shared in slavery and afterward. Her experience revealed the wilderness not as something to be overcome or conquered but as a place of refuge. In her first wilderness experience, Hagar

> meets *her* God for the first time. Her experience with this God could be regarded as positive by African Americans because God promises survival, freedom and nationhood for Hagar's progeny. The African American community has, all of its life, struggled for survival, freedom, and nationhood.[3]

But Hagar's experience, like that of most slave women, does not end here. She is forced to return to the wilderness as a free woman with her child but without resources of any kind, just as the slaves experienced a "freedom" in the name only at Reconstruction's end as they had nothing but themselves.

Like African American people, Hagar and her child are alone without resources for survival. Hagar must try to make a living in the wide, wide world for herself and her child. This was also the task of many African American women and the entire community of black freed people when emancipation came.[4]

Williams continues:

> The post-bellum notion of wilderness (with Hagar and child as its content) emphasized black women's and the black community's negative economic experience of poverty and social displacement....This post-bellum African American symbolic sense of wilderness, with Hagar at its center, makes the female figure symbolic of the entire black community's history of brutalization during slavery; of fierce survival struggle and servitude after liberation; of children being

> cheated out of their inheritance by oppressors; of threat to the life and well-being of the family; of continuing search for a positive, productive quality of life for women and men under God's care.[5]

It is not known how many of the millions of Africans who endured the middle passageway to the Americas were Catholic Christians (converted and baptized by the Portuguese from the fifteenth century on), Muslims, or followers of the traditional African religions. What is known is that they brought with them a shared world view that, when later syncretized with the Christian faith of their captors, enabled them to persevere, sustained by their belief in a "wonderworking" God who would, in God's own time, free them from the unmerited captivity in which they passed their weary existence.

Brought from the western lands of Africa, people of many tribes, cultures, and languages shared a world view that enabled them to survive four hundred-plus years of slavery, segregation, discrimination, and second-class citizenship. This world view was sacred, resisting the dualistic separation of the sacred and secular domains that their captors/enslavers sought to instill in them. African women and men "knew" God intimately as active, either as Godself or through intermediaries, in their everyday lives, and that knowledge nurtured and sustained them. Religion was seen as all-pervasive, surrounding them on all sides. The holy was a constant presence in their lives and all of life was sacred, from womb to tomb, before and beyond, weaving a web of connections that encompassed both the living and the dead. This religious understanding helped them to create community, for individualism was not a part of their self-understanding. Rather, the "I" of the individual was seen to exist and persist only in the "we" of family and friends—blood and fictive kin who played substantial roles in their lives and the lives of their descendants. They took this understanding and wove it into their reception of the God of Jesus Christ who, they believed, had suffered like them and shared in their pain. This God, who had himself been whipped and lynched, had freed others wrongly enslaved, and despite the insistence of their owners that God had willed their captive status, they knew that God would in time free them as well.

Those Who Were Before Us

Black women are the critical part of this understanding for they are the "bearers of culture," those who passed on the stories, songs, prayers, and memories of the people. They were able to form a connection that, rather than being broken, was strengthened and expanded in the Americas to encompass all who were enslaved.

> [Women] were the heads of their communities, the keepers of the tradition. The lives of these women were defined by their culture, the needs of the community, and the people they served. Their lives are available to us today because they accepted responsibility when the opportunity was offered—when they were chosen. There is the element of transformation in all of their work. Building communities within societies that enslaved Africans, they and their people had to exist in, at least, dual realities. These women, however, became central to evolving the structures for resolving areas of conflict and maintaining, sometimes creating, an identity that was independent of a society organized to exploit natural resources, people, and land.[6]

These structures remain to this day as symbols of the strength, courage, and steadfast faith of these nameless and unknown African women who laid the foundation for the millions who followed them.

The majority of black Catholics came speaking Spanish or French as well as their native languages except for those, fewer in number and later in their arrival, who came with the English Catholic settlers to the colony of Maryland. Most came long before others from Africa, beginning as early as the sixteenth century, and were both free and slave.

> The first Africans to arrive in what is now the continental United States were Spanish-speaking and Roman Catholic. The Spanish government introduced in 1565 the colony of St. Augustine in northern Florida....The baptismal registers, which began with the colony and are the oldest ecclesiastical documents in American history, witness to the presence of

> Blacks among the first inhabitants of St. Augustine. In these registers, Blacks and mulattos are clearly designated as such, along with the indication of whether the individual was slave or free.[7]

Today we are just beginning to uncover and explore the histories and the stories of the women of this and other Catholic colonies. They are our mothers, our "sheroes," women who somehow, despite all of the forces arrayed against them, were able not simply to preserve a culture but to pass it on to those coming after them. We know very little about black Catholic women, free or slave, except for the names found in old baptismal and marriage records. But, as Fr. Cyprian Davis has indicated, these clearly noted who was black or mulatto, quadroon, or some other mix of Africa with the native people of this "new world" to which they had been brought as well as the blood of their captors and oppressors, the Europeans, whether French, Spanish, or English speaking. We know they were co-founders of cities, but we also know them as women who worked long hours and seemingly impossible jobs in order to keep their families intact, their children baptized and catechized, and their faith strong in the face of opposition from so many within their own church as well as society.

The full story is not yet written, partly because the stories of all women, regardless of race or ethnicity, have historically been ignored for centuries. In the case of black Catholic women, however, it is also because there were so few able to recover or interested in recovering these histories. It is only in the aftermath of the Second Vatican Council that we began to see, as a result of increasing numbers of black Catholic women entering into theological programs of study, efforts to uncover, recover, and proclaim these and other critical stories. It is vital that we do so, for they are the foundation for the black Catholic community today: women who worked side by side with black Catholic men, but who also had the courage and foresight to come together as women in the church today to struggle for change.

They were lay and religious, slave and free, women like Henriette De Lille and Elizabeth Lange, founders of religious orders who chose to live lives of obedience to God rather than as concubines or servants, whose stories have finally been written and published. They also include women like Coincoin, a former slave and successful plantation owner who, after receiving her freedom and that of one of her ten children, spent the rest of her life purchasing the freedom of the remainder as well as all of her grandchildren. We also call forth the names of Ellen Terry, who established Catholic settlement houses in the East and Midwest, and Dr. Lena Edwards, the first board-certified African American female obstetrician and gynecologist. We can say that they all had a dream, a dream of a time when Catholics of African descent would not only be welcomed in their churches as full and equal participants in God's mission but would also be leaders, honored for their contributions to the life of the church at every level. Through their perseverance in faith, these women, the "bearers of culture," as all women are, gave birth to a people and a world that persist to this day. As Fr. Cyprian Davis affirms, speaking of black Catholic religious women:

> In an era when black people were accorded little or no respect or esteem, in a time when black women were degraded by slaveholders or abused by white employers, in a society where black women were considered to be weak in morality, black sisters were a counter sign and a proof that the black Catholic community was rooted in faith and devotion, for vocations arise from a faith-filled people. Lest it be forgotten, the two black sisterhoods were not European transplants; they were very much American in origin.[8]

These women were mothers in the fullest sense of the word, one not limited by biological or blood ties. They were mothers to an entire people, seeking through the work that they did to enable them to survive and thrive. As Fr. Davis states, "The African American religious sisterhoods helped lay the faith foundation of the black Catholic community....As pioneers, they often worked without encouragement or support and too often in the face of indifference and antipathy. Without them, the black Catholic community would not be what it is today."[9]

But the sisters were not entirely alone in their struggle. They were joined and supported by black Catholic mothers who, within their families, the domestic church, not only planted the seeds of faith but nurtured them until they bloomed into black Catholic men and women determined to carve out a niche for themselves and their people, not only in the

Catholic Church but in the United States as well. It is the lives of faith of these women that serves as the source from which Catholic womanist theology springs forth.

The Birth of Womanist Theology

Womanist theologians use the "stuff" of women's lives to spin a narrative of their persistent effort to rise above and beyond those persons and situations that attempt to hold them down. Their sources are social, political, anthropological, and especially, literary.[10]

Womanist theology, a theology of, by, and for black Christian women acting to build (and rebuild) community, emerged at a critical time in the history of Christianity and the world, a time of revolutionary change in which "the least among us" began to take charge of their own lives and, as a result, of how their stories were told and their faith life presented. It is a theology that seeks to give women of African descent in the United States a voice by enabling them to speak the truth of their historical and contemporary experiences as black and Catholic women, a truth both bitter and sweet, a truth that relates how they were able to "make it through." The term *womanist* comes, of course, from the poet and author Alice Walker, who sought a descriptive term for "audacious, courageous, bold and daring" black women that neither restricted them with definitions already developed and concretized by others who had not shared their experiences, not required them to place a "color" before their names to distinguish them from normative society. To be womanist is to be black; to be black is to be womanist, at least, as the term has been developed and deepened by black female Christian theologians such as Delores S. Williams, Jacqueline Grant, and Kelly Brown Douglas, among others. As a critical response to the absent voice of women of color in both feminist (normatively white) and black (normatively male) liberation theologies, womanist theology seeks to bring the presence and activity of black women to the forefront, rather than the background, of the church's awareness and dialogue.

Both Protestant and Catholic theologians have helped to deepen our understanding of this term, in keeping with the ongoing endeavor in which all theologians are ostensibly engaged—the effort of "faith seeking understanding" in such a way that the faith can be explicated for others. It is an exercise in "doing" theology, praxis rather than merely "thinking," without putting the results of that reflection into action. It is an exercise that engages heart, mind, and spirit in the effort to correlate the historical experience of all black folk, man, woman, or child, with the gospel. Thus, womanist theology is also a theology of liberation, one that both liberates those *doing* that theology, turning them from the objects they have been made into by others into subjects of their own histories, as well as liberating theology from the rigid, top-down strangle-hold of abstraction and objectivity that, for centuries, has held it in captivity. This approach enables theology to speak on behalf of those unjustly wronged and dehumanized as Jesus himself did.

Womanist theology starts with black women, women of African descent, in their own particular situations. It engages their historical experience and seeks to reorient reality through the eyes of a black woman. Womanist theologians, Protestant and Catholic, seek to speak a new language, a God-talk, thus, springs from centuries of denigration and dehumanization, from the denial of our female persons and the right to control our own bodies, minds, and spirits. It is a struggle that continues into the present day, to articulate what it means to be a black woman and, more particularly for me, to be a black Catholic woman in the world and in the church today. It is also a theology that seeks to confront not just race or class or gender or sexuality or any other forms of oppression that continue to flourish into the twenty-first century but to confront all of these at the same time and to eliminate the dualistic separation of various forms of oppression that have kept people who share in oppression in their own bodies and lives, in their families and communities. Oppression cannot be dealt with singly; it must be attacked like the virus it is, one that simply mutates and changes form as it moves from one place and one people to another. It can be eradicated only when it is attacked from an angle that addresses all of this venomous reality.

The Challenges Womanist Theology Raises

As women of African descent, we look first to Africa as the cradle of our history, culture, and traditions, seeking to tap into the river of spirituality that flowed through our ancestors and enabled them to survive the middle passage, Jim Crow, segregated pews and segregated sacraments, and still speak a word of life and hope to those coming after them.

There is a "generational continuity" (the passing on of cultural values and personal history), traditionally the domain of women, that can be seen to continue today as black women writers, for example, focus "on Africa not only as historical ancestor, political ally, and basis for ideological stance but as part of a continuum in which Black women, before the slave trade and since, have recorded cultural history and values through their stories."[11]

A "cultural continuity" also exists in the perpetuation of African values and customs in the Americas. "The cultural mores and values systems are passed down through the female members of the society, especially through and to the children."[12] Continuing this tradition, African American communities have attempted historically, through their women, to retrieve, regather, and repair the often scattered and torn-apart roots of their African culture and reshape them in ways that are renewing and reviving for their people today. This is the wellspring out of which womanism pours forth. It reveals a critically different understanding of values and individual and communal responsibility.

Catholic womanist theologians seek to explore the intersection of race, class, gender, sexuality, and religion in an effort to reveal the role the Christian religion, especially Roman Catholicism, has played in affirming, exploiting, perpetuating, and upholding understandings of social constructs that have served to provide not only a language but a pervasive, hegemonic ethos of subordination and oppression of women and persons of color. Grounded in the neo-platonic dualistic separation of the sacred and secular worlds, such an understanding has enabled the spread of a race-based hierarchical/patriarchal system that supported the enslavement not just of other human beings but of other Christians, the dehumanization of women and persons of color, and a stance that supports rather than challenges the oppression of so many.[13]

The challenge today is to look at these social constructs, including religion itself, as they have come to be constituted in the United States, through eyes that have been opened by the recognition of the "other-createdness" from which they emerged. Dualistic systems allow for the emergence of an "either/or" understanding of life, knowledge, morality, and society. Dualism enables the differentiation of human beings into "us and them," into "human and nonhuman," into those we recognize as friend and "others" by whom we feel threatened. It speaks a coldly sterile language of negativity, dualism, separation, subordination, and alienation.

Three examples can serve to demonstrate how a womanist critical lens can take a story that we have heard countless times and see it and its significance very differently. We can begin with the models of womanhood and femininity that have historically been such a significant part of our church's teachings on women. Mary, the mother of God, is contrasted eternally with either Eve, the alleged cause of humanity's fall into sin, or Mary Magdalene, the repentant sinner. Are these women as strikingly different from each other as they have been portrayed? First, a disclaimer: I am not a scripture scholar; you might say that I am simply attempting to recover the rest of the story. And when we read Genesis 2 and Luke with a critical womanist eye, we do begin to see something quite different from the story to which we are accustomed.

Beginning appropriately with the text of Genesis and the second Creation story, a careful reading finds no mention in that story that Eve committed a sin (her son Cain, the first murderer, is the first sinner), nor is she cursed by God (the serpent is), nor can it be said that she seduced or in any other way forced Adam to eat of the fruit of the tree in the garden's center. She is, ironically, the first person in the Bible to serve someone food, something women have been doing from then on. But she and Adam are expelled from the garden because they have acquired knowledge, that is, they have become thinking, aware human beings. It could be said that they have become fully human.

Yet many if not most interpretations of this story place fault solely with Eve, the gateway, as she and all women have been called, of hell, a woman guilty—if of anything—only of seeking greater knowledge than was deemed good for her. From a womanist perspective, as the descendant of a people forbidden to learn how to read and write at pain of death but also, ironically, stigmatized as incapable of learning, being only at best "bright monkeys," Eve's story for black women is not one of sin but of courage and boldness, of persistence in the pursuit of knowledge, a persistence to learn under almost impossible conditions after a day of backbreaking labor—but a pain deemed worthy of repeating over and over again (as women do by bearing more than one child, and as the slaves and freed slaves did when persisting in their efforts to gain an education despite whippings, beatings, and being burned out of their homes and schools). The pain is overcome by reward, greater knowledge, a goal historically deemed worthy of pursuit only by men, and white men at that.

Mary Magdalene has also been maligned down through the ages. For centuries venerated as the Great Apostle and the Apostle to the Apostles because of her unique role in being present at the resurrection as well as being commissioned by Jesus himself, the resurrected Christ, to spread the good news, the gospel, to others, she was unceremoniously demoted and commingled with other unnamed women in the New Testament as a prostitute and repentant sinner. This is a stigma that remains to the present day despite the church's *sotto voce* reversal of that commingling. This appears in a footnote in the *Roman Missal* and in John Paul II's acknowledgment of her, once again, as the Great Apostle. From a womanist perspective, the Magdalene speaks for and to countless unnamed black women, slave and free, who were condemned for their allegedly "sluttish" behavior, a lie put forth by the very men, Christian for the most part, who used their positions of power to rape them and even profit from the offspring produced as a result of the rape. Black women today must still live down the slander of being "Jezebels," women with uncontrollable sexual appetites, as well as "Sapphires" or "sistas with attitude," in the newest permutation of the same aspersion, that is, women who are willing to stand on their faith in themselves and their God in order to speak words of truth to their people, and anyone else who needs to hear, words that may seem harsh and at times unloving but that are spoken out of love and the effort to give life, as Mary Magdalene did.

Finally, there is the Virgin Mary. For two millennia we have been taught as women to revere and model ourselves after a Mary, meek and mild, who humbly bowed her head and submitted unquestioningly to the will of God. Feminist theologian Elizabeth Johnson notes in her recent book about Mary the words of author Mary Gordon:

> Mary was a stick to beat smart girls with. Her example was held up constantly: an example of silence, of subordination, of the pleasure of taking a back seat....For women like men,

> it was necessary to reject the image of Mary in order to hold onto the fragile hope of intellectual achievement, independence of identity, sexual fulfillment.[14]

For Gordon and many like her, Johnson notes that "the Marian tradition is accused of distorting women's reality, of promoting a restrictive idea of human fulfillment, of constricting women's social roles, of blocking their access to God's blessing in the fullness of their lives. It has presided over the evil of sexism rather than challenged it."[15]

Once again, let us look at the story from a womanist perspective. In today's understanding, Mary is still a child, barely if at all into her teens. She is betrothed to a much older man, as was the custom of the day. She is approached by the angel Gabriel, who speaks words to her that are both mysterious and frightening. She does not simply accept what the angel has to say to her; she questions him for she is understandably "troubled" by his words. She is then told that, having found favor with God, she will conceive and bear a son whom she will call Jesus. Like many slave women, Mary is basically being told what her life will be. Yet she again, probably to the angel's amazement, questions him. As yet she has not been very meek or submissive; she wants to know *how* this is possible, *how* it will come about. Gabriel's response is intended to resolve her fears and confusion once and for all, but at the same time to remind her of the power of God. To further convince her, he tells her that her cousin Elizabeth, whom Mary knows is not only barren but also beyond her child-bearing years, has also conceived and is in her sixth month of pregnancy. Only then does Mary agree to the miracle about to unfold within her.

What is the significance of all this? First, like Hagar, Mary is being spoken to directly rather than through a man such as her husband, father, or uncle. At the same time, she has not sought and does not seek permission from a man for her response, her "let it be done." Remember now, Mary, though betrothed, is still quite young and a virgin. But she knows the customs of her people and the harsh consequences for being found pregnant prior to having been wed. She would be taken outside of her village and stoned to death. She knows that what she is being asked to agree to (and she *is* being asked, because Gabriel, as we saw, has to convince her that all that he has said is possible) could cost her life and would certainly derail her engagement to Joseph, who, as we later read, does intend to break off the engagement once he discovers that she is pregnant.

We read the annunciation story in just a few minutes, but for Mary it surely took more time to make such a momentous decision. God does not force anyone; we, as humans, freely acquiesce to God's will, but we do so, not blindly, but knowing that saying a yes to God will irrevocably change our lives. There will certainly be consequences. And, indeed, the life of this young woman is changed forever, as is all of history.

It can also be argued that, still unsure and even perhaps a bit disbelieving of all that has taken place, she quickly goes to visit Elizabeth to see for herself evidence of God's word. It is only when she encounters a heavily pregnant Elizabeth that she proclaims her faith in God in a magnificent song that stands to this day as a proclamation not of passivity or humility but of revolution, of a reversal of the status quo and the breaking forth of God's righteous justice into the world in the form of her son. Mary's song, like other songs by women in sacred scripture, is not a song of pious submission but one of righteous judgment and vindication for all who, like Mary and her son, are born poor and oppressed and unjustly victimized. She is prophesying the coming kingdom of God, a time and place where those who are poor will receive God's bounty and those who are hungry will be fed while the rich and arrogant, those who are unjust, will be cast away. Is it any wonder that her son Jesus makes an almost identical prophetic statement in his first sermon (Luke 4:16–30)?

By saying yes to God, Mary breaks open human history and subverts it, turning all of reality upside down, for she affirms and acknowledges that the miraculous work of God brought about through the Holy Spirit will result in a new reality for all of humanity. She stands, therefore, as a symbol, of hope and courage for so many women, poor and invisible, who, by their actions throughout history, by their willingness to stand up and walk out on faith, like so many black Catholic women have done, can bring about a new and better world for all humanity. They and their children serve as catalysts for change in the world and for hope beyond it. Mary, therefore, is a sign of contradiction, and a model not of passivity or voicelessness but a bold, daring, audacious, and courageous model for black Catholic women. She is a source of hope for young pregnant girls of today, children giving birth to children, for in her coming to voice through the intervention of her God, they can see the possibilities that exist in what would otherwise for so many seem a hopeless situation.

Existentially, Mary's response carries with it a fundamental definition of her personhood. Facing a critical choice, she sums herself up

> in one of those great self-constituting decisions that give shape to a human life....This young woman's decision is not a passive, timid reaction but a free and autonomous act [that] encourages and endorses women's efforts to take responsibility for their own lives. The courage of her decision vis-à-vis the Holy One is at the same time an assent to the totality of herself.[16]

These three women—Eve, Mary of Magdala, and Mary the Mother of God—are only a few of the women in sacred scripture who speak words of womanist wisdom and dare to become other than what they have been told they should be. Seen holistically rather than dualistically, seen through the dark eyes of their black Catholic sisters who have borne the burden of rape, forced sterilization, children sold away or taken away by the state, loss of name, history, husband, family—all that makes up a human life—and denied their very humanity, yet these women told God it would be all right if he changed their names. For to be a woman named by God was to be a woman who changed the world. They are sisters in solidarity rather than opposition who speak words of black wisdom and live lives of black hope, courage, and faith in a world that saw them as nothing.

> Catholic womanist God-talk is rooted in the cycle of life and death rather than in death alone. It seems always to bring forth life from that which was seen as lifeless, inhuman, or despised. It is the effort constantly to speak truth to life, knowing, as poet Audre Lorde knew, that "we were not meant to survive."[17]

In so many ways these women, along with Hagar, Deborah the judge, Dinah the daughter of Jacob, and many others named and unnamed down through the ages, were not meant to survive. At least their stories, as they would have them told, were not meant to survive in their original form but would be rewritten, too often by others with a different agenda who knew nothing and probably cared even less of their pain and fears, their hopes and dreams. Theirs are stories that must be retrieved and retold "in memory of them" and countless other women, whose spirits dwell among us still.

The Challenges Black Women Face

For Catholic womanist theologians, the ongoing challenge is to recover and reclaim these and the lives of so many black Catholic women, and men as well, whose stories cry out to be told. We must proclaim their lives boldly so that others may learn of and follow them. The task is not an easy one, for there are many other challenges that confront us as well. One of these, a critical one, is gaining the right to speak out in academia and the church from within our particular context, that is, specifically as black Catholic women. Patricia Hill Collins speaks of black women, especially those now in professional fields, as "outsiders-within."[18] Our positions as women with degrees at the master's or doctoral level, especially in institutions of higher learning, provide us with an "insider's" status, enabling us to participate to a certain degree in academic discourse and have an impact on others in those institutions. At the same time, however, because of our personal situations as black women, we are also "outsiders" whose views are not always welcomed and whose input is often trivialized. We find ourselves straddling two worlds, that of academia or other professions, and that of the black community with its own perspective. In order to belong truly to one or the other, it is assumed that we must give up our existence in the other, as they are not complementary. These assumptions, however, are cynically grounded too often in issues of power, control, and manipulation, yet again, of the black woman's reality.

The exclusion of black women's ideas from mainstream academic discourse and the curious placement of African American women intellectuals in both feminist and black social and political thought have meant that black women intellectuals have remained outsiders within all three communities. The assumptions on which full group membership are based—whiteness for feminist thought, maleness for black social and political thought, and the combination for mainstream scholarship—all negate a black female reality. Prevented from becoming full insiders in any of these areas of inquiry, black women remain outsiders within, individuals whose marginality provides a distinctive angle of vision on the theories put forth by such intellectual communities.[19]

Attempting to survive in these often contradictory worlds is a constant and often enervating challenge that often leaves us feeling as if we are being torn in several directions, required to make choices that have severe consequences not only for self-identity but also for the work that we are trying to do.

As womanist theologians we seek to remove the masks that cover up the inherent illegitimacy of the existing forms of society and their use of language to exclude and restrict.[20] We do this by revealing other more holistic world views that serve to bring about unity rather than division, harmony rather than discord. As black women we have come to realize that in order to authenticate ourselves and legitimate the work that we do, we must also remove the masks that have covered the many worlds in which we find ourselves. Only in so doing can we then reveal these masks to public view and develop a unified challenge to them and to those worlds with which they appear to conflict. The words *appear to conflict* are used deliberately, for the reality is that they do not necessarily conflict but are made to appear so by those who are in some way threatened by them.

This means claiming the legitimacy of our being as black female professionals and working to develop a critical understanding of both past and present in order to participate in building a more holistic future, one in which persons will no longer be required to deny the totality of their being in order to "belong," but can embrace and be embraced for what they bring to intellectual and personal discourse in both the public and private areas. In so doing, in company with my sister womanists, I seek to speak in ways that are understandable to these communities but with a preference toward the black and other marginalized communities, recognizing that as a result I may be accused of being too *popular*, a term often used to denigrate the language of persons of color, women, and those lacking a string of letters after their name. As Patricia Hill Collins has noted:

> My choice of language…typifies my efforts to theorize differently. A choice of language is inherently a political choice. Writing…in a language that appears too "simple" might give grounds for criticism to those individuals who think that the complex ideas of social theory [and theology] must be abstract, difficult, and inaccessible. Populist ideas become devalued exactly because they are popular. This position reflects a growing disdain for anything deemed "public" and for the general public itself.[21]

Black women, as their community's bearers of culture, have, historically, been the forgers of new ways of being and speaking in the world. They recognize with Collins that "privatizing and boarding ideas upholds inequality. Sharing ideas through translation and teaching supports democracy."[22] It is our task today as Catholic womanists to speak life into the future, a future inclusive and representative of all. We do so by working to redefine what it means to be male and female in language that complements the actual experiences of those engaged in living out maleness and femaleness, in ways inclusive of both heterosexual and homosexual understandings. In our stories, songs, prayers, and God-talk (theologizing), black women speak life into being, not a stunted growth unable to flourish and condemned to premature death, not one confined to dry, dusty tomes read and understood by only a privileged few, but a life that is fruitful and representative of a diversity created, not by human hands, but by divine ones.

Black women have, historically, worked to make community, a desire deeply rooted in their African ancestry and made even more important by their experiences in the United States.

> "Making community" means the processes of creating religious, educational, health-care, philanthropic, political, and familial institutions and professional organizations that enabled our people to survive. In the early eighteenth and nineteenth centuries, Black women…made community…through the building and shaping of slave culture. Later the process of "making community" was repeated in post-emancipation agricultural areas and then in urban industrial societies….It was

> through "making community" that Black women were able to redefine themselves, project sexual respectability, reshape morality, and define a new aesthetic....Black women came to subjecthood and acquired agency through the creation of community.[23]

Today we who name ourselves womanists do so not in opposition but in creation, seeking to "make community" wherever we find ourselves. We define ourselves not over against but in solidarity with, affirming that new ways of self-definition must emerge, not as hand-me-downs or cast-offs or shaped by others' self-understanding, but created out of the fabric of our own lives. In so doing we are creating a new language of liberation that is open to any and all who are willing to speak plainly without assuming their language will give them power and/or authority over another. As womanists, we see as our challenge the gathering of the myriad threads of the richly diverse black community and breathing into them renewed life that can serve as a model of life for our world. That model is centered on the co-createdness by God of all, regardless of efforts to separate by the arbitrary use of divisive language and beliefs that restrict rather than encourage the fullness of life and its possibilities.

All who are oppressed share in solidarity with each other, a solidarity that should not be laid aside for individual desires or "battles." The struggle is communal, not individual, and can be worn only if experiences are shared, stories are told, songs are sung, histories are reclaimed and restored, and a new language emerges that speaks words of peace and unity, that unites, that recalls both the pain and the joy of our different heritages and leads us into a brand-new day.

Notes

1. Darlene Clark Hine, ed., *Encyclopedia of Black Women in America* (Bloomington: Indiana University Press, 1994), 457.

2. Hine, *Encyclopedia of Black Women in America*, 259–60.

3. Delores S. Williams, *Sisters in the Wilderness: The Challenge of Womanist God-Talk* (Maryknoll, NY: Orbis Books, 1993), 118.

4. Williams, *Sisters in the Wilderness*, 118.

5. Williams, *Sisters in the Wilderness*, 119.

6. Bernice J. Reagon, "African Diaspora Women: The Making of Cultural Workers," in *Women in Africa and the African Diaspora*, ed. Rosalyn Terborg-Penn, Sharon Harley, and Andrea Rushing (Washington, DC: Howard University Press, 1987), 167.

7. Cyprian Davis, "God of Our Weary Years," in *Taking Down Our Harps: Black Catholics in the United States*, ed. Diana L. Hayes and Cyprian Davis, OSB (Maryknoll, NY: Orbis Books, 1999), 20.

8. Davis, "God of Our Weary Years," 30.

9. Cyprian Davis, OSB, *The History of Black Catholics in the United States* (New York: Crossroad, 1990), 115.

10. Diana Hayes, "And When We Speak," in Hayes and Davis, *Taking Down Our Harps*, 106.

11. Gay Wilentz, *Binding Cultures: Black Women Writers in Africa and the Diaspora* (Bloomington: Indiana University Press, 1992), xii.

12. Wilentz, *Binding Cultures*, xv–xvi.

13. See Kelly Brown Douglas, *Sexuality and the Black Church: A Womanist Perspective* (Maryknoll, NY: Orbis Books, 1999), 25–29; and Hayes, "And When We Speak," 102–19.

14. Mary Gordon, cited in Elizabeth A. Johnson, *Truly Our Sister: A Theology of Mary in the Communion of Saints* (New York: Continuum, 2004), 10–11.

15. Gordon, cited in Johnson, *Truly Our Sister*, 11.

16. Johnson, *Truly Our Sister*, 257.

17. Audre Lorde, "A Litany for Survival," in *The Collected Poems of Audre Lorde* (New York: W. W. Norton, 1997), 255–56.

18. Patricia Hill Collins, *Black Feminist Thought: Knowledge, Consciousness, and the Politics of Empowerment*, Perspectives on Gender, vol. 2 (New York: Routledge, 1990), 11–13.

19. Collins, *Black Feminist Thought*, 12.

20. In 2008, e.g., we are confronted by an administration that claims to be acting on behalf of peace by instigating war, to be helping the poor and unemployed by providing tax cuts and write-offs for the rich, and to be helping students by requiring standardized tests for children as young as three and cutting back on loans and grants for higher education. The language is cast in words familiar and soothing, but the effect of the actions behind them is oppressive and life-threatening to many.

21. Collins, *Black Feminist Thought*, xxi.

22. Collins, *Black Feminist Thought*, xxiii.

23. Darlene Clark Hine, *Black Women and the Re-construction of American History* (Bloomington: Indiana University Press, 1994), xxii.

List of Contributors

Dean Baker is a co-founder of the Center for Economic and Policy Research based in Washington, DC.

Mary Jo Bane is the Thornton Bradshaw Professor of Public Policy and Management, America, at the Harvard Kennedy School.

Alison Benders is Senior Lecturer in Systematic Theology and Associate Dean at the Jesuit School of Theology of Santa Clara University.

M. Shawn Copeland is Professor Emerita of Systematic Theology at Boston College.

Charles E. Curran is the Elizabeth Scurlock University Professor of Human Values at Southern Methodist University and the co-editor of this volume.

Robert DeFina is Professor and Chair of the Department of Sociology and Criminology at Villanova University.

Lisa A. Fullam is Professor of Moral Theology at the Jesuit School of Theology of Santa Clara University and the co-editor of this volume.

Katie M. Grimes is Assistant Professor in the Department of Theology and Religious Studies of Villanova University.

Lance Hannon is Professor in the Department of Sociology and Criminology of Villanova University.

Diana L. Hayes is Professor Emerita of Systematic Theology in the Department of Theology at Georgetown University.

Kristin E. Heyer is Professor of Theology at Boston College.

Mary E. Hunt is the co-founder and co-director of the Women's Alliance for Theology, Ethics, and Ritual in Silver Spring, Maryland.

Mary Jo Iozzio is Professor of Moral Theology in the School of Theology and Ministry of Boston College.

Ada María Isasi-Díaz was Professor of Ethics and Theology Emerita in the Theological School of Drew University.

Michael P. Jaycox is Assistant Professor in the Department of Theology and Religious Studies of Seattle University.

M. Therese Lysaught is Professor at the Neiswanger Institute for Bioethics and Healthcare Leadership and the Institute of Pastoral Studies at Loyola University Chicago.

Julie A. Mavity Maddalena is Assistant Professor of Philosophy and Religion, Ulrich Ethicist in Residence, and chaplain at Lakeland University.

Bryan Massingale holds the James and Nancy Buckman Chair in Applied Christian Ethics at Fordham University.